The Great American Banking Snafu

Mary L. King
San Francisco State University

Lexington Books
D.C. Heath and Company/Lexington, Massachusetts/Toronto

Library of Congress Cataloging in Publication Data
King, Mary L.
  The great American banking snafu.

  Bibliography: p.
  Includes index.
  1. Banks and banking—United States—History.
2. Banks and banking—Sweden—History.   I.Title.
HG2481.K595   1985   332.1'0973   84-48080
ISBN 0-669-09127-8 (alk. paper)

Published simultaneously in Canada
Printed in the United States of America on acid-free paper
International Standard Book Number: 0-669-09127-8
Library of Congress Catalog Card Number: 84-48080

Contents

Preface

T his book is the product of curiosity: first, as to why the U.S. banking system is so racked by crisis and instability and its payment system is so backward, and, second, as to whether the United States could benefit from the experiences of Sweden, whose stable system is recognized as one of the world's most technologically advanced. Because banking historically has been the most regulated of all industries, government policies can mean the difference between success and failure for financial institutions. But anything involving money and politics is inextricably bound up with the whole gamut of human strengths and frailties, with some plans that succeed and more that go awry, and with people's universal fears about security, privacy, and crime. Hence, the answers to the questions were to be found in social and political, as well as economic and technological, forces.

In addition to studying all the pertinent material available in the United States, I learned the Swedish language in order to overcome the problem of penetrating what one scholar has described as "the largely self-congratulatory views typically offered by Swedes for foreign consumption."[1] Then I spent seven months in Stockholm, conducting interviews and poring through hundreds of books and documents.

A historical orientation is taken because, rather than treat policy as a choice made at some time X, isolated from social and structural context, the book shows policies resulting from an accumulation of past events, political and organizational constraints, and values with roots reaching back into time. Five separate but overlapping areas of significance to the industry—structure, competition, technological cooperation, consumer protection, and employment—are examined, with sufficient behavioral detail provided to permit some conclusions about the reasons for the policies adopted and their effectiveness.

Chapter 1 outlines the development of the banking and payment systems in the two nations and the political, cultural, and economic environments in which they evolved. It reveals the role of the Swedish and U.S. governments in running and regulating banks and the public attitudes and values that led to the emergence of that not-so-silent partner of all bankers, the government.

In chapter 2 the major payment mechanisms in both nations are described to facilitate understanding of the remainder of the book, which focuses not so much on what payments systems nations have as why they have them. The role of crime in Sweden's early adoption of cashless payment mechanisms is related, along with the story behind the giro, which in Europe is called "the poor man's bank."

Structural issues are examined in chapter 3, including the populist politics behind the thorny branching and interstate banking problems in the United States, which prompted banking by loophole and culminated in the anomalous "nonbank banks" of the 1980s. The background to the invasion of the "money snatchers" is described, as well as the mayhem resulting from the lopsided 1980 deregulation legislation. By contrast, the development of Sweden's stable structure is depicted, along with its all-in-one agency and more cooperative approach to supervision of the industry.

Chapter 4 covers competitive issues, with an explanation of how forty years of oppressive U.S. regulation stifled innovation and competition in the industry. Both Swedish and U.S. cartels are described, plus the mass money migration in the United States when the government-imposed cartel was cracked by securities firms followed by retailers, placing U.S. financial institutions in the unique position of having to compete with unregulated companies. The secret to the success of small Swedish savings and cooperative banks in competing with large ones is revealed, as well as how the Federal Reserve competes with some U.S. banks.

Technological cooperation is identified as a key to Sweden's lead in electronic funds transfer systems (EFTS) in chapter 5, which tells how the Swedes came up with a futuristic national EFTS plan in 1972, including home banking. However, while in recent years the Swedish bankers have become less cooperative and more independent as a result of self-confidence about EFTS, the Americans have just entered the stage of cooperation. Surprisingly, the chapter shows how the Americans relied on their government to take the lead in developing EFTS, while the more socialistic Swedes did it on their own.

An expert on privacy law has said, "Although the United States is the most advanced nation in the world in the field of computer science, we must look elsewhere to find comprehensive legislative proposals for solving the computer-privacy problem."[2] In chapter 6, Sweden's creation of the world's first national computer privacy law and its successful implementation are described, along with consumer protection in general, security, the massive wave of credit card fraud, and the effects of electronic banking on employment.

The final chapter summarizes and analyzes the material present earlier to explain how Sweden's system dynamically progressed to excellence while that of the United States lagged behind, with the problems that set back the United States spoofed in "The Team That Couldn't Win." It is followed by evidence that the United States has never had a sound banking system, with the crisis of the 1980s but one of a long series of crises over the years. Thus, it is argued that since Congress over the course of more than a hundred years has failed to secure a sound system for the nation, it is time for the public to take the lead in demanding reforms to achieve one. To deal with some of the major problems besetting the industlry and disturbing the American public, a series of pragmatic, if perhaps controversial, proposals are presented. If they stimulate debate that leads to corrective measures, this book will have served its purpose.

Notes

1. Thomas J. Anton, *Governing Greater Stockholm: A Study of Policy Development and System Change* (Berkeley: University of California Press, 1975), p. 135.
2. Arthur R. Miller, *The Assault on Privacy* (Ann Arbor: University of Michigan Press, 1971), p. 227.

Acknowledgments

Τhis book would not have been possible without the gracious cooperation of over one hundred men and women in Sweden and the United States who provided voluminous information and candid opinions in exchange for an assurance of anonymity. Special thanks also are due to Bo Gunnarsson of the Swedish Bankers Association, Rudolf Jalakas, chief economist for Svenska Handelsbanken, and Harry Karlsson of the Bank Inspection Board for their invaluable help with research work in Stockholm and to Robert W. Eisenmenger, senior vice-president and director of research, and Steven D. Felgran, economist, both of the Federal Reserve Bank of Boston, for their assistance in facilitating the gathering of U.S. data.

1
Building Blocks of the Past

For a part of the time, we rested in the imaginary security of ignorance; for another part, we seemed indifferent to our plight; and for
the remainder of the time we were afraid to apply the remedy lest
we interfere with the processes and profits of a privileged class.[1]
Honorable Carter Glass

Written some sixty years ago to describe the government's reaction
to the instability of the banking system in the years preceding passage of the Federal Reserve Act, the words above just as aptly
depict the background to the upheaval of the U.S. banking industry in the
1980s as nondepository institutions captured a major share of the nation's
financial services and congressional gridlock precluded legislative remedy.
The blanket of protection the government laid on the industry when it
banned the payment of interest on checking accounts and set interest rates
on deposits below market rates provided only "imaginary security." Moreover, the blanket smothered the industry by stifling competition and innovation so that while in other countries banking was transformed to an electronic information system, U.S. banking remained mired in an anachronistic
check-based payment system.

There was "ignorance" of the fact that technological advances had made
it possible for any firm with computer capability and a few phone lines to get
into payment services. And they did. By the end of 1984, economic guerrillas
had funneled $214 billion into 332 money market funds, and only $297 billion remained in savings accounts in the banks and thrifts. By the time regulators overcame their "indifference" and authorized competitive products for
the industry, it was too late: the public had found not only higher rates of
return for deposits but also an alternative to standing in line and sullen service. That demolished another source of "imaginary security": the carefully
nurtured myth that, given the choice, the public would always choose the
safety of insured funds.

The "remedy" Congress applied to the hemorrhaging industry in 1980
with deregulatory legislation ignored the reality that its structure had already
been shattered into only two segments: the regulated and the unregulated.
Trying to preserve the old compartmentalized structure was about as mean-

ingful as rearranging deck chairs on the *Titanic* after it hit the iceberg. The legislation was, moreover, little more than a Band-Aid, since it deregulated only the deposit side of the banks' operations; it increased their funding costs without enabling them to diversify their product lines. To cover the higher cost of purchased funds, the regulated firms sought higher yields by investing in riskier ventures. With the premiums for deposit insurance unrelated to the riskiness of assets, the financial institutions gambled on being bailed out if they got into trouble. And they did. In 1983 there were ninety-five failures and arranged mergers of savings and loans (S&Ls), and when in 1984 the nation's largest S&L suffered a liquidity crisis, the Federal Savings and Loan Insurance Corporation (FSLIC) could not rescue it because the agency's $6.3 billion of insurance funds could not cover the thrift's $12 billion of insured deposits. More banks failed in 1984 than in any year since the Great Depression, and the government virtually nationalized Continental Illinois to avert its collapse. Not surprisingly, public confidence in the banking system declined, thereby jeopardizing the regulated firms' one competitive advantage: trustworthiness.

With an unblemished trustworthy image, a card base larger than Visa's, and 813 stores linked by a powerful computer system, Sears, Roebuck by then had expanded into financial services, along with J.C. Penney, American Express, stockbrokerages, and insurance companies. Those firms were to banking what the Japanese interlopers had been to the U.S. auto industry, and Continental was the Chrysler of the banking industry. Like the Japanese automakers, they had lower costs: they used computerized products, were not hampered by interstate and branching restrictions, and were not burdened with noninterest-bearing reserves, low-interest mortgages, or nonperforming loans. Like the U.S. automakers, the bankers sought protection from the predators. But at the same time, they sought permission to expand into the insurance and securities fields, which prompted those industries to demand protection. In the ensuing melee, regulators clashed with one another and with Congress, which lapsed into paralysis, afraid to anger any of the special interest groups that constitute the "privileged class" of the 1980s.

As a harsh reminder of what this chaos was costing the public, an international survey of retail banking castigated the U.S. payment system as "very backward" and "one of the least efficient" in the developed world, while Sweden's was rated the most efficient.[2] Indeed, while in 1984 U.S. banks advertised "the beginning of electronic trade payments and the end of checks," those payments in Sweden have been made without checks since 1925 and electronically since 1964. The Swedes have had direct deposit of pay since the late 1950s and have had two nationwide networks of cash dispensers since the 1970s. No depositor there has lost a cent since 1929, and since the industry was deregulated in 1968, savings and cooperative banks have offered the same services as the commercial banks. Moreover, while the cost of federal banking regulation alone in the United States increased 48 percent between 1980, when deregulation began, and 1984, one Swedish agency with sixty people supervises over 570 banks at no cost to taxpayers.[3]

How could a nation the size of California but with only 8.3 million people have the top-rated retail banking and payment system in the world? Just as Japanese management styles have been studied in efforts to learn the secrets of that nation's success in manufacturing, this book comparatively examines the evolution of the banking and payment systems in Sweden and the United States to see what lessons about financial services can be learned. Because such systems reflect the economic, social, and political conditions that have prevailed throughout a nation's history, the study begins with a review of the foundations on which the two systems have been built. In the process, striking patterns of commonality, as well as differences, emerge.

Sweden's Extraordinary Early Monetary History

In retrospect, it makes sense that the country that was the laughingstock of Europe in the seventeenth century because it had the heaviest coins in recorded history should be a world leader in weightless electronic funds transfer systems in the twentieth century. It took a while, but the Swedes finally got the last laugh.

It all began back in the days when Sweden had a monopoly on copper, in which the government had a vested interest as part owner of the largest mine. Hence, in an effort to maximize his return on investment, the king in 1624 replaced the silver standard with a bimetallic standard based on silver and copper. Since Gresham's Law had not yet been translated into Swedish, the king was surprised when the copper coins drove the silver ones out of circulation and dismayed when the resulting overissue of new coins depressed copper prices.[4] Although it was conceded that the scheme had been based on a miscalculation, the standard survived until 1776.

Meanwhile, there were those coins. Since the price of copper was barely 1/100th that of silver, the ten dollar coin was a record-breaking 43 pounds. The most common coin, the two dollar piece, measured about 9.5 inches diagonally and weighed over 8 pounds. People had to use horse carts to haul the large, rectangular slabs when making major payments. Although foreigners found the sight of the natives staggering about under the weight of the coins on their heads and backs a real sideshow, the stolid Swedes never saw the humor in the situation. A Swedish historian has characterized as "rather malicious" the comments of a Danish diplomat who in 1720 wrote home: "Four riksdalers (dollars) would be a terrible punishment for me if I had to carry them a hundred steps; may none here become a thief."[5] One unintended consequence of the large coins was their stimulus to the development of Sweden's transportation infrastructure. Roads had to be built so that treasury agents could use the wagons necessary for hauling in the cumbersome tax collections from the countryside.

Actually Swedish coins can be traced back to the Viking age, although a barter economy prevailed then. Fortunately, they were not made of copper, or their ships probably never would have made it out of the harbor, thereby denying history those adventuresome sagas. The earliest recorded comments on Swedish monetary policy can be found in the Stockholm chronicle of 1592–1593, in which the city clerk noted that too many bad coins had been struck during the preceding year, and "contempt of money swiftly rose . . . so lately nobody has wanted to sell his goods for the bad and soft money."[6] Thus, the nation returned to a barter economy, which endured there for centuries longer than in other European countries. Certainly the cumbrous copper coins did little to enhance the concept of money, but they had another unintended consequence that did: the introduction of Europe's first paper money in 1661.

In 1656 a Livonian named Johan Palmstruch obtained a charter to establish a bank in Stockholm, although he had been imprisoned in the Netherlands for economic espionage before coming to Sweden. His innovative, if ultimately fatal, idea was to issue bank notes as receipts for deposits of the bulky copper coins. Within a year this inspired another innovation—in crime: the world's first forged bank note.[7] However, the weary-armed Swedes embraced the paper money with no less enthusiasm than did the banker, who was enjoying interest-free deposits. Palmstruch, then, in the words of a historian, "lost both common sense and decency": he issued more notes than could be redeemed in hard cash.[8] When word spread that the notes had been depreciated, it caused a run on the bank. To quell the panic, the government closed the bank, sentenced Palmstruch to death, and banned foreigners from bank ownership, a law still in effect in 1984. The first paper monetary system failed with a crash and produced a distrust of bank notes that persisted for almost a century. Everyone agreed, however, that the bank had been useful, so Parliament took it over. Thus, the Riksbank, the oldest existing central bank in the world, was established in 1668.

At the end of the seventeenth century, the king's financial adviser launched yet another innovation: light copper dollars adapted for the pocket. But they were easily counterfeited and were, moreover, issued without limitation so that they depreciated wildly. Since the Swedes take monetary matters seriously, the adviser was beheaded in 1719 for "ruining public credit by imaginary money" and for having given the king bad advice.[9] That put a damper on innovation in the monetary area for a century or so.

During a money crisis in 1773, a discount company was chartered, an event that marked the beginning of commercial banking history in Sweden. The firm was so successful that the king could not resist the lure of its profits. Although its charter had not yet expired, the state acquired it, thereby creating its first commercial bank. Three private discount companies were also founded, and they prospered until the crisis at the end of the Napoleonic wars when the government had to step in to help them. Although the rescue effort succeeded, discount firms were never the same again. By this time, the national affliction commonly known as "Royal Swedish Envy" had given rise to criticism of the firms' high profits, which had provided dividends of 24 to 28 percent even during the worst years. To make bad matters worse, auditors discovered that one company had made sizable illegal loans to the city's biggest businessman. When news of the scandal got out, there was a run on all discount houses, and the state shuttered them. After the fall of the discount houses, which are regarded as Europe's first commercial banks outside Great Britain, Sweden lacked full banking activity for a long time.

The average Swede then could not have cared less. The burning problem was not capital acquisition but widespread poverty. This was a country that in 1632 had hesitated to invite foreign dignitaries to the funeral of its fallen king for fear that "they will see how poor we are."[10] During the eighteenth century, untold thousands of Swedes died of starvation, and the so-called last great starvation was not to occur until 1868.

The poverty may seem perplexing, since at the time Palmstruch founded his bank Sweden was regarded as a first-rate military and political power; however, its power has been described as a "colossus on feet of clay."[11] Although the copper industry provided financing for the wars that raged from 1600 to 1720, during the next hundred years wars were paid for with paper money. It resulted in heavy financial obligations, which led Europeans to refer to the country as "the fortified poorhouse."[12]

The country's social problems came to a head when humiliating defeats in the war with Russia in 1808–1809, during which Sweden lost all the land it had won in earlier wars, led to the deposition of the king and a demand for a new form of government. The result was the Constitution of 1809, which, after the U.S. one, is the oldest written constitution in the world. Yet while philosophers hailed it as the freest constitution in Europe, the Swedish masses did not receive the right of political participation until the end of the nineteenth century. Although the peasants constituted a majority, the bulk of the country's wealth was concentrated in the hands of a small number of families. Hence, as Sweden emerged from its last long century of warfare, the uneven distribution of economic and political power caused an undercurrent of disquietude.

Beginning of the U.S. Monetary System

In search of a better life, a boatload of Swedes emigrated to the United States in 1638 and founded New Sweden, near what is now Wilmington on the Delaware River. Like other early settlers, they used barter for trade as they had in the old country. Later, as commerce developed, the colonists used coins of other nations, which they acquired through trading. Although the British forbade the coining of an American currency, when a serious shortage of money disrupted business activity in 1652, British colonists in Massachusetts built a mint to turn out silver shillings and operated it until the British closed it in 1688.

Although checks did not become popular in England until the end of the eighteenth century, they were introduced into the American colonies with an experiment that began in 1681. Called "The Fund at Boston in New England," the scheme was developed by a group of Boston businessmen to compensate for another shortage of hard currency. They mortgaged their land and commodities to the fund in return for credit against which they could draw checks. The checks were soon replaced by paper currency, however, which was better suited to the needs of the time.

The development of paper currency in America, as in Sweden, followed that of coins, albeit not initially as a solution to a weighty problem. Like the later issue of notes in Sweden, however, the colonial paper money was created more in response to the needs of the war than those of business. The first American paper money was printed to finance the 1690 expedition against the French from Massachusetts.[13] One promoter of paper currency was Benjamin Franklin, who published "A Modest Enquiry into the Nature and Necessity of a Paper-Currency" in 1729. His argument in the book was so compelling that it won him the job of printing some money, which he embellished with a pattern of leaves. Since the art of counterfeiting had reached the New World by then, the pattern was intended to discourage practitioners of the trade that had been invented in Sweden. Another deterrent was Franklin's imprinted warning, "To Counterfeit is DEATH."[14]

Inasmuch as the Bank of England had been established in 1694 and the British banking system had developed considerably in the intervening years, that system was proposed as the ideal pattern for every colony to emulate. But a vastly different system developed in America. Rather than found a few large banks, which then could serve the country through a widespread network of branches, the United States developed a system made up of a great many individual banks, with branching rigidly controlled. To a large extent, the U.S. system can be viewed as a reflection of two value orientations so strongly ingrained in the culture that to some Europeans they appear to be phobias: a fear of big business and a suspicion of banks.

In order to provide funds for the beleaguered Continental Army, a group of patriotic merchants formed the Pennsylvania Bank in 1780. Congress pledged to protect its subscribers against losses, even though it was a private firm. But it operated only until late in 1781, when the United States' first real bank, the Bank of North America, was chartered. The bank's equity capital included loans and gifts that the ubiquitous Benjamin Franklin obtained from the French treasury. Reminiscent of Sweden's early experience with coins, it took sixteen teams of oxen two months to haul the funds from the port of Boston to Philadelphia. The bank made loans, took deposits, and issued paper currency, which circulated in the East. In the wooded mountains of eastern Tennessee, however, where the State of Franklin existed from 1784 to 1788, the backwoodsmen used animal furs as official coinage, with the governor paid in deerskins and assembly members reimbursed in raccoon skins.

The evolution of the U.S. banking system, like that of Sweden, differed from those of many European countries in that banks of issue were founded without the nation's first developing a private banking system. In this regard, it was based more on the model of the Bank of England than on the British private banking system. The reason was that the young nation needed money, and since banks create money, it needed banks. At the same time, however, there was strong political opposition to banking. Hence, banking was treated as a quasi-state monopoly, with legislatures giving rights to banks based on the notion that they were responsible to government. Therefore, banks in America, as in Sweden, have never enjoyed true laissez-faire; the government has always been a dominant figure in the industry.

Prior to 1828 the approval of Congress or a state legislature was needed for a charter, and regular reports to public officials were required almost from the beginning. By 1800, however, chartered banks were complaining about the same issue that bedevils them in the 1980s: unfair competition from unregulated competitors. By then, schools, canal companies, and other businesses had learned that they could go into debt profitably by issuing notes that looked like money and circulated like money. In response, New York State, among others, passed restraining legislation to ensure its six chartered banks a monopoly on their rights. The law made it illegal to conduct banking activities without legal authorization and provided a bounty of $500 for the conviction of unauthorized bankers.

Growth of the U.S. Banking System

Although Secretary of the Treasury Alexander Hamilton was fully aware of the deep distrust of banks and "moneyed interests" by many Americans, in 1790 he presented a plan for a national bank. To assuage the fears of those who envisioned a European-type central bank, he proposed that it would not have a large number of branches and would be under private rather than public control. Hamilton wanted the bank because it could provide financial services to the federal government; its note-issuing powers could convert the national debt into a useful medium of exchange; and it could provide additional short-term credit to the business community. Moreover, as a mercantilist, Hamilton believed in a strong central government that would actively promote industry and commerce. Opposition to the bank came from the agrarians, including Secretary of State Thomas Jefferson, who advocated self-reliance and distrusted centralized government, industry, and banking. Perhaps the only issue on which the two cabinet members ever agreed was the decimal system of currency, which Jefferson proposed and Hamilton implemented. Hence, Jefferson advised the president that the act to establish the bank was unconstitutional. But Washington accepted the opinion of his secretary of the treasury, and the First Bank of the United States was created in 1781.

Before long, the bank had branches in the major cities, and its paper currency was circulating throughout the country. In time, the government discovered an unforeseen benefit of the bank: by calling for the redemption of the state banks' notes and checks, the national bank could restrict the overextension of credit. In effect, it was both a regulator and a competitor, not unlike the central banks of other countries at that time.

At the time the First Bank of the United States opened its doors, there were only 5 banks in the country; by the time its charter came up for renewal in 1811, there were nearly 250. When it was chartered, the Federalists who represented the moneyed interests were in control; when it expired, the Jeffersonians were in power. By then opposition to the bank came not only from the agrarians who fundamentally disliked all banks but also from the state bankers who resented the redemptions pressed on them by the bank. Moreover, in the eyes of many, the bank was the last monument of Federalism. Hence, its charter was not renewed.

Before the charter expired, a group of New Yorkers who held stock in the bank laid plans to convert it into a state bank that would be the largest in the country. They anticipated strong opposition to their proposal because their bank would succeed one that had an image as Federalist and British, and since war with England then was considered imminent, their timing could hardly have been worse. Sensitive, however, to the PR aspects of their endeavor, they hired lobbyists and a staff of what were described as "mostly low and worthless fellows," including an Irish preacher.[15] To sweeten the deal, the bank's organizers agreed to pay the state a bonus of $600,000 and lend it $2 million. But in spite of an uproar over charges of bribery to four members of the lower house, the bill cleared the legislature. Following a trial on bribery charges, the two leading lobbyists were acquitted, but the preacher was sent to the slammer. Thus, in 1812 the Bank of America in New York was chartered. In 1928 it was acquired by A.P. Giannini as the eastern terminus of his short-lived transcontinental banking network, and in 1931 it became part of what is now Citibank.

Machiavellian machinations, murder, and sex colored the origins of another major New York bank. Until 1799, the only banks in New York were a branch of the national bank and the Bank of New York, which effectively blocked the chartering of a competitor for years. But after the city suffered an outbreak of yellow fever in the summer of 1798, Aaron Burr forged a coalition of liberals and conservatives to found a banking company to finance and construct a waterworks for the city. In considering the proposal, some legislators questioned the rationale for a clause in it that would permit the firm to use surplus capital to engage in monetary transactions. But after Burr explained that it was the only way to remunerate the stockholders properly, a perpetual charter was granted, and both the city and the state bought stock in the company.

Although the Federalists later charged that Burr had used the waterworks as a ruse to obtain a charter for a bank, the company actually did build and operate one. In fact, the construction project attracted sensational attention when the body of a young woman "of easy virtue" was found in a well the workers had dug. In what later seemed supremely ironic, the man accused of the dastardly deed was defended by the team of Burr and Hamilton, who won an acquittal for him before their relationship deteriorated into the duel that cost Hamilton his life. Although other banks were set up to build canals, railways, and roads, they usually did not survive the projects they funded. But the Manhattan Company (now Chase Manhattan) concentrated on banking and in time let the waterworks go down the drain.

In response to President James Madison's proposal that another national bank be formed to develop a uniform national currency, Congress in 1816 chartered the Second Bank of the U.S. Like its predecessor, it was not a true central bank, since the government was only a minor stockholder; however, both banks were influential because of their size and the fact that they were creditors of state-chartered banks.

State banks by then were flourishing, but there were abuses in issuing notes. The first bank failure in the United States occurred in 1809 when a Bostonian, who owned a bank in Rhode Island that issued $800,000 in notes based on $45 of capital, gave what has been described as "the first American demonstration on how to ruin a bank."[16] Between 1811 and 1816 the amount of paper money in circulation increased from $80 million or $90 million to $200 million, an amount that has been characterized as "more money than could possibly be redeemed." [17]

By 1820 there were over 300 banks, and four years later the Suffolk Bank of New England introduced a system by which it regulated the extension of credit and provided clearing services, central reserves, and the management of notes for country banks that were required to maintain specie balances with it. Those concepts later were incorporated into the National Bank Act of 1863 and the Federal Reserve Act of 1913. Another major innovation was the formation of the New York Safety Fund in 1829, which, because it in-sured the circulating note liabilities of banks, is regarded as the forerunner of the Federal Deposit Insurance Corporation (FDIC). The fund enabled New

York banks to be the first to resume payments in specie after the Panic of 1837, which earned the city recognition as the nation's financial center. Based on the idea of banks as a system rather than free agents, the fund authorized the first bank inspections in the nation. This, as one Federal Reserve official noted later, marked the beginning of the banking bureaucracy that "has resulted in complexity, duplication, confusion, cost and hypertrophy."[18]

When the charter of the Second Bank of the U.S. came up for renewal in 1831, it was attacked by state banking advocates as unconstitutional because the bank's branches crossed state lines, thus usurping state powers of chartering. There were other charges of reckless operations and abuses of power, such as its "retainer" fees to Senator Daniel Webster. But, above all, the bank was big, and public policy in the Jackson era favored small unit banks. Hence, the bank became a victim of agrarian populism: Congress voted to recharter it, but the president vetoed the bill. When the bank closed in 1836, there were nearly 600 banks, one-third of which had opened in the preceding three years.

Sweden's First Banks

There were more banks in New York City than in all of Sweden in 1817 when a Swedish legislator proposed the creation of a state-run savings bank, based on the idea that through saving, poverty could be alleviated; the slogan was "Help through self-help." Inherent in it was a strong strain of moralism, since the upper classes believed that adversity was God's punishment for bad living. Later one of the founders of the Social Democratic party was to describe the plan with biting irony as "the millionaires' recipe for the art of becoming rich through work and saving."[19] The motion was rejected because Parliament believed such work should be done by private patriotic men. To stimulate such patriotism, the king ordered that a report be prepared on the subject. If no one else was moved by his indoctrinating efforts, the author was: he founded two savings banks in the next two years. During the next decade, some thirty others were established, some with the character of pawnshops in that they granted loans on watches and jewelry. But ten years later, there was disappointment in the effectiveness of the savings banks in relieving the widespread poverty. And there was some poor management. As a historian wrote, "The lovely principle that savings banks in no form could provide profits to founders or members of management . . . was scarcely suited to stimulate energy within leadership."[20]

In 1824 Parliament decided there should be no state support for commercial banks because it would entail heavy responsibility for government.

Therefore charters would state that no bank could expect any public aid, even if in distress, but, by the same token, there would be no regulation aside from quarterly reports. The response was underwhelming: no one applied. The reason was that people then thought that a bank could not be profitable with only its capital and deposits. As a contemporary journalist commented, "A bank without bank notes is like an army without weapons."[21]

Finally, however, in 1830 a charter was granted to a priest to open a provincial bank, and within two years it was issuing notes, even though that was illegal. The finance minister did not protest, though, because by then he too had decided that note issuing offered the only way to get a banking system established. Gradually the number of commercial banks grew, but since they regarded deposits as an encumbrance that merely incurred heavy interest costs, they did not represent a competitive threat to the savings banks. But they did to the Riksbank. When Parliament wrote its 1824 edict, it expected commercial banks to be opened in the cities. But since note issuing was their bread and butter, the private banks did not want to be where the central bank was, and vice-versa. Meanwhile, the state bank uneasily watched the erosion into its previous monopoly on the issue of notes. At the end of 1850, its note issue was about 34 million kronor, while private notes amounted to some 15 million. But as time went on, the order was reversed, so that in 1870 the figures were 26 and 40 million, respectively.[22]

The 1840s were marked by growing hostility toward the private banks. Granted, their hours were not too good—usually three hours on three days of the week. And because some bankers would not stoop to handling money, borrowers had to deal with employees or middlemen. This, plus the fact that the employees were paid very little, led to embezzlements. The image of the savings bankers as friendly folks was not enhanced, either, when one tight-lipped, flinty-eyed priest who ran a rural thrift institution with patriarchal authority was prosecuted for flogging borrowers who defaulted on payments.

It was, however, the banks' high profits from issuing notes that engendered the greatest opposition. In an 1840 parliamentary debate, the peasants termed bankers "vampires who suck the arm of society's body."[23] They demanded that the Riksbank be given a monopoly on note issuing so that the profits could help the poor. The Liberals, however, wanted no monopolies; they said the situation called for more competition. The bankers, meanwhile, sanguinely discussed the idea of having only one private bank for the whole country. As opposition to the private banks mounted, Parliament passed the Bank Act of 1846, which sought to guarantee the redeemability of private bank notes by regulating their issue. The brouhaha climaxed in 1848 when Parliament proposed to end private banking completely; the banks escaped extinction only because the Riksbank did not have enough silver to take over their assets.

Sweden's Maturing System

The prevailing public opinion in Sweden at that time, as in the United States, was that when it came to banks, small was beautiful. Thus, in 1856 Parliament imposed a maximum on the capital funding for commercial banks, which in three years produced an increase in the number of banks from 12 to 29. The growth in the number of savings banks was even more dramatic: from 136 in 1860 to 378 in 1890. Their market coverage was truly remarkable. In 1861 there was one for every 20 people; in 1871, one for every 10; and in 1892, one for every 4.8.[24] And small they were. The press of business was such that although one rural thrift had seven branches, its main office was open only on the second Wednesday of each month from 10 A.M. to noon.

When Stockholms Enskilda Bank was founded in 1856, it changed Swedish banking from a narrow issuing-and-lending business to a full-service one by taking deposits. Although note issue was its main source of profits initially, the bank strove to replace cash with other means of payment. It introduced money orders and encouraged checking accounts, which other banks found too costly because they left the funds idle for fear of large withdrawals.

The nature of the industry was, however, more significantly altered by the establishment of the first joint-stock company banks, Skandinaviska Bank and Svenska Handelsbank, which based their operations on their own capital and on deposits rather than on note issue. In effect, it marked the beginning of the end of note issuing by private banks, which for thirty-four years had constituted a distinguishing feature of the Swedish system.

The first Swedish banks had been modeled after the Scottish ones because government officials had been impressed by the stability of that system in which bankruptcies were very rare, compared to those in England and the United States, where there seemed to be a never-ending series of runs, collapses, and panics. Furthermore, although Scotland, like Sweden, was a poor country, it had nevertheless created a banking system that had thrived for over a hundred years and had contributed to that nation's development.

The early Swedish system, however, also was consistent with the agrarian philosophy advocated by the Jeffersonians in the United States in that the banks were not in cities or financial centers but in the rural areas, where they primarily met the needs of the agricultural sector. Industrial credit needs in those early years were handled by merchants and brokers who acted as financial intermediaries; for major capital needs, Sweden sold bonds abroad.

Public policy also played a major role in discouraging the early banks from seeking deposits. Until it was repealed in 1864, a legal limit of 6 percent on the interest rate for loans forced the banks to offer such low rates on deposits that they were not competitive with the open market where the ceiling could more easily be evaded. To say that the banks were disinterested would be an understatement. At one provincial bank, not only did depositors get no interest but they had to pay for the privilege of putting their money in the bank.

While in some countries the inspection of banks has been a response to crises that resulted in heavy losses to the public, such as in Germany in the early 1930s, the Swedish Bank Inspection Board evolved along with the banking system. The reason was that government leaders believed that the sanction inherent in the banking charter should entail certain guarantees as to the soundness and security of the banks so as to protect depositors. This was to be achieved partly by certain restrictive regulations governing the banks' loans and deposits and partly by regular inspections. Thus, in 1868 a special official in the Department of Finance, who in 1877 was formally designated bank inspector, was given the responsibility of examining the banks' operations. The logistics of the assignment proved a bit overwhelming, however, since at the time there were 44 commercial banks, which had 210 offices. But it was the idea that counted.

As governments learned long ago, giving out notes is preferable to paying interest on deposits. Hence, because note issuing was so profitable, bankers were reluctant to surrender their right. Moreover, they had found a kind of sport in intercepting Riksbank notes. They would pick out its notes from in-payments and convert all out-payments to their own notes. By 1860, the bankers had most of the Riksbank notes in their hands, and by the end of the decade, its notes were completely out of circulation. But the printing presses kept rolling. The number of private notes, which amost tripled between 1860 and 1900, consistently outstripped that of the Riksbank. The variety of notes issued not only caused confusion but also led to a considerable amount of counterfeiting. Tellers had to scrutinize each note presented, which caused delays and lines of irritated customers.

Another problem associated with the proliferation of paper money was one that has continued to this day: finding a way to transport it safely. One bank in a coastal town regularly sent notes to Stockholm by steamboat in a specially constructed iron chest. One time, during pleasant summer weather, the captain of the boat decided to make the trip by night. In the dark, the vessel went aground, and the chest filled with money was almost heaved overboard as the crew tried to lighten the load.

Looking back, it seems remarkable that the system lasted as long as it did. But in 1897 the exclusive right to issue notes was vested in the Riksbank, which in turn discontinued its commercial business and became a true central bank.

Meanwhile, confidence in the savings banks plummeted after state-ordered audits revealed widespread mismanagement and embezzlements. Included among the scandals were cases involving an officer of one thrift who fled to the United States with depositors' money, a parish vicar who purloined the funds intended for an organ and school, and an accountant who committed suicide after his embezzling was discovered. Moreover, the auditors found that 70 to 90 percent of the loans on the books lacked sufficient security and that access to the institutions was inadequate, since only 5 percent of the offices were open all day and one-fourth were open only once a month. A government commission concluded that the thrifts were not meeting the needs of society and proposed a postal savings bank.

While the idea of a state-owned savings bank had been rejected earlier, now there was a new element: fear of the poor. Supporters of the postal bank wanted to increase the number of property owners, believing it would provide better protection against attacks on ownership than increasing the number of policemen. The peasants contended that since the private savings banks had become linked to the capitalists, a postal bank was needed to serve the proletariat. In general, sentiment for creation of the postal bank was strengthened by the phenomenon of the mass emigration, which reached its peak in the 1880s. Sweden lost over one-fifth of its population, a dramatic expression of discontent with prevailing conditions. Hence, despite objections from those who feared it would drain money from the country to the cities, the Postal Bank was established in 1884.

Between 1880 and 1896, the bank inspector considered it improper for one commercial bank to compete with another in the same area. At that time a bank was regarded as a semiofficial institution that should not have to put up with competition in its territory. In effect, the Swedish banking system became a regional one—for a while.

Of Wildcat Banking and Locofocos

Much like the Swedish system in that period, the monetary system in the United States from 1836 to 1863, when there was no federal regulation of banking, was a checkerboard of currency as some 1,600 banks issued 10,000 or so different kinds of bank notes.[25] Counterfeiting was rife; one catalog in 1858 described 4,500 fraudulent notes in circulation when there were only 7,000 authentic ones.[26] Uncertainty led to discounting when notes were presented outside their area of issue, requiring catalogs called bank note detectors to establish exchange rates. Although the proliferation of notes issued by Swedish banks at that time also produced confusion and some counterfeiting, there were two big differences: the Swedish government exercised control over note issuing, and the number of banks was much smaller. Due to the imprecision of the monetary clauses in the U.S. Constitution, debate ensued for years about the legality of states issuing notes, a practice that Chief Justice John Marshall termed unconstitutional. But after his death, the Supreme Court in *Briscoe* v. *Bank of the Commonwealth of Kentucky* in 1837 held that they were legal.

For the first two decades or so of their use in the United States, bank notes were not money but promissory notes to pay the holder either on demand or at some specified date. People who tried to redeem them, however, often encountered resistance because payments reduced the reserves required for local lending. Thus, small town residents viewed with alarm city slickers who strode into their banks with suitcases full of notes bought at discount, which they would exchange for specie. To prolong the length of circulating time, U.S. bankers developed a variation of the Swedish game of swapping notes whereby they would exchange blocks of notes with colleagues in distant cities and pay them out to customers.

An extreme version of this was "wildcat banking," a term first used in Michigan to describe unscrupulous operators who set up banks so deep in the woods that few holders of their notes could find them to redeem the paper—and armed guards kept them at bay. The coin reserves some wildcatters showed state officials were only kegs of nails with a layer of coins on top, and while the examiner was tromping through the brush to the next bank, the keg would be whisked ahead for display there. Such operations were the result of "free banking" laws passed by fourteen states after the Panic of 1837 soured the public on banking. While intended to remove abuses in chartering, the ease of entry the laws provided led to such bad banking experiences that many states, including Texas, banned banking completely.

The agrarians and laborers who made up the radical wing of the Democratic party called the Locofocos wanted all banks abolished, and in a manifesto much like those of the Swedish peasants, termed New York's banking system "a hydra-headed monster whose overthrow was essential to human rights."[27] In fact, animosity to banking was widespread; people lost a lot of money through wildcat currency and bank stock that proved worthless. Antibank feelings erupted into rioting in Cincinnati in 1842 when mechanics learned a bank had suspended payment on notes they held. After throwing the desks, counters, ledgers, and unsigned sheets of bank notes out on the street, they demolished the lobby with crowbars and sledge hammers. When the sheriff showed up, they threw him out too, and when a lawyer tried to read the riot act, the mob of 300 men chased him off before going on to destroy other banks and the office of a note-issuing broker.[28]

In response to public sentiments, Indiana, Missouri, and Iowa limited banking to state-controlled monopolies, as did Illinois, although two Banks of Illinois failed. Wisconsin initially banned note-issuing banks but later adopted free banking, only to repeat Michigan's experience with speculators cranking out notes and setting up shop in the woods and even on Indian reservations. This proved too much for Chicago bankers, who in 1858 refused to accept the notes of twenty-seven Wisconsin banks, which, they claimed, were inaccessible. All told, in 1861 over $200 million of state banks' currency was in circulation, but it could not legally be accepted in payment to the federal government.[29] By the advent of the Civil War, the inadequacies of the banking system, if it could be called that, demanded reform, but it took the exigencies of the war to goad Congress into action.

Birth of the Dual Banking System

The primary purpose of the National Bank Act of 1863 was to create funding for the war. In addition, the bill was intended to ensure sound currency by restoring to the federal government control of the nation's monetary system and to create a uniform system of commercial banking. There was no enthusiasm for the bill because Congress then, as in subsequent times, did not want to deal with banking legislation. Because banking touches almost every segment of society, issues in the industry become politicized easily, resulting in intense pressure on lawmakers from a diverse set of constituencies. Thus, state bankers led the opposition to the bank act because they viewed it as an obstacle to their privilege of unrestricted note issuing. The Democrats opposed it because of their antibanking sentiments, and the New York Clearing House bankers opposed it because they preferred to maintain control through their own strong regional operation, which had ended speculative banking in that state. But due to the war emergency, the bill became law.

The act created a new class of banks, chartered and regulated by the federal government, and it limited the note issue of any national bank to the amount of its paid-in capital. To ensure a sound system, it set stringent capital requirements and provided for bank examinations by creating the Office of the Comptroller of the Currency. The act has been criticized for creating a defective reserve system that permitted pyramiding by allowing some banks to count deposits in other banks as part of their reserves.[30] Hence, the system was not as strong as it appeared and was subject to strain when demands for currency relative to demand deposits suddenly increased.

Although Congress had expected that state banks would convert en masse to national charters after passage of the act, they failed to do so and voiced objections to some of its terms. To encourage conversions, Congress revised the act in 1864. One significant, if little noted, change in the amended version was the elimination of the right of national banks to establish branches, although it permitted state banks seeking national charters to retain their existing branches. By 1865 more than 1,000 new national banks had been organized, bringing the total to 1,601, yet 700 new national banks were chartered before the conversion of the first state bank.[31] Frustrated in its efforts to bring them into the fold through accommodation, Congress in 1865 unleashed its most devastating weapon in an all-out effort to destroy the state banks: it imposed a 10 percent tax on state bank notes. Since many bankers did not believe they could survive without issuing notes, this brought about half the banks to their knees. The other, hardier half continued to flourish as state banks because Congress had failed to realize that it had deprived them of what was only one part of the monetary supply: it had overlooked the growing importance of deposit credit.

The state banks survived by aggressively implementing an innovation called checking accounts. Even though checks had been introduced almost two centuries earlier, it was passage of the punitive 1865 federal legislation that motivated the state banks to promote aggressively acceptance of checks as a major medium of exchange. Thus, because checking accounts replaced note issuing as the most important source of funds and the conditions imposed by state laws on banking were less restrictive, the trend to national charters soon was reversed. By 1871, the deposits of state banks were virtually the same as those of the national ones, a condition that prevailed for many years. Ironically, the legislation that had been written to create one national banking system had the unintended consequence of producing fifty-one: one federal and fifty state ones.

As the U.S. economy grew larger and more complex over the next half-century, a cyclical pattern of booms and busts reflected the shakiness of the financial structure. The last decade of the nineteenth century was marked by manifestations of labor unrest and the emergence of the Populist party, which believed that the wealth and power of the eastern banking and financial community resulted in exploitation of the masses. It earned one-twelfth of the votes in the presidential election of 1892 and prevailed on Congress to create the Postal Savings System in 1910. The system, however, never had a significant amount of savings until the Great Depression, when its share of thrift funds grew to 13 percent as a result of the public's distrust of the banking system.[32]

In the wake of a massive depression in 1893, followed by panics in 1903 and 1907, pressure mounted for public control of the banks. Legislators studied other countries' systems, with special interest in Canada's, which, with a structure of a few banks with very large branch networks, enjoyed stability and an absence of bank failures. A debate raged between those who favored centralization and those who, primarily because they feared large financial institutions, insisted on decentralization. With the Democrats controlling both houses and Woodrow Wilson in the White House as plans for the Federal Reserve System were shaped, strong support for decentralization led to the idea of a number of reserve banks with a Federal Reserve Board to exercise some national coordination. In the battle over the bill, bankers decried the framework of government regulation dominated by political appointees, which a Texas banker denounced as a "communistic idea."[33] The agrarians protested that the bill did not provide for "those who toil, produce, and sustain the country." Those who argued for state banks, which outnumbered national banks three to one, said a unified national banking system would increase the monopoly power of big banks and threaten small unit banks with extinction.

After passage of the Federal Reserve Act in 1913, the large state banks did join the system, but the majority of small ones did not. Thus, the system of correspondent relationships, which had begun nearly a century before, was extended under the act's dispensation for a dual banking system. To provide for the needs of nonmember banks, the national banks created a sort of private reserve system of their own. The founders of the Federal Reserve System thought they had ensured that there would never be another banking crisis; in fact, it had already been established that prognosticating about the effects of legislation on the U.S. banking system was an exercise in futility.

Crises and Consolidation in Sweden

The first decades of the twentieth century in Sweden, as in the United States, were marked by social and political unrest along with economic growth. Huge fortunes were being amassed by the nation's new class of industrialists, with the result that in 1908, 25 percent of Sweden's private property was in the hands of 1 percent of property owners.[34] While the uneven distribution of income provided great infusions of capital for investment, it also provided grist for the mill of politicians preaching protest against exploitation of the masses. There was, moreover, discontent about more embezzlements in the thrifts, especially after depositors in one institution lost 30 percent of their funds. Yet when a proposal was made to open the annual meeting of the savings banks' association to the public, an association official refused with these words: "A bank's reputation is as easily damaged as a woman's, and these internal personal affairs must therefore not be dragged before the public."[35]

As a result of the small capital requirement the government had set to stimulate the formation of non-note-issuing banks, their number grew to a historic peak of eighty-four in 1908, after which the number of banks declined while the number of offices grew.[36] In consonance with the tenor of the times, in 1912 a group of Social Democratic leaders founded a workers' bank. But it never attracted more than 1 percent of total deposits, and after its major shareholder was forced to resign in 1917 for doing business with the Bolsheviks, the bank lost deposits and significance.

Because demand deposits could not provide the capital needed for expansion, the banks bid for long-term funds and, to get around the law, set up subsidiaries to make loans on securities. Toward the end of World War I, however, inflation and speculation combined to produce an unprecedented volume of such loans. When the boom collapsed, the country suffered a devastating depression in which businesses failed, unemployment soared, and banks foundered. By 1930, there were only thirty banks left, one of which had set up a department to operate five steel works, three paper mills, and a fleet of ships of which it had become the owner.[37]

The crisis was blamed in part for a steep rise in crimes of fraud, including the greatest scandal in Swedish banking history when some $16 million was lost in the looting of a group of profit-oriented savings banks owned by high-level politicians. Not only did they divert depositors' funds to their own spec-ulative ventures, but they also voted themselves golden parachutes before being prosecuted in 1929. Because losses were suffered by virtually every or-ganization in Sweden as well as individuals, the government was pressured to cover them partially. Moreover, when people saw the headlines, "Savings Banks Crash," runs ensued on even the soundest of the real savings banks. With public confidence badly shaken, the government imposed supervisory control on savings banks too. Since then, no Swedish depositor has ever lost money in a bank or thrift institution.

Toward the Cashless Society

Before the scandal dominated the headlines, the nation's newspapers had been filled with news about a major innovation in Sweden's payment system: the Postal Giro. To reduce the country's heavy dependence on cash, Parlia-ment in 1922 had debated a proposal for a postal giro system such as other European countries had adopted. Because the banks had failed to develop checks as a payment mechanism, businessmen strongly supported the con-cept, which was promoted as "cashless." The banks, however, vehemently opposed the bill, and it was rejected by the Social Democratic government on grounds that the state should not incur expenses to help business. Two years later, though, after the new right-wing government repackaged the ser-vice as a means of rationalizing state payments and of tightening audit con-trol of public funds to reduce the rising volume of forgeries, it was passed. To win acceptance of the new system, it was launched with the most intensive advertising and PR campaign in the nation's history and to a large extent was based on sensationalism and fear. "Use Postal Giro to Prevent Embezzling," said ads, referring to news accounts of such crimes by civil servants and union officials.[38] Indeed, by 1930 the giro had 1,000 municipal accounts, thanks to state auditors' having mandated them. For the Swedish Postal Giro, crime *did* pay.

There were also a couple of surprises. Early in the first year, officials learned that the "cashless" system led to increased, not decreased, streams of cash at post office counters because so long as there was a small number of accounts, direct transfers were limited. People who formerly had stood in line at utility offices to pay bills now stood in line at post offices. As one wag observed, with their money and queues, the post offices began to look like banks. When the banks found they could save time and money by using the giro instead of insured service to send excess cash to the Riksbank, they started dumping it all in the post offices, where clerks were swamped by the task of counting and sorting notes. In retaliation, the postal workers started sending that cash, plus their own excess notes, to the banks to buy bank money orders for sending it all to the Post Office account in the Riksbank. To end this exchange in which the notes were being fingered to pieces, the two sides worked out a compromise: both sent all their excess cash to the Riksbank, uncounted. Thus, from 1925 to 1930, Riksbank workers watched with mounting horror as the inflow of cash from post offices increased by 1,000 percent.

Meanwhile, a drama was unfolding within the postal service involving illegal loans and embezzlements, which officials at first tried to hush up. After deep probing, auditors made the startling discovery that the chief perpetrator was the head of the bank and giro—the man who had used the specter of crime to promote the giro. He resigned in 1933.

Politics, Growth, and More Politics

In 1932, Sweden's "golden years," which had begun in 1924, ended as abruptly as Ivar Kreuger's life when the country's most famous industrialist—and swindler—shot himself in Paris. The securities on which much of the good times had been based proved less substantial than the matchsticks on which his fraudulent "empire" supposedly had been built. He left behind losses that forced the nation's second-largest bank deeply into debt and so many shattered dreams that, coming as it did after a series of crises, the event tarnished the concept of capitalism itself. In response to the crash, Parliament repealed the banks' right to own or acquire stock, although they were permitted to continue their trading in securities.

While nothing had come of an earlier proposal to nationalize the banks, in the wave of radicalism that swept over Sweden after World War II, the left wing of the Social Democratic party (SDP) renewed the demand. As a compromise, a state-owned commercial bank named Kreditbank was formed in 1951. Although it was not supposed to have any special privileges, most government accounts were transferred to it, so that its assets grew twice as fast as the other banks' in the next eight years. Then in 1970, as a counterproposal to renewed efforts for nationalization, the government passed a law giving the government the right to appoint one of more representatives to the commercial banks' boards of directors.

But when the SDP radicals again demanded a takeover of the banks a few years later, the more conservative party leaders effected a more spectacular compromise: they created in 1974 a state bank that was the largest bank in Scandinavia by merging the postal bank into Kreditbank. The official announcement said its purpose was to sharpen competition on equal terms, but many questioned the consistency of that goal with the bank's exclusive access to the widespread post office network. Fearing financial losses because postal savings for years had subsidized a large part of giro costs, the giro people referred to the break-up as a "painful wound."[39] In fact, the only favorable response to the proposal came from the dominant trade union. But as an observer later explained, "The criteria for choice of viewpoints against inevitability must be vague and arbitrary."[40]

Having heard that the SDP at its 1975 convention had proposed seating more public representatives on the banks' boards, the chairman of one of the largest banks stopped a top labor union leader who was emerging from the meeting hall to ask if it really was necessary to do that. The union executive stepped close to the banker, playfully grabbed the lapels of his suit coat, and whispered, "Why, if I'd been in the men's room at one point this morning and not in the hall, your bank would have been nationalized. You should be glad it's only a little change in your board."[41] Hence, in the following year Parliament extended public representation to regional bank boards and gave local community delegates the right to choose people for the banks' 850 local boards. While bankers interviewed said that the effect of the public board members has been mainly cosmetic, one placed his tongue in cheek and observed, "It may be good to have a few people from Parliament on the board; maybe we can teach them something about banking."

In discussing how the banks react to the recurring threat of nationalization, one banker who reads American novels jocularly confided, "It's a kind of rubber hose they periodically use to beat us into submission." Yet they not only survive but excel.

U.S. Banking Crisis

In the more free-wheeling climate of the United States, as state banking authorities competed with their federal counterparts in the first two decades of the century, the number of commercial banks grew from 12,427 to over 30,000.[42] By offering less restrictive conditions and greater operating freedom, the states chartered 76 percent of those new banks. Even labor unions got into banking in the 1920s, much as Swedish unions had done earlier. The Brotherhood of Locomotive Engineers formed a holding company to create a system of banks, as did the Amalgamated Clothing Workers of America, although only the latter endured for more than a short time.

But as is often true, a period with a sudden increase in competition often precedes a banking crisis marked by bank failures. Between 1921 and 1929, over 5,700 banks failed, with losses to depositors of $564.7 million.[43] In addition to the competitive pressures engendered by the vast number of new banks and by rising interest rates, an agricultural depression and the speculative boom also contributed to banks' problems. However, because state banks accounted for 85 percent of the failures between 1910 and 1925, nearly paralleling their record during the 1907 panic, national bankers attributed blame to the states' leniency in granting charters. An economist's evaluation of the societal effects in the United States of the decade's economic events is intriguing because it could as well have been written about the situation in Sweden: "The market performance of the 1920s accentuated the public mistrust and criticism of banking that have characterized its history in this country."[44]

In November 1930, 256 banks failed, and in the next month, 352, including the Bank of the United States, which, with over $200 million of deposits, was the largest bank failure in U.S. history until then. [45] Its collapse especially eroded public confidence because, due to its name, many thought the bank was associated with the government. Although Congress established the Reconstruction Finance Corporation (RFC) in 1932 to support the banks, the agency failed to stem the tide of failures, partly because the flow of funds fell short of the massive infusions needed and partly because banks feared applying for its loans, knowing that their names would be published. That could touch off a run by depositors because in effect it announced that the bank was in trouble. In Michigan, amid mounting unemployment and home mortgage delinquencies, the RFC appealed to Henry Ford for a last-minute rescue of two tottering banking companies. Although they had over 80 percent of the state's national bank resources, the automaker said, "Let the crash come," believing a shake-out was in order.[46] The banks did fail, and the state had to declare a four-week banking holiday.

Other financial institutions were collapsing too. Between the end of 1929 and the end of 1933, 526 S&Ls failed.[47] To provide aid to them and home owners with mortgages, the Federal Home Loan Bank Board was created to grant emergency loans to S&Ls. The mutual savings banks, however, escaped the ravages of the depression. But for the commercial banks, the early 1930s represented a virtual collapse of the banking system. The nationwide banking holiday for one week in March 1933, during which all commercial and Federal Reserve banks were closed, was unprecedented in the nation's history. By the end of 1933, the number of U.S. banks had been reduced by more than one-fourth, and the costs to stockholders, depositors, and other creditors of the over 9,000 banks that failed between 1930 and 1933 was some $2.5 billion.[48]

With the safety of the system exposed as a myth, Congress in 1932 responded to demands for reform by imposing far greater regulation on commercial banks than ever before. Within three years, it passed twenty bills amending the Federal Reserve Act, thereby providing a framework for regulation of the banking system that prevailed until 1980. The Banking Act of 1933 (Glass-Steagall) introduced new restrictions at the same time that it extended special protection to some parts of the financial industry. To reduce the instability of the system, it permitted a national bank to merge with another bank located outside its home city so that strong banks could absorb weak ones. Based on the belief that the practice of paying interest on demand deposits led banks to acquire risky investments to offset the costs of obtaining the funds, the act prohibited such payments. Because during the 1920s depositors' funds had been used to finance the operations of affiliated companies, the act forced banks to divest themselves of security trading affiliates. It also authorized the government to set interest rates on time deposits. Like the ban on paying interest on demand deposits, the measure was intended to protect the banks by restraining competition within the industry, but it later became an albatross around their necks when they needed to compete.

Of major significance was the creation of the FDIC to provide safety for depositors and liquidity in the payments mechanism. The initial bill gave only provisional coverage to nonmember state banks on condition that they join the Federal Reserve System within a given amount of time. But even though the grace period was extended three times, the state banks held out. So in the end, when the government realized it could not withdraw the coverage without causing public panic, a new lease on life was given to the dual banking system.

Into the Electronic Era . . . by Buggy

The regulatory environment in which the U.S. banking industry operated until 1980 was written in response to the banking panic of the 1930s. Subsequently those laws had been undermined by change. Multinational business developed; the urbanization process was completed; the industrial age gave way to the information age; and by the 1970s the transformation of banking from a paper-based commercial lending operation into an electronically driven retail business was accomplished in most developed nations.

The regulations of the 1930s were meant to limit the competitive powers of the financial institutions; they did, to the extent that unregulated money market funds were able to drain billions of dollars out of the depository institutions while the banks and thrifts stood by with their hands tied. The requirement of noninterest-bearing reserves for Federal Reserve membership was meant to facilitate monetary control, but as rising interest rates made the rule too burdensome, the attrition in membership swelled from a trickle to a flood, with the result that reserve funds plummeted to a fraction of what they had been. The specialization of the thrifts in long-term mortgages was based on the assumption that the savings deposits they held also were long-term; but when interest rates rose and disintermediation occurred, their viability was threatened by the imbalance between the cost of funds and the return on their low-interest mortgages.

Reluctant to deal with the conflicting demands of state versus national bankers, thrifts versus banks, money center versus small banks, and unit banks versus branching advocates, Congress procrastinated for years by appointing a series of commissions to study the banking system. But as the basic instability of the system was revealed through the liquidity problems suffered by the thrift institutions beginning in the late 1960s, Congress finally was forced to act. The result was the Depository Institutions Deregulation and Monetary Control Act of 1980 (DIDMCA). Hailed as the most significant banking legislation since the 1930s, the act changed many rules that had become obsolete. Yet although sweeping in nature, it was pothole legislation in that it addressed immediate problems while failing to chart a course for the future nature and structure of the financial services industry.

Having finally dealt with the prickly area of banking, Congress hoped that that would be it for another half-century. But there seems to be no end to problems. The complex web of rules and regulations governing the industry was predicated on the belief that they would promote stability, yet the costliest failures in the FDIC's history have occurred in the 1980s. With the United States lagging behind other nations in the development of electronic funds transfer systems (EFTS), the federal government has encouraged adoption of the technology; yet outdated laws reflecting territorial protectionism lead courts to rule that automated teller machines (ATMs) are bank branches, and some banks' efforts to share ATM networks have been blocked by federal regulators. The Federal Reserve System was meant to support banks; now it competes with them in clearing services. Interstate banking is illegal; yet banks make a mockery of the law by operating offices all over the country. Often the Comptroller of the Currency makes a ruling that is at odds with the Federal Reserve and/or a state, all of which in time are superseded by court decisions.

Buffeted by tremendous pressures from competing interest groups, Congress in 1984 delayed the enactment of legislation needed to deal with the industry's problems. But there is no holding back the economic and technological forces that continually change conditions for the industry. An assessment from a study of electronic banking coauthored by a law professor who has served as head of the Antitrust Division of the Department of Justice astutely summarizes the policy environment for modern banking as symbolized by EFTS in the United States:

> Rather than a coherent, planned, intelligent approach which one would expect in the late twentieth century, with the resources of the best-educated

populace in the history of this nation, the availability of generating information for decision making through never-before-available computer technology, and the experience of other nations who have led in the introduction and implementation of this new technology, we have made a hash of it.[49]

Notes

1. Carter Glass, *An Adventure in Constructive Finance* (New York: Arno, 1975), p. 60.
2. Patrick Frazer and Dimitri Vittas, *The Retail Banking Revolution* (London: Michael Lafferty Publications, 1982), pp. 288–289.
3. Murray L. Weidenbaum, "Regulatory Reform: A Report Card for the Reagan Administration," *California Management Review* 26, no. 1 (Fall 1983): 17.
4. The economic principle that "bad money drives out good," named for English financier Sir Thomas Gresham (1519?–1579).
5. A Mr. Bircherod, quoted by Eli F. Heckscher, *An Economic History*, trans. Göran Ohlin (Cambridge: Harvard University Press, 1954), p. 90.
6. Ibid., p. 75.
7. F.P. Thomson, *Money in the Computer Age* (Oxford: Pergamon Press, 1968), p. 47.
8. Kurt Samuelsson, *From Great Power to Welfare State* (London: George Allen & Unwin, 1968), p. 27.
9. Alexander Del Mar, *History of Monetary Systems* (London: Effinghams Wilson, Royal Exchange, 1895), p. 326.
10. Ingvar Andersson, *Introduction to Sweden* (Stockholm: Swedish Institute, 1949), p. 16.
11. Samuelsson, *From Great Power*, p. 13.
12. Joseph B. Board, *The Government and Politics of Sweden* (Boston: Houghton Mifflin, 1970), p. 14.
13. Bray Hammond, *Banks and Politics in America* (Princeton: Princeton University Press, 1957), p. 15.
14. Thomas Fleming, ed., *Benjamin Franklin, A Biography in His Own Words* (New York: Newsweek, 1972), 1:127.
15. Hammond, *Banks*, p. 162.
16. Ibid., p. 176.
17. Ibid., p. 236.
18. Ibid., p. 557.
19. Hjalmar Branting's comment cited by Kurt Samuelsson, *Postbanken—postsparbank och postgiro (1884–1925–1974)* (Stockholm: Postverkets tryckeri, 1978), p. 18.
20. Emil Sommarin, *Vårt sparbanksväsen. 1834–1892* (Lund: Gleerup, 1942), p. 36.
21. An unnamed journalist quoted by Sven Brisman, *Sveriges affärsbanker* (Stockholm: Svenska Bankföreningen, 1924–1934), 1:79.
22. Sommarin, *Vårt sparbanksväsen*, p. 167.
23. Brisman, *Sveriges affärsbanker*, 1:161.

24. Statistics from Sommarin, *Vårt sparbanksväsen,* pp. 147, 284.

25. Robert A. Hendrickson, *The Cashless Society* (New York: Dodd, Mead & Co., 1972), p. 223.

26. *Nicholas Bank Note Report* (1858).

27. Cited by Hammond, *Banks,* p. 493.

28. *Philadelphia Public Ledger,* January 18, 1842, cited by ibid., pp. 609–610.

29. Robert P. Sharkey, *Money, Class and Party* (Baltimore: Johns Hopkins, 1959), p. 224.

30. See, for example, Robert C. West, *Banking Reform and the Federal Reserve, 1863–1923* (Ithaca: Cornell University Press, 1977), pp. 29–30.

31. Sharkey, *Money,* p. 229.

32. Milton Friedman and Anna J. Schwartz, *A Monetary History of the United States, 1867–1960* (Princeton: Princeton University Press, 1963), p. 173. The system was discontinued in 1967.

33. This and the following quotation cited by Roger T. Johnson, *Historical Beginnings . . . The Federal Reserve* (Boston: Federal Reserve Bank of Boston, 1982), pp. 28–29.

34. Samuelsson, *Postbanken,* p. 38.

35. A savings banks' association official quoted by Emil Sommarin, *Vårt sparbanksväsen 1893–1945* (Lund: Gleerup, 1945), p. 63.

36. Lars-Erik Thunholm, *Svenskt kreditväsen,* 10th ed. (Stockholm: Rabén & Sjögren, 1969), p. 41.

37. Karl-Gustaf Hildebrand, *Banking in a Growing Economy,* trans. D. Harper (Stockholm: Svenska Handelsbanken, 1971), pp. 38, 58.

38. Karl Wilhelmsson, *Svenska postgirot 1925–1949* (Stockholm: Postverkets tryckeri, 1950), p. 41.

39. Gösta Hultin, "Re-organization of the Banking Activities of the Swedish Postal Administration," in *Union Postale,* no. 6 (1975): 111A.

40. Samuelsson, *Postbanken,* p. 119.

41. This and following quotes in section from interviews.

42. Almarin Phillips, "Competitive Policy for Depository Financial Institutions," in *Promoting Competition in Regulated Markets,* ed. Almarin Phillips (Washington, D.C.: Brookings Institution, 1975), p. 340.

43. FDIC data.

44. Phillips, "Competitive Policy," p. 343.

45. Friedman and Schwartz, *Monetary History,* p. 308.

46. Cited by Marquis James and Bessie R. James, *Biography of a Bank* (New York: Harper & Row, 1954), p. 364.

47. Phillips, "Competitive Policy," p. 348.

48. Friedman and Schwartz, *Monetary History,* pp. 167, 351.

49. William F. Baxter, Paul H. Cootner, and Kenneth E. Scott, *Retail Banking in the Electronic Age* (Montclair, N.J.: Allanheld, Osmun, 1977), p. 180.

2
The Makeup of Payment Systems

Because many individuals in addition to tax dodgers, members of the Mob, and those anticipating a visit by the tooth fairy have been worried about what will happen if all cash is displaced by electronic impulses, in this chapter such concerns will be alleviated by placing the various payment mechanisms into perspective culturally, economically, and technologically. The scope of inquiry will be broadened beyond the United States and Sweden to include information about the payment systems in other major European countries and Japan.

Although payment systems have not on the whole been planned in any nation but rather have evolved along with banking systems, in the United States the Federal Reserve System has strongly influenced the growth and direction of payment systems by establishing standards, providing facilities for expediting the movement of checks and funds, and creating a schedule of funds availability in the banking system. In fact, the Fed participates far more extensively in the clearing and funds transfer process than the central bank in any other country. In Sweden, for example, the Riksbank has not sought to exert any influence over the payment system, nor is the functioning of the payment system there governed by any kind of special legislation. To a great extent, the Fed's involvement has been necessitated by the size of the United States and the vast number of banks resulting from the dual chartering system and branching restrictions. But in general governments play a role in payment systems because of their historic role in providing cash as a means of payment.

Instruments of Payment

Basically there are only three instruments of payment: cash, consisting of notes and coins; paper transfer documents, including checks, giro forms, payment orders, and plastic card vouchers; and electronic funds transfers. Although plastic cards are sometimes referred to as a payment mechanism, they merely serve to identify the customer, authorize the transaction, and create a financial message, which then must be recorded and transmitted either on paper or electronically in order to access the buyer's assets. Hence, cards have actually represented a link between the paper-based and electronic systems.

Cash: Down But Not Out

The emergence of central banks was rooted in their early involvement with the issuing of notes, and today's central banks retain a monopoly on that profitable enterprise, which is made possible only by the willingness of citizens to hold cash without receiving interest on it. The banking system itself has evolved from the role of safekeeper of cash to the role of provider of payment services. While a study of payment systems in eleven developed countries revealed a decrease in the use of cash over the last thirty years, the cashless society predicted in the early 1960s has failed to materialize.[1] Cash is still used for 85 to 95 percent of the total volume of payments in most countries because it is ideally suited for small retail transactions; it remains the only totally hassle-free medium for buying.

The cash orientation of nations varies from those in which currency is used only for retail transactions to those in which wages and pensions are still doled out in notes and a new suitcase rather than a microprocessor represents an innovation in the transit of the wherewithal for buying a house or making a business deal. Nor do people in those countries carry around cash-stuffed valises only to dodge tax collectors or the police; often it is because their payment systems are underdeveloped. According to one study, Italy is the most cash oriented of the European countries.[2] Japan is as dependent on cash as Italy, albeit for different reasons. Although most Japanese salaries now are directly deposited, cash is needed because payment by check there is almost nonexistent. In England, 44 percent of the workers were still being paid in cash in 1981, although that marked an improvement over the 75 percent who were paid in currency in 1969.

Generally a much larger proportion of the money supply is held in the form of cash in European countries with giro systems than in Britain or the United States. Thus, since World War II, currency has comprised only about one-fourth of the total money supply in the United States, compared to about half in Sweden, with the remainder made up of demand deposits.[3] Surprisingly, although the population of Sweden has not grown and its businesses and government units have virtually ceased making payments in cash, the volume of currency in circulation grew at a faster rate between 1977 and 1981 than it did between 1968 and 1978.[4]

In the United States, by contrast, currency as a percentage of gross national product (GNP) declined from 7.8 percent in the early 1950s to 4.8 percent in 1976.[5] Nevertheless, because the average American makes over 1,000 cash transactions annually, the provision of cash is an important banking service. Since World War II, the growth of coin-operated vending machines has contributed to a marked increase in the volume of coins outstanding, while a combination of inflation and the burgeoning underground economy—estimated to be somewhere between 10 and 33 percent of GNP—has produced a sharp increase in the use of larger denomination notes. Even after discounting the inflation factor, in constant dollars the demand for $100 bills grew by 73 percent from 1970 to 1978 while the demand for small denomination notes ($1, $2, $5, and $10) declined 39 percent.[6] Moreover, as an indication of the use of cash for purposes of tax evasion, illicit operations, and a desire for financial secrecy, the proportion of $100 bills returned to those issued in 1978 was only 22 percent, compared to 86 percent in 1960, while the corresponding figure for small denomination notes declined only from 98 percent to 87 percent.

A study in the 1970s suggested that about 20 percent of all cash in the possession of individuals does not enter normal banking channels; another 15 percent is lost or inactive. Thus, only two-thirds of the money issued is actually circulating.[7] Moreover, Federal Reserve data indicate that about 42 percent of the notes returned are unfit. This brings up the point that while cash may be cheap, anonymous, and efficient, it does have costs of its own. The storing, counting, guarding, and transporting of cash is estimated to cost approximately 2 to 7 percent of its value, with the total Federal Reserve costs for coins and currency in 1978 recorded at $182.5 million.[8] In addition, in 1972 the Federal Reserve let out contracts to three companies to develop a machine that would automatically verify the count accuracy of currency deposits, check each note for authenticity, denomination, and fitness, restrap notes in multiples of one hundred, and destroy unfit notes by shredding. After six years, two viable high-speed currency systems were produced at a development cost of approximately $4.9 million.[9] But note issue does constitute interest-free lending to the government and is especially lucrative when one has a monopoly. Although there are no available data on the costs borne by banks in handling currency, there is the cost of holding stocks of a nonearning asset. But for society as a whole, the greatest cost in using cash is that stemming from crime.

Violent crime was virtually unknown in Sweden until the mid-1960s; between 1950 and 1963, there were only 7 bank robberies.[10] Between 1971 and 1978 the number of robberies doubled. In 1978, there were 3,000 robberies, of which about 0.05 percent were of post offices and banks. But employees of those institutions became alarmed when the number of post office and bank robberies went up 85 percent between 1970 and 1972, and joint efforts were launched by bank and government officials, unions, and police to thwart the attacks. Anxiety intensified in 1973 after four employees of the state-owned commercial bank were abducted during an armed robbery and held hostage for six days; that led to the formation of a state crime commission. But while steps were being taken to prevent the robberies, the thieves adopted a new modus operandi: after finding it too tedious and time-consuming to fish out the contents of night depository boxes on the walls of banks, they turned to that famous Swedish invention, dynamite, and started blowing up the boxes, wall and all. In 1977, of 147 depository boxes robbed, 121 were blown up. After the banks started using color dye pillows in the boxes to splatter the money indelibly if the containers were opened improperly, the incidence of the crimes declined for a while but then went up again.

The director of the bank inspectorate reported in 1978 that direct losses from robberies in recent years had been about $2.2 million annually but that indirect costs for security measures were more than five times higher.[11] The discrepancy between actual theft and the cost of allaying fear quantified to some extent the psychological effects of this shattering change, in what had hitherto been a safe and secure society, on attitudes toward the object of all that crime and violence: cash.

Many years earlier, however, a desire to reduce the volume of cash in use had been manifest in the creation of the Postal Giro. Indeed, the first specific government expression of its commitment to the value of the "cashless" concept appeared in the 1924 edict creating the giro, in which it stated that its purpose would be to "promote such payment methods which are intended to reduce the use of cash."[12] The Swedish government has had two basic reasons for encouraging the move away from cash: first, in its role as a generator of large volumes of payments to cover the womb-to-tomb care provided by the social welfare state, it seeks efficiency, and, second, in its role as arbiter of the social costs and benefits of the nation's payment system, it seeks to eliminate vulnerability to crime.

Checks in the United States: The Paper Blizzard

Because banks have dotted the landscape for so long and banking today is accepted as a basic part of everyday life in the United States, it is easy to forget that only in the past twenty-five years or so have most U.S. households had banking relationships. Although paychecks had been commonly used since the mid-1950s, they were more often cashed then in grocery stores, drugstores, and bars than in banks. To this day, supermarkets cash about the same number of checks as do banks. One large chain has found that about 37.5 percent of the value of the checks it takes in are for cash in excess of the purchase.[13] Moreover, in spite of a process that customers find just a shade less intrusive than the Spanish Inquisition, bad checks cost the grocers on average 0.05 percent of gross sales, which can equal 5 to 10 percent of a store's profit.[14] As a result of intensive marketing efforts by the commercial banks to expand beyond their traditional business market into the consumer area, the proportion of households with checking accounts grew from less than half in the late 1960s to over 80 percent in one decade.[15]

Small wonder. The banks' strategy for attracting this substantial new customer base was elementary: there was no charge. One would be hard pressed to find anywhere in the annals of business history another example of an industry that had a monopoly on its only unique product, one that could be used to advantage by most every household in the country, and that then gave it away for half a century. The banks hoped that customers would maintain other accounts with them that would be profitable, and they implicitly offset some of the costs by not paying interest on checking accounts and by paying below-market rates on savings accounts. But Americans, knowing a good thing when they saw it, went off on a check-writing binge, using checks for over 90 percent of their cashless transactions. They wrote on average twenty checks a month, 40 percent of which were for less than $25, so that volume during the 1970s rose 7 percent a year.[16] The flood of paper reached 65 million checks daily by 1981 as Americans busily wrote about half the checks in the world and was racing along toward tidal wave dimensions when its momentum was checked by a basic economic fact of life: checks ceased being free—to the banks.

Until then, the Federal Reserve had processed checks free of charge, except for the implicit price of the banks' having to maintain interest-free reserves with the Federal Reserve Banks. The end to the government's subsidization of checking services—and probably the end of the heyday of checks in the United States—was spelled out by the Depository Institutions Deregulation and Monetary Control Act of 1980, which required the Fed to charge banks explicitly for its services. Although technological developments have kept costs down—and the growth of productivity in check handling has exceeded that of U.S. productivity growth as a whole—the total cost of writing and processing checks has been estimated at 1 percent of GNP.[17] With each check on average transferred ten times, the full cost of processing a check is somewhere between 40¢ and 90¢, with the range reflecting the lack of relevant data, differing assumptions as to allocation of overhead costs, and the vast difference in operating efficiencies of various banks.[18] The logistics involved, moreover, in moving funds between two of the more than 115 million accounts in some 15,000 commercial banks, excluding accounts in the 29,000 thrift institutions and credit unions, requires an extensive infrastructure, which is part private and part public.[19] Before the Fed was created, check clearing and settlement were done entirely by the private sector. Although check clearing is not a traditional activity of central banks, the Fed became involved due to dissatisfaction with certain practices and because it alone has a national structure and authority to ensure the uniformity and standardization needed for the clearing process to function smoothly. Hence, the Fed employs 5,000 people to handle checks and operates a transportation network that includes the "Fed Airline," which every night ferries checks to its forty-eight processing centers around the country.

The complexity of the system, along with the fact that some 1 percent of the 100 million checks deposited daily bounce, has led banks to deny customers the use of funds from checks deposited for periods of from several days to weeks.[20] With a more sophisticated populace aware that financial insitutions earn interest on the float—the time between when the check is deposited, is collected, and is credited to the depositor's account—federal and state legislators held hearings in early 1984 into the practices. After testimony revealed that banks were delaying crediting even Social Security, welfare, tax refund, and other checks written on the U.S. Treasury, some states took action to prescribe limits on the delays. Even those maximums would shock Europeans: two days for checks drawn on banks in the same city, four days for those from cities in the same state, and six for out-of-state paper, with overnight crediting mandated for government checks and those for less than $100.

The 1 million a day bad checks constitute a tip-of-an-iceberg-type problem, which has defied technological solution. In part, the problem is inherent in the check itself, which literally is a backward payment mechanism. The check is a debit transfer, meaning that the recipient must take it to his bank, which usually does not credit the depositor's account immediately unless it is drawn on the same bank. Instead, a hold is placed on the funds while the check enters the collection process, which routes it back to its originator's bank. There the amount for which it is written is deducted from his account (that is, it is debited)—assuming there are sufficient funds in the account. If not, it becomes what is called a return item and enters into a labyrinth of costly and labor-intensive steps in which it flows back through the clearing system with manual inspection of each endorsement to reverse all previous provisional credits. In 1978 the cost per returned item was 5.5¢, compared to 0.9¢ for a good check.[21]

The bad check problem is rooted in the failure of U.S. banks to develop an effective national check guarantee system, even though the country's payment system depends more heavily on checks as a means of transferring deposits than any other in the world. The humiliating complexities involved in trying to cash a check in most cities suggest that the future of the check for shopping transactions is cloudy at best. Although Swedish bankers faced the same problem a decade ago, they did solve it, as have continental European bankers. In the words of two researchers, "It is ironic, but perhaps not surprising, that banks in traditionally giro-based countries have perfected the cheque as a retail banking instrument, whilst the banks from traditionally cheque-based countries have presided over its relative decline."[22]

Checks in Other Countries

Consumers in Australia, Canada, France, and the United Kingdom also make the bulk of their cashless payments by check. Perhaps because the British have been using checks since 1659, the six London clearing banks have developed a system so efficient that large checks are cleared in one day and others in two days. However, although the banks there started issuing check guarantee cards in 1966, they, like their U.S. counterparts, have been plagued by fraud losses, which have been increasing at about 50 percent a year. The use of checks by Australians and Canadians on a per capita basis is second only to that of Americans and, like their neighbors to the south, the Canadians lack a good guarantee program. But while the Australian central bank participates in the clearing system, the Canadian one does not. After one hundred years of being operated by the Canadian Bankers Association, the system now is run by a group comprised of representatives of all types of depository institutions. In spite of the size of the country, through the use of ten regional clearing centers, their system permits customers' accounts to be credited with cleared funds on the very day checks are deposited.

With their penchant for adding a soupçon of drama to the mundane, the French for years evoked envy in the hearts of bankers from other check-oriented countries because they really put the screws into people who passed bad checks. There, instead of using credit bureaus and ad hoc procedures as U.S. banks do, all bank branches make an on-line or overnight inquiry to the central bank when a customer wants a checkbook. Hence, by maintaining a file of people who wrote bad checks, they could deny them access to a checking account for a year. Additionally, transgressors were subject to publicity and penalties ranging from a fine of 6 percent of the amount of the check to five years' imprisonment and a fine of about $8,000 for willful fraud. But in a show of Gallic insouciance toward the authorities, the list grew to over a million (the population is under 54 million), whereupon the government passed a new law that banks must warrant checks for amounts up to about $22. From 1971 to 1981 the volume of checks written in France more than quadrupled as a result of intensive bank marketing campaigns, retailer acceptance due to the laws cited, and an old law that obliges employers to pay wages above a certain amount by check or transfer to a checking account. When that amount was generally exceeded with public acceptance in the 1970s of a program that encouraged monthly wage payments, it resulted in over 90 percent of adults having a checking account.

Ironically, although checks are not a major payment mechanism there, German bankers in 1968 invented Eurocheques, which have become a major means of payment on the Continent. The system enables over 41 million Europeans to get cash and make purchases in twenty countries by using a standard check, made out in local currency, together with a card that guarantees payment by their bank. In 1971 the guarantee was extended to retailers, hotels, and restaurants, which now total some 4.5 million.[23] By restricting the number of Eurocheques issued to each card holder, the issuing banks can simultaneously control credit and fraud risks, with the result that Europeans regard the checks as the safest means of payment. Cooperatively owned by the banks, the system is completely integrated into the banking system so that it requires no central administrative office, and its operations are directed by delegates from the member countries. Since 1974 banks in fifteen countries have replaced their bank guarantee programs with uniform Eurocheques and cards, and in the Netherlands, for example, they represented 58 percent of all checks used in 1981.[24]

Checks are heavily used in Denmark, with the average householder writing twelve to sixteen a month, and are so widely accepted that they can even be used for taxi fares.[25] The heavy usage can be attributed to the guarantee extended by the banks, which is the equivalent of $50. Losses under the program have been described as modest, due in part to the use of an identification card, aided and abetted, most likely, by the fact that it is a very small country. There, as in most European countries, checks are not returned, and 95 percent are truncated at the branch where cashed; that is, they are filed there and not sent back to the bank office on which drawn.

Belgium is often referred to as having the most advanced system of check truncation. But since it applies only to checks below $700, it is not as comprehensive as the Swedish system. However, the high degree of cooperation that characterized the development of the system and the idea of competing in terms of quality of service while sharing use of the technological infrastructure are the same as the Swedish approach. It began in 1970 when the commercial banks, private savings banks, public credit institutions, and postal giro, at the urging of the central bank, started working on a coordinated plan. In a period of a year and a half, they changed all the numbers of their accounts in order to create a uniform structure. Then they standardized the giro documents and checks and adopted the Eurocheque norm. Thus, since 1974, both commercial and savings banks' customers have had only one checkbook to use at home and abroad. Belgium decided to truncate because the large financial institutions no longer were checking signatures on giro forms and small amount checks anyway, and aside from the signature, the other data are numerical. They have found it less expensive to run the small risk of challenge than transport checks and set the threshold for the sake of limiting risk.

Sweden's Late Adoption of Checking Accounts

The check has survived for over 300 years because it has intrinsic merits as a payment mechanism: it can be used to send payments through the mail and to pay people who have no bank accounts; no information about the payee is needed; payment can be stopped; and although writing a check takes longer than paying by cash, it eliminates the risk of carrying around large amounts of cash. Hence, the failure of checks to achieve wider acceptance in

Sweden for so many years provoked considerable attention. In a Swedish bankers' journal in 1944, the situation was described as remarkable because Swedish bankers imposed no fees on checking accounts but instead paid interest on them, advantages not offered in countries where checks were popular.[26] Thus, the writer argued, the reason had to be the fact that because so many bad ones were passed, checks were not accepted in payment; indeed, even the banks were reluctant to cash checks drawn on other bank offices. The problem was laid in the lap of the banks themselves, which, according to the author, failed to screen people properly when opening accounts and were reluctant to prosecute for check fraud in spite of a 1932 law that prescribed stiff penalties as a deterrent. Names were not printed on checks, nor was there any standard form of identification in cashing them. Moreover, because the banks did not return checks, letters of remittance sent with payments had to be followed by letters of acknowledgment, and because of the loose procedures in their use, checks had to be sent by registered mail, which was expensive. The writer also cited giro service as a reason for checks' not being popular.

While the giro certainly was a formidable competitor then, some twenty years after its founding, it had been the failure of the banks to fill the gap in the payment system by providing a safe, simple cashless way of carrying out transactions that had sparked the efforts to create the Postal Giro. Earlier studies had shown that while in England and the United States bank deposits consisted of 80 to 90 percent checks, in Sweden checks made up only 27 percent while money orders (issued by banks and the post office) comprised 36 percent and currency, 37 percent.[27] But by 1945, the picture had changed significantly. By then, checks accounted for only 12.2 percent of the number of cashless payments—but 52.7 percent of the value—while bank money orders had declined to 1.7 percent; postal money orders comprised 10.4 percent and bank transfers, 0.6 percent; but giro payments made up 75.1 percent.[28]

The writer's analysis also failed to include a major reason stated earlier: very few individuals then had bank accounts. Until the 1960s, Swedish factories, businesses, and even banks paid wages weekly in cash, from the managing director on down. Most people did not have much disposable income; they got it, they spent it, and then they got some more. What little was left over was put aside into a savings bank for the proverbial rainy day. They did not need checks. This simple cycle was transformed by both economic and technological changes, including the spread of prosperity, the incursion of commercial banks into retail banking, and the advent of electronic data processing (EDP), all of which were linked. The relatively early entry of the Swedish commercial banks into the retail market strongly supports the theory that the most important force for change in banking has been the rise in the standard of living in industrial countries, since Sweden experienced a growth rate in the last hundred years that was second only to Japan's.[29]

The commercial banks' sudden interest in the household sector was prompted by a triad of forces: between 1954 and 1956, as their lending commitments continued to grow, the government tightened its credit policy at the same time the previously profuse business savings showed a tendency to decline. Fortuitously, during that decade the rising standard of living in the country had made the households rich sources of deposit funds for the first time. As they sought a strategy to tap the sizable and stable source of revenue in the personal market, the bankers considered salary accounts. Although the concept had the potential to be a powerful catalyst for change, the idea was not new.

Salary Accounts and Widespread Checking

Thirty years earlier the Postal Giro had only half-seriously suggested the accounts for state employees; but during World War II, it handled direct deposits of military salaries. Then in 1955, postal management rejected a government proposal to use the giro for paying state workers' salaries because they feared that the system could not handle the 83 percent increase in accounts it meant. But where the Post Office saw problems, the commercial banks saw the key to the workers where the savings banks had a stronghold. Because of the populace's strong cash orientation, the banks began their campaign by promoting to larger companies that employed white-collar workers and to city governments the administrative advantages of paying by check. To encourage acceptance of checks by employees and retailers in those early days, some municipalities paid their employees at first with commercial checks guaranteed by the cities. After the checks themselves were accepted, the banks proposed taking over the whole job of preparing paychecks for their employer customers and opening accounts into which the employees' salaries could be deposited. The first recorded use of salary checking accounts in Sweden was by a company that tested the concept in 1956 with its salaried staff and later expanded it to all employees.

The task of enrolling millions of workers in salary accounts was not as difficult as it might appear because of the Swedes' propensity for joining organizations. Not only are the workers tightly organized in their labor unions, but employers also have their own associations. Hence, the banks' strategy focused on lining up support from both those groups. Since they already had companies as customers, strong impetus for the change from cash to checks came from the employers' groups, which promoted to their members the reduction in payroll processing costs and lower security risks provided by the accounts. The leaders of the employers' associations, moreover, worked closely with the union leaders in presenting the new pay plans to employees, who had the concept presented to them virtually as a fait accompli. Nevertheless, to overcome workers' resistance to the newfangled idea, the banks dressed up the special accounts by providing unlimited check-writing privileges, charging no fees, and, beginning in 1961, paying interest on them.

This invasion of their turf did not go unnoticed by the savings banks. In 1958 they investigated the accounts to see if they were profitable; although not convinced that they were, the thrift institutions decided to offer them anyway. Just as the commercial banks viewed the accounts as a way to penetrate the consumer market to which they previously had no access, the savings banks perceived them as a way to get their foot in the door of corporate business. They had an advantage, moreover, in that since blue-collar workers constituted their largest group of customers, some of the trade unions had savings clubs in their banks, with accounts that could be converted to salary accounts. Another advantage savings banks had was that since they financed housing, many consumers wanted an account relationship with them that could provide access to a home loan. Hence, when the accounts were first introduced, there was a problem because although many workers preferred the savings banks, the companies wanted the accounts in their commercial banks to facilitate payments. The two banking groups later resolved the matter by agreeing that the companies would be able to choose the bank for the workers' accounts, but the employees would have the right to transfer their funds to another bank if they so desired. Hence, according to bankers interviewed, about 25 percent of salary accounts today are what they call passthroughs.

In 1960 a newspaper reported that 500 companies had introduced the accounts, and the unions were promoting what they accurately called "bookkeeping" payments.[30] Then a state commission investigating measures to stimulate saving reported that not only did salary accounts promote saving, but there also was no cheaper way to pay salaries. Since its studies suggested that by using them, administrative costs would be only about 10 percent as high as with cash payments, the commission proposed that the state adopt the system for its workers. The commercial banks responded by informing the Minister of Finance that they were prepared to make their system available through the state-owned commercial bank, Kreditbank. Whereas until then the postal officials had been viewing these events phlegmatically from the sidelines, now they were galvanized into action. Thus, within a short time, the Postal Giro announced its own salary accounts.

Growth and Growing Pains with Checks

By 1961 stories about bad checks being passed in banks, restaurants, and businesses were appearing in the press. To encourage use of the payment mechanism, the banks had agreed to cash each others' checks up to about $200 and to honor, under certain conditions, those checks retailers accepted that lacked cover or were forged. Because so many checks were being presented, tellers stopped calling to verify their validity, and abuses went penalty-free because the agreements made prosecution almost impossible.

Whereas in 1956 there had been only some 170,000 checking accounts in Sweden, by 1963 there were 714,000, of which 87 percent were salary accounts.[31] The first computers arrived just in the nick of time as the growth in the number of accounts led to an explosive rise in transaction volume: in ten years, the number of checking account transactions went up nearly 400 percent. This phenomenal growth of the payment mechanism and the attendant publicity attracted the attention of Parliament, which in 1964 requested state auditors to study the account systems. They reported that the accounts were highly efficient and promoted saving. However, the concomitant rise in fraudulent use of checks prompted a recommendation that a separate inquiry be made. That commission in turn proposed intensified education of the public about proper use of checks.

While the government was studying the unanticipated societal impacts of direct deposit of pay, the commercial banks also were examining them, but from an economic perspective. They had known when they started offering the accounts that there would be some losses in the form of overdrafts on customers' checking accounts. But with experience they found that they had badly underestimated not only those but, "above all, losses through unauthorized withdrawals from others' accounts." [32] While a 1962 analysis had projected losses at roughly 22 cents per account annually, by 1965 the actual losses from check abuse were running about three times that for each of the 717,000 accounts, or about $473,000. Three years later, a bank journalist observed: "We have in our country a checking system internationally viewed as unusually liberal, which was meant to be as convenient and generally useful as possible."[33] The government, however, was concerned and ordered another investigation. Meanwhile, determined to overcome what was perceived as foreign criticism of their earlier failure to achieve widespread use of checks, the banks kept signing up firms for salary accounts.

But when check frauds soared to a new high in 1970, the police took the initiative. In meetings with banking officials, they demanded strict control measures and an end to the retailers' agreement. When the banks acceded in the following year and told the merchants that forged checks would no longer be honored, they responded with a boycott. Thus, in 1972, while about 1.1 million wage earners had checking accounts, they could not use checks in stores or restaurants. The boycott ended in early 1973 after the banks provided identification cards and personalized checks to customers, guaranteed checks to a maximum of about $100, and imposed a fee on small checks. The last move was intended to reduce the number of checks presented so that cashiers could do a more thorough job of verifying each check. It produced results immediately. Where before, checks under about $10 represented 40 percent of total check volume, afterward they made up only 3 percent.[34] By

October 1974 about 7 percent of store purchases were by check, and for the year, check frauds were only one-eighth as numerous as in 1970.[35]

By 1978 the banks found they had bitten off more than they could chew: the volume of transactions had increased to the point where processing costs were becoming prohibitive. They proposed raising the fee on small checks and imposing a limit on the number of checks written each month. The unions, however, were instrumental in blocking the latter on grounds that while the banks had only a few years earlier talked the workers into using checks, now they wanted them to stop using them so much. But since the bankers were able to authenticate the cost problems in the indiscriminate use of checks for small payments, they succeeded in raising the fee on those. They also negotiated an agreement with retailers to limit the value of checks they cashed to a certain amount above the purchase price to discourage people from using stores as banks for cashing checks. To contain the costs of check processing itself, the banks developed a truncation system.

The success of direct deposit of pay in spreading the banking habit is attested to by the fact that by 1982 nearly 91 percent of the working population of Sweden had a salary account, and for a population of 8.3 million, there were an estimated 6 million checking accounts.

Payment Orders

Before there were checks, when people could not use cash or a giro for payments, they relied on payment orders. These include postal and bank money orders and checks that can be purchased from banks, such as travelers' checks and guaranteed or certified checks, with the latter used primarily when a customer has to pay a large amount to a creditor who demands a guaranteed payment. For years in Sweden, postal money orders were the most popular means of cashless funds transfer and were used by the state even for tax collection. In 1924, when cost-free postal money orders could be used in some 820 locations, 19 million were purchased.[36] But after the founding of the giro, money orders were made more expensive to encourage their displacement by the new mechanism.

They not only refused to go away, however, but also became big loss producers for the Post Office, which was reluctant to raise the fees for them because of competition from the banks. A 1945 study of payment mechanisms showed that they still accounted for 10.4 percent of payments by volume although only 0.9 percent by value, reflecting their use primarily for smaller amounts.[37] In fact, the instrument seems indestructible. In 1978, there were approximately as many payments made with them as with credit cards, and in 1980–1981, money order transactions constituted 5.5 percent of all such post office counter business, considerably exceeding check transactions.[38] Private purchases, however, accounted for only 14.7 percent of them;

it was the state that used most of them for pension, family allowance, and social insurance payments. Since then, the government has been converting those payments to direct deposits into recipients' accounts.

Although the money order may seem something of an anachronism in today's world, it continues to play a role as a payment mechanism in other countries as well, especially for people without bank accounts in such check-oriented nations as Canada, the United States, England, and Australia. Because money orders are prepaid, they are instantly negotiable, an advantage in countries without effective check guarantee systems. In the United States, moreover, they are of value not only to the estimated 15 percent of households that lack checking accounts but also to those with them who need to have payments credited without waiting for checks to clear. This is of special importance in getting payments to a distant area of the country where the inefficiencies of the postal system, which cannot be avoided, compound those of the banking system, which can be, albeit at the cost of standing in line at a post office. Because the volume of payments in the United States is so enormous, the percentage of money orders used is minuscule, but in Australia, the 1 percent they comprise represents 11 million payments. In England, where 40 percent of the populace have no bank account, the 89 million postal orders in 1981 made up 2.7 percent of total payments.[39] That relatively large British volume can be attributed in part to the use of postal orders for millions of football pool payments each week.

Due to the restrictions on interstate branching and the lack of a national check guarantee system, Americans use more travelers' checks per capita than people in any other country. For reasons that are less clear, the market for the instruments has been increasing in Europe, even though Eurocheque enables travelers there to write guaranteed checks in the currency of the country they are in. Although a number of companies now issue travelers' checks, American Express is the oldest and largest company in the business. It began selling money orders over a century ago and introduced its travelers' checks in 1891. Still innovating, the firm in 1976 began dispensing its checks through automated machines located primarily at U.S. airports, hotels, and American Express offices. The machines are activated by the American Express card, with the charge made against the cardholder's bank checking account through a separate agreement. Although the checks are easily negotiable in Europe and are supposed to be as good as cash, in a manifestation of the sort of pettiness that sets the teeth of consumers to grinding, some U.S. banks refuse to cash travelers' checks other than the brand that they sell. Cashier's checks are also supposed to be readily negotiable, yet some U.S. banks now put a five-day hold on them even when drawn on a bank just two blocks away.

Convenience of Giro

Even older than payment orders are giro systems. While historians have found evidence of the ancient Egyptians and Greeks making payments through their grain banks by transferring credit from one account to another without using money, the first European giro banks appeared in the thirteenth century, and the Amsterdam city giro was founded in about 1609. The word *giro* comes from the Greek, meaning a ring or circle, representing the circulating of claims to and from a center. Basically it is a bookkeeping system whose purpose is to transfer payments between individual accounts without a physical transfer of funds. A giro payment is more like a money order than a check in that the availability of funds on receipt is assured by the fact that it is a credit rather than debit transfer.

In Europe it often is referred to as "the poor man's bank" because payment also can be initiated by mailing or delivering a payment to a bank or post office for transfer if one does not have a giro or bank account. Although the giro is usually thought of as the most distinctive feature of Western European payment systems, Japan also has had a postal giro-type payment system since 1906. Originally introduced there to accommodate mail order businesses, now it is used primarily for making monthly installment payments and for remittances to distant locations. But while it does not constitute a major element in Japan's payment system, the Dutch postal giro for many years served as that nation's primary payment system, and the Netherlands, Austria, Germany, Sweden, and Switzerland are still regarded as giro countries.

Today's giro systems are based on a service developed by the postal savings bank in Austria in 1883 as a promotional gimmick. The bank had been opened the year before for the same social reasons that led to the founding of postal banks in other countries in that era. The response from the public was so underwhelming that its managers feared that the imbalance between the small size of its deposits and the large size of its administrative costs spelled imminent doom for both the institution and their positions. Convinced that the only way to draw in significantly more funds was by attracting merchants and businessmen, they decided to offer free interest-bearing checking accounts if a customer would maintain a certain minimum balance in his savings account—a nineteenth-century version of the NOW account. Since bank checking accounts were not widely used then on the Continent, it was an enterprising venture.

In the following year, giroing became possible when the bank gave customers the right to write on the back of checks that the amount should be credited to another account. Through that device and the granting of free postage for mailing payment orders to the bank, the groundwork was laid for the basic procedures still followed today. The innovation was a big hit; within one year, the bank's deposits were more than seven times larger, with almost three-fourths of the total made up of the new giro accounts. When word of the success spread, it was not long before other countries adopted giro systems: Hungary in 1890 and Switzerland in 1906, followed by Germany, Belgium, the Netherlands, France, and Denmark.

By 1911 the head of the Swedish Post Office was sufficiently curious about the giro systems to dispatch a postal official to France and Belgium to investigate them. After a report to Stockholm's Chamber of Commerce on his return, banking officials immediately expressed their opposition to the idea of a giro for Sweden while representatives of business and industry were more favorably impressed. That pretty much set the tone for what ensued over the next fourteen years, as various studies and proposals were made in the usual Swedish style of in-depth research and seemingly endless venting of opinions before adopting a new idea.

With unemployment high and government income down due to the depression, many questioned the wisdom of creating a new agency that could produce losses, even though its advocates projected a 14 percent rate of return from its annual activities. Opponents fretted about creating a "large bureaucracy," although the Post Office planned to hire only twenty-five new people. The bankers were horrified by the idea of the giro's paying interest and snobbishly pointed out the difficulties inherent in training postal employees to calculate the amounts. It was, moreover, not needed, according to those champions of oligopoly, since people had cost-free postal money orders as well as bank money orders. In view of the massive crime wave triggered by the bankers' failure thirty-five years later to develop safeguards before inundating the country with checks, it is ironic that they caustically derided the security procedures proposed for the giro out-payments and warned that the system could lead to disorder through misunderstanding. But in the end, the proponents prevailed.

In countries with giro systems, a standardized invoice form containing the account number of the creditor is sent to the debtor, who indicates on the form how the funds are to be transferred—either from account to account or by a cash or check in-payment—and then delivers or mails it postage-free to the giro where the transfer is made. In the early days of the service many payments were made with cash, but as more accounts were opened, true giroing began with simple bookkeeping transfers made with no cash involved. The advantages to giro payments include the fact that where with a check each payment has to be addressed, with a giro a number suffices. Giro payments eliminate the need for dating and signing, writing cover letters, providing envelopes, paying postage, and balancing a checkbook. For the recipient, there is no need to take care of remittances arriving in the mail; they do not have to be endorsed and sent to the bank; and there is never any worry about insufficient cover for the amount. Finally, not only are there post offices all over, but they are open longer hours than banks, and on Saturday too. In addition to its basic in- and out-payments and credit transfers domestically, transfers can be made between Swedish Postal Giro accounts and those in not only European nations but even Japan and Algeria.

For the transfer of funds between checking accounts, the Swedish commercial banks in 1950 initiated a decentralized bank giro service, which at the time was mainly directed to businesses. Then at the end of the decade, the cooperative and savings banks joined the commercial banks in forming a consortium called Bank Giro, which reorganized the system, standardized all documents, and centralized procedures to create an integrated system for transferring funds from one bank account to another.

Those Proliferating Pieces of Plastic

While giroing is unexcelled for paying bills, it is not suited for shopping, and there plastic cards have found a niche in payment systems. Although the cards have been called "plastic money," most of them only identify a person and an account which is accessed after the card is used to emboss a paper sales slip or provide data that generate an electronic funds transfer. When the card is used in connection with the purchase of goods or services or a withdrawal of cash from a machine, a debit is made to the cardholder's account. Similarly, when merchandise is returned or a deposit is made to an account, the card assists in creating a credit transaction. This is true whether it is called a debit or credit, check guarantee, retailer, bank, or T&E (travel and entertainment) card. The only cards whose function differs from this general definition are the stored value cards, which are tantamount to electronic cash because, like currency, they directly pay for goods and services. For that reason, each card is limited to a debit function, with its balance constantly being reduced by use.

The most widely used card, the credit card, is a hybrid payment instrument in that it uses credit as an intermediate step to final payment and also serves as a substitute for cash and checks at the retail level by aggregating payment transactions into monthly payments by consumers and daily or weekly payments to merchants. In 1978, it was estimated that the use of bank credit cards produced a net saving in payments equivalent to 3 percent of check volume in the United States.[40] Not only do Americans hold 80 percent of the world's credit cards, but their use as a proportion of cashless payments is significantly higher. The per capita use in 1981 in the United States was 11 percent, compared to 5 percent in Britain and 3 percent in Sweden.[41] After the United States, the countries with the heaviest use of cards are Canada and the United Kingdom, reflecting the fact that cards generally are used more in check-oriented countries where there is a need for an identification mechanism that is universally accepted for retail purchases.

Although many people think automatically of Visa and MasterCard when the term *credit card* is used, the bank credit cards they typify comprise fewer than half the number of cards issued by U.S. retailers and fewer than those of the oil companies as well. Japanese retailers also issue credit cards extensively, but in Europe credit has never been used extensively as a promotional device for sales. German bankers have maintained an iron grip on the provision of consumer credit, even to the extent of waging a hard-fought battle to keep Visa cards out of their country. Their moral suasion in inculcating the norm that it is not right for retailers to offer credit has been subtly reinforced by the control the commercial banks exercise over the major store groups through substantial stock ownership. Since the Dutch banks have adopted a position like the Germans', credit card use there is negligible, as was true formerly in France. But use there has been growing, with Carte Bleue dominating. A cooperative product of the largest commercial banks, the card was linked to Visa in 1973 and functions as a cash dispenser access card as well. Although most bank credit cards are affiliated with one of the two big organizations, banks in some countries, in efforts often imbued with a touch of xenophobia, have joined together to promote nationwide cards. This is true in Denmark and also in Japan, where the government did not permit cards that could be used outside the country until 1978. A different scenario unfolded Down Under when, in 1981, the Australian trading banks, whose Bankcard has 62 percent of the market and whose distribution is more than twice as large as that of all the retailers' cards together, ended a brief affiliation with Visa and MasterCard in high dudgeon over the firms' plans to issue their cards for domestic as well as international use.

The bank credit card is a child of the computer, conceived by the desire of California bankers to find new uses for the data processing equipment they acquired to handle the burgeoning volume of checks in the postwar boom years. Since over one-half of a bank's operating expenses other than interest on savings deposits is incurred in the payments function, as the use of checks doubled in two decades, the banks faced a major cost problem. It was compounded by persistent staffing problems, marked by back office turnover rates of over 100 percent a year. Hence, the early adoption of computer technology by the large California banks was said to reveal "a little-suspected propensity to innovate. It may be only that opportunities for innovation in the payments field were rather limited before the advent of automation."[42]

To offset the large initial investment and high fixed costs of EDP, the banks sought new products to increase income and turned to credit cards, even though many regarded them as a highly risky venture. The Bank of America first considered issuing a card in 1946, but it was 1958 before it issued 2.5 million BankAmericards, which evolved into today's Visa cards. The cards were so successful that to compete with them, four other major California banks in 1966 formed an association that introduced the Master Charge card. In the following year, they joined forces with other regional bank card groups to form Interbank Card Association, which prospered with its card that in 1980 was renamed MasterCard.

The risk inherent in the card schemes was manifest on the East Coast, where the nation's first bank card had been offered by Franklin National Bank in 1952. In the following years, hundreds of banks with dreams of high profits emulated its card plan, only to have them turn into nightmares of losses. Chase Manhattan Bank introduced its card plan the same year as Bank of America, and by the end of 1959 there were over forty different plans, mostly in New York and on the West Coast. But New York bankers faced major problems with restrictive branch banking laws, which prevented them from attaining the necessary cardholder bases, and from tough retailers whose tenacious grip on their own credit plans limited the volume of bank card purchases. Thus, after sustaining losses for years, Chase in 1963 was forced to abandon its plan. The unusual cooperation displayed in the subsequent formation of regional card associations was a reaction by chastened bankers to the lesson learned vicariously from the giant New York bank's abortive effort in the card field.

Between 1965 and 1970, after Bank of America started to license other banks to issue its cards and as Interbank affiliations grew, the number of banks offering credit cards increased from 79 to 8,900 and the number of cardholders grew to 30 million.[43] By the end of 1981, Americans held about 114 million bank credit cards. Exceeding those were some 119 million cards issued by oil companies, which along with some large department stores, pioneered in the introduction of the cards in the United States around 1914. While issued then only to the stores' most valued customers, by 1981 the retailers had some 277 million cards in the hands of their broad customer bases. By comparison, in 1981, 57 percent of U.S. households had a Sears, Roebuck card; 53 percent had a Visa card; and 11 percent an American Express card.[44] American Express is the largest of the T&E cards and in just seven years after it was created in 1958 overtook the original T&E, Diners Club, which in 1950 was the first nonoil company to issue charge cards on a large scale.

Visa and MasterCard did not arrive in Sweden until 1978–1979 and have small market shares compared to the two nationwide credit/debit/cash dispenser cards, one of which is offered by the savings banks and the other by the commercial and cooperative banks. Retailers' cards enjoyed phenomenal growth in Sweden between 1974 and 1979, when the volume of card credit increased by a factor of 19 and the number of card plans tripled. The surge resulted from a government crackdown on the use of installment credit and resulted in the use of card credit increasing inversely to the decrease in the use of the older form of credit. What happened then reads like history repeating itself:

> The development was watched by politicians, authorities and mass media, and questions about the social benefits of card credit for consumers came under debate. . . . The number of crimes involving credit cards rose alarmingly fast during 1977. . . . The causes of this primarily were lack of control and identification.[45]

Subsequent investigations indicated, however, that there actually was a smaller percentage of consumers having problems in handling credit than before 1975, and in time, with better control, the crimes declined just as they had with checks. Neither of those problems hurt the industry as severely as restrictions the government imposed on consumer credit in 1981 and 1982: they cut the use of credit cards between 10 to 20 percent.

Electronic Techniques

Electronic Communications Technology in Sweden

A payment system is a series of links between customers and their financial institutions, and electronic funds transfer occurs when the links are operated electronically. An EFT system contains four main elements: (1) terminals at which instructions are entered into the system and messages are received; (2) computers that carry the messages; (3) telecommunications lines that link terminals and computers; and (4) software programs that guide the operations of the system. Although all terminals convey instructions to a computer in a form that it can read, not all communicate directly with it, that is, online. In off-line operation, the information is stored on magnetic tape within a cassette or on a floppy disk. A terminal with a keyboard is used to enter data; other types of terminals read the information and convert it into the digital impulses that activate the computer. For the automatic reading of data from a document, Swedish banks, like most others, use a system called Magnetic Ink Character Recognition (MICR), but the Postal Giro used Optical Character Recognition (OCR). Although the apparatus to encode in MICR is very expensive, OCR can read typewritten information, so that customers can write their transfer instructions in a readable computer form.

Since the essence of EFT is the transmittal of information between customers and bank computers, implementation of the technology is highly dependent on a nation's telecommunications system. In the 1960s, the use of mainframe computers in central locations compelled banks to use batch processing, the concentration of a day's transactions into a short period of off-peak telephone time. The more costly alternative of leased lines, dedicated to one link between a bank branch and its data processing center, was adopted for links bearing especially heavy traffic. But the costs of on-line operation were reduced in 1981 when the Swedish Telecommunications Administration (STA) introduced a digital network for data communications that operates on a circuit-switching principle, with the link between users established only while transmission is in progress. Since it is intended primarily for customers with geographically scattered data units that send relatively frequent but short data messages, the system is ideally suited for bank offices and cash dispensers (CDs) in checking balances before withdrawals.

The special need for security in bank data transmissions has led Swedish banks to join 900 others in the Society for Worldwide Interbank Financial Telecommunications (SWIFT), a private data network using leased lines. Although banks have on-line links to it, it does not carry out transactions but rather conveys instructions for doing so. Through the system, banks send customer payments to recipients in foreign countries, pay for the purchase of foreign exchange, and make settlements with foreign banks.

Terminals and the Easter Holiday Caper

According to a team of English researchers, "Spending on computers and automation per bank employee in Sweden is the highest in Europe, if not the world."[46] Certainly the conversion to electronic technology began early there. The installation of on-line, real-time teller terminals began in 1972, and by 1977 virtually all the commercial banks had completed their networks. The savings banks began installing off-line teller terminals in 1972 and two years later started linking them directly to their shared computer center, SPADAB. Formed in 1962 to provide data processing services to a small group of thrifts, SPADAB today has on-line links to 133 of the 162 savings banks and serves the smallest ones on a batch-processing basis. Through a data communications network covering the country, teller terminals in some 1,000 savings banks' offices are connected to SPADAB. Moreover, by mid-1983 nearly half of the post offices had counter terminals, and about half of those were on-line to the central computers of the Postal Giro and the PK Bank.

In the transition to a fully electronic funds transfer system, the teller counter terminals play a key role in that they record account activity immediately, automatically screen check transactions against a daily warning bulletin stored in all the banks' central computers, and halt the flow of paper at the counter. Although the payment instructions have to go to the back office for copying on microfilm and filing, the essential information for effecting a transfer is captured at the point of entry into the system.

If a transaction entered into a teller terminal involves an account in another bank, it is routed through Bank Giro, which functions as an automated clearinghouse (ACH). Since it is an off-line system based on the exchange of magnetic tapes, its computers merely sort the details of transactions from one tape onto other sets of tapes, one for each bank involved. A higher level of sophistication is achieved in the configuration involving counter terminals in the post offices, which are linked on-line to two separate computer networks. At an even higher level is a switching center used for CDs when more than one bank is involved in an on-line system, and one reason Sweden's payment system is so highly regarded is that it has had two shared nationwide networks of on-line CDs in operation for years.

In an about-face from their philosophy in the early decades of the century when technical innovations were often opposed as unsuitable, the savings banks have pioneered with automated retail banking services in Sweden. The first CD in the Nordic countries was a prototype installed by the Uppsala Savings Bank in 1967, and a network of savings banks' off-line CDs was in operation by 1969. Two years later the commercial and cooperative banks, together with the Postal Bank, formed a consortium, Bankomat Center, to handle the purchase of equipment and management of the new service for them. Their first CDs were installed in 1972 and, like the savings banks' units, were operated by inserting a punched card and using a numerical code. Data about withdrawals were recorded on punched tapes, which at the end of each business day were sent to SPADAB or Bankomat Center, which did the sorting, bookkeeping, and clearing of the transactions. Bankomat Center also maintained a security control with a list of blocked card accounts.

The interest today in those first CDs from a historic standpoint would seem to exceed that of the public at the time; even the image-conscious Swedish bankers concede that few customers used them due to inadequate technology and poor marketing. Perhaps just as important, people who had only recently been warmly welcomed into the vaulted halls of banks through salary accounts were being asked to go back outside into the wind and snow and conduct their banking business with strange machines, even stranger punched cards, and confusing codes. However, a few people found the devices irresistibly attractive.

The longest bank holiday of the year in Sweden is the four-day one celebrating Easter and the promise of spring, especially appealing to a northern people emerging from months of dark days and long, frigid nights. The Easter weekend of 1977 will long be remembered as the one when the Swedish savings banks had a record-breaking number of withdrawals from their hitherto unpopular CDs. By Tuesday morning not a note was left in any of their machines in the entire country; they had been ripped off by a gang of enterprising crooks who had emptied the lot of them using duplicated punched cards they had made during the drab, dreary winter. After four days of marathon driving over the length and breadth of the California-sized nation, they had misappropriated approximately a third of a million dollars, without anyone being any the wiser. The Easter Holiday Caper probably would have gone down in history as a perfect crime except for a chance occurrence. On Monday night, the mastermind of the plot was waiting in the crowded parking lot at Malmö for the ferry to Europe, with his ticket to freedom in hand, when a passerby noticed what appeared to be a gun sticking out from under a blanket in the back seat of the car. The startled citizen reported his suspicion to the skeptical police who, upon checking, were astounded to find not only a gun but piles of bank notes stashed under the covering on the seat and floor.

Compared to armed robberies and forgeries, this incident marked the attainment of greater sophistication in crimes against Swedish financial institutions and dramatically heightened the awareness of bankers to the vulnerability of off-line units. Within a year, the savings banks introduced Sweden's first on-line CDs, which are linked to SPADAB by leased telephone lines. They were followed in 1981 by on-line Bankomats, which use the new data network and are activated by cards that, when inserted into a CD, dial into their bank's computer system. That tie at the time of the transaction enables banks to block the use of lost or stolen cards and to control the use of account balances, thereby permitting larger withdrawals. With the total number of CDs approaching 1,000, withdrawals from them now equal about one-third the number of checks written for cash each year.[47] Moreover, since they also provide a large number of balance inquiries, they handle a significant part of customer bank transactions. However, since they primarily provide cash more conveniently, they perpetuate reliance on that most primitive element in the payment system.

A point-of-sale (POS) system does the opposite. Through terminals that link retail stores to financial institutions, they eliminate cash by verifying checks, authorizing credit purchases or transferring funds from customers' accounts to the merchant's, and also eliminate paper in the last-named direct debit transaction. That concept has proved highly popular in Sweden where in 1979 oil companies negotiated agreements with banks and the Postal Giro so that they could issue debit cards to their customers. For years, over 85 percent of the gas pumped there had come from currency-accepting pumps; then the company that made them developed new units that would accept cards. Now the customer inserts the oil company card in the terminal on the pump, keys in an identifying number, and pumps the gas. When done, the card comes out, and the purchase is registered. Transactions are routed on-line to the companies, which batch them and enter them into the Bank Giro system, which routes them to the account-holding institutions. No receipt is issued at the time of purchase, but the companies send out statements about every ten days, and the debit also appears later on the bank or giro account statements. Since 1983 several oil companies have been testing the service in the United States.

Better Methods for Making Regular Payments

The potential for improving the U.S. payment system is most clearly revealed in a comparison of the methods for making regular payments here with those abroad. While most Americans receive wages and other income payments by check and then troop off to stand in line at a bank to deposit them, in Western Europe such payments have been directly deposited for decades. Since the 1960s it has been mandatory in the Netherlands that wages and government benefits be credited directly to a depository account, and the Swedish government in 1981 stopped paying out cash benefits due to increased robberies and proposed that all be converted to direct deposit by 1983. While salary accounts there at first were paper-based, they were early candidates for conversion to automation, and payors now deliver magnetic tapes or other data media to financial institutions' computer centers or transfer the data by direct terminal connection for crediting to employees' accounts.

The volume of transactions made through telephone bill-paying systems, which are unique to the United States, reached 36 million in 1982.[48] They are considered precursors to home banking through videotex, which links modified television sets or home computers to banking computers via phone lines. Following some twenty experiments that began in 1979, a New York bank began selling a home banking service in 1983 and had 4,000 customers by 1984; however, a Florida videotex system launched in the same year laid off one-fifth of its staff in late 1984 due to slow acceptance of the service.

Two major problems that have hindered the acceptance of home banking service in the United States are the retarded development of ACHs and the failure of banks and firms to adapt their systems to handle electronic payments. Home banking has proved more acceptable in countries with highly developed giro systems where both individuals and institutions are used to making and receiving direct fund transfers. The French successfully tested a system in 2,500 homes at the end of 1980, and a small thrift institution offered the first home banking service in England in 1982. But it was Germany's tiny Verbraucherbank that became the world leader in home banking with the comprehensive service it introduced in 1981. While it proved that the size of the bank does not matter when offering the service, Verbraucherbank subsequently has enjoyed spectacular growth.

Most Americans pay recurring bills by check; Europeans use paper-based giro transfers or electronic standing orders for fixed payments on predetermined dates and direct debits for fixed or variable amounts on payment dates that can be varied each month. Both authorize the bank or giro to transfer the sum due automatically, and itemized statements about the payments are sent periodically. In Germany, where they have been using them since 1963, direct debits comprise 30 percent of cashless payments, half of which are electronic—the highest proportion in Europe. By comparison, the percentage of noncash payments that are electronic in France is 11 percent; in Sweden, 37 percent; in the United Kingdom, 18 percent; and in the United States, 1 percent. The use of paper giro transfers makes up 38 percent of the volume in Germany; 35 percent in Sweden; 13 percent in the United Kingdom; but only 1 percent in France, where the use of checks is almost as high as in the United States.[49]

No Western nation can match Japan's dramatic progress directly from a heavily cash-dominated payment system until the mid-1970s into the world's most technologically advanced electronic transfer system. With the use of checks by individuals practically nonexistent and credit card use low, the need for cash there led to the introduction of off-line cash dispensers in 1969 and on-line CDs in 1972. Today there are four shared CD networks, and half of all withdrawals are from them. The array of machines was augmented in 1971 with the installation of automatic depositors that automatically count notes and present a total to the customer who has a choice of accepting it or getting the money back. They were followed in 1978 by ATMs, which differ from other nations' customer terminals in that they operate with either a card or a passbook and, in addition to more customary functions, can make on-line electronic payments to other accounts, thus providing "the world's first self-service, mass market" EFTS.[50] For thirty years, the Japanese have been using direct debits for paying recurring bills to utilities and insurance firms, and they now comprise 57 percent of cashless payments. The banks regard it as an "extra service" to customers to handle the paying of tuition, taxes, and bills either on an individual payment basis or by preauthorized agreement. To transmit such payments, customers can use the paper-based system, which makes up 29 percent of the volume, or the Zengin system, the world's fastest, which completes electronic transactions within an hour. The telecommunications system, which began operations in 1973, can also be accessed directly by customers through ATMs to pay bills.

While such technological prowess is impressive and intriguing, the descriptions of payment systems are intended to provide perspective for the central focus of this book, which is concerned not so much with what payment systems nations have as why they have them. Hence, to achieve the in-depth background to attain that goal, the following chapters dealing with policy issues will be more limited to scrutiny of Sweden and the United States and the public policies surrounding their systems.

Notes

1. Bank for International Settlements, *Payment Systems in Eleven Developed Countries* (Basel: BIS, 1980), p. 7.

2. Patrick Frazer and Dimitri Vittas, *The Retail Banking Revolution* (London:

Michael Lafferty Publications, 1982), pp. 29, 31, 250 for numerical data in paragraph.

3. BIS, *Payment Systems,* p. 57; Mark J. Flannery and Dwight M. Jaffee, *Economic Implications of an Electronic Monetary Transfer System* (Lexington, Mass.: D.C. Heath, 1973), p. 35.

4. Sveriges Riksbank, *Statistical Yearbook 1981* (Stockholm, 1982), pp. 28–29.

5. George W. Mitchell, "Opening Remarks," in National Commission on Electronic Fund Transfers, *International Payments Symposium* (Washington, D.C.: NCEFT, 1977c), p. 76.

6. BIS, *Payment Systems,* p. 277, for these and following currency data.

7. Arthur D. Little, Inc., *The Consequences of Electronic Funds Transfer.* (Cambridge, Mass.: ADL, 1975), p. 48.

8. Carl M. Gambs, "The Cost of the U.S. Payments System," *Journal of Bank Research* (Winter 1976):243; BIS, *Payment Systems,* pp. 276, 282.

9. BIS, *Payment Systems,* p. 256.

10. Crime data from interviews and documents at Svenska Bankföreningen, Stockholm.

11. Sten Walberg, "Brott och säkerhet i banklokaler" (paper presented at annual meeting of the Swedish Savings Banks Association, Stockholm, October 19, 1978).

12. Karl Wilhelmsson, *Svenska postgirot 1925–1949* (Stockholm: Postverkets tryckeri, 1950), p. 181.

13. Donald R. Buchanan, "Remarks," in Federal Reserve System, *Papers and Comments of the International Conference on Banking and Payment Systems,* Atlanta, April 2–4, 1980, p. 167.

14. Arthur D. Little, *Consequences,* p. 174.

15. Frazer and Vittas, *Retail Banking Revolution,* p. 30; Mitchell, "Remarks," p. 76.

16. "Fed Check Clearing Role Creates Inequities on Costs," *American Banker,* November 28, 1983, p. 29.

17. Gambs, "Cost," pp. 242–243.

18. "Electronic Banking," *Business Week,* January 18, 1982, p. 74; BIS, *Payment Systems,* p. 283.

19. BIS, *Payment Systems,* p. 256.

20. "The Banks Had It Coming," *Business Week,* April 23, 1984, p. 124.

21. BIS, *Payment Systems,* p. 257.

22. Frazer and Vittas, *Retail Banking Revolution,* p. 71.

23. Eckart van Hooven, "Remarks," in Federal Reserve System, *Papers,* p. 131.

24. Frazer and Vittas, *Retail Banking Revolution,* p. 228.

25. Mogens Munk Rasmussen, "National P.O.S. Schemes: The Danish Project," in European Financial Marketing Association, *Texts of the Presentations,* EFMA Conference, Monte Carlo, March 21–24, 1982 (Paris: EFMA, 1982), p. 172.

26. "Några synpunkter på checken som betalningsmedel," *Ekonomisk revy* 1 (February 1944): 182–183.

27. Ibid., p. 182.

28. Ragnar Ivestedt, "Den svenska betalningsvolymens sammansättning," *Ekonomisk revy,* no. 2 (April 1945): 95.

29. Frazer and Vittas, *Retail Banking Revolution,* p. xii; for Sweden's growth rate, see Assar Lindbeck, *Swedish Economic Policy* (Berkeley: University of California Press, 1974), p. 1.

30. "Checklön införd hos 500 företag," *Svenska Dagbladet* (Stockholm), February 19, 1960; Sveriges verkstadsförening, "PM" (April 26, 1960), p. 1.

31. Data in paragraph from Svenska Bankföreningen records.

32. Olov Ernsell, "Checklöneräkningen—ett räntabilitets problem," *Ekonomisk revy* 2 (1965): 93–94, for quotation and data in next sentence.

33. "Checkar och legitimation," *Ekonomisk revy* 6 (1968): 343.

34. Thomas Glück, "Remarks," in Federal Reserve System, *Papers,* p. 234.

35. "Checkbetalningar i butiker ökar," *Ekonomisk revy* 4 (1975): 198–199.

36. Kurt Samuelsson, *Postbanken—postsparbank och postgiro (1884–1925–1974)* (Stockholm: Postverkets tryckeri, 1978, p. 46.

37. Ivestedt, *Svenska betalningsvolymens,* p. 95.

38. Data from Swedish Post Office annual reports.

39. Frazer and Vittas, *Retail Banking Revolution,* pp. 138, 259.

40. BIS, *Payment Systems,* p. 269.

41. Frazer and Vittas, *Retail Banking Revolution,* p. 36.

42. Richard E. Towey, "An Evaluation of the Payments Mechanism in California," in Hyman P. Minsky, *California Banking in a Growing Economy: 1946–1975* (Berkeley: Institute of Business and Economic Research, University of California, 1965), p. 340.

43. Flannery and Jaffee, *Economic Implications,* pp. 51–52, for earlier data; Frazer and Vittas, *Retail Banking Revolution,* p. 284, for 1981 data.

44. "The New Sears," *Business Week,* November 16, 1981, p. 143.

45. Harry Karlsson, "Elektronisk betalningsförmedling och konsumentskyddet," Institutet för Rättsinformatik-rapport 1981:1, Stockholm, p. 22.

46. Frazer and Vittas, *Retail Banking Revolution,* p. 233.

47. Bo Gunnarsson, "Elektroniska betalningsjänster nu och i framtiden," Svenska Bankföreningen, November 4, 1982, pp. 5–6.

48. "Electronic Banking," p. 76.

49. Data in paragraph derived from Frazer and Vittas, *Retail Banking Revolution,* pp. 184–185, 36.

50. Ibid., p. 215.

3
The Shaping of Industry Structure

The wrenching structural stresses to which the banking industry in the United States has been subjected in the decade between 1975 and 1985 contrast sharply with the strength and stability of the industry in Sweden in that period. In this chapter, the effects of public policies and their implementation by regulators on the makeup of the industry and the distribution system for payment services in the two countries is traced to determine the causes of those significant differences.

Structure of the Swedish Depository Institutions

The Swedish banking structure resembles that of many other European nations in that it is made up of commercial, savings, and cooperative banks, plus a Postal Giro, which provides only payment services. All three types of bank are full-service institutions that provide nationwide service through CDs, branches, and full reciprocity to customers of other banks. The fourteen commercial banks consist of four banks with nationwide branching networks, three of which have 70 percent of commercial bank assets; six provincial banks, which on average are about one-sixth as large; two small local banks; and two that serve as central banks for the savings and cooperative banks. The sector is highly concentrated as the result of a long process of mergers. Skandinaviska Enskilda Bank (S-E Bank), the product of a merger in 1972, was the largest until 1974 when the larger PK Bank was formed by the merger of the Postal Bank with the state-owned Kreditbank. By 1983, however, S-E Bank had reassumed the lead, and PK Bank had been relegated to third place. This prompted the government to announce that it was planning to sell 15 percent of the bank because the country's huge deficit precluded giving it the capital infusion needed to expand its operations.

The merger process has cut even more deeply into the number of savings banks, which had fallen to 160 by 1983 from 451 in 1950. Legally they are foundations and may not distribute any profits they make but must reinvest them. Like their counterparts on the Continent, they have strong links to local authorities, and half of their trustees are appointed by the government of their community. In terms of size, they vary greatly, with the fifteen largest accounting for about half of all their assets.

The cooperative banks, which until 1974 were called agricultural credit associations, date back only to 1915 when Parliament established them to provide loans to farmers. In their early years they had government support in the form of equity capital, which now consists of members' dues and retained earnings. They have a three-tiered structure, which at the base has 399 local banks that cover the country with 694 offices. At the midlevel are 12 regional banks, which oversee and assist the local banks; and they in turn are members of the Federation of Swedish Cooperative Banks, which supervises overall operations. Their change of name reflected the broader mandate they obtained through the 1968 uniform banking laws, and since opening their doors to all, their membership has more than doubled.

Although it seems foreign indeed to Americans who do not have the same degree of confidence in their postal system, in Sweden as well as most European countries and Japan, the security and speed of the postal service have made it an integral part of the delivery system of banking services. Because the Swedish post office network constitutes the primary structure for the Postal Giro and strongly supports PK Bank, postal workers, including rural carriers, function like bank tellers. Through them, people make deposits, give payment orders, cash checks, open accounts, apply for loans, and buy and sell shares in the stock fund of PK Bank.

In a newsworthy departure from the seemingly inexorable process of consolidation, the Bank Inspection Board in 1982 gave its blessing to the formation of Sweden's first new commercial bank since 1927. But while that was unusual, the government in 1984 made a major policy change when it decided to let bygones be bygones three centuries after Johan Palmstruch's disastrous banking experience and proposed letting foreign banks set up Swedish subsidiaries in 1985. The ban has led to a situation in which twenty-four foreign banks do business from representative offices but are not subject to government regulation. Hence, although Swedish bankers anticipate tougher competition, most favor the change because then all will operate on the same terms. Said one, "They're welcome; as soon as they start taking deposits, they can start helping to finance the national debt, too. We need all the help we can get."[1]

Hand of the State in Shaping Structure in Sweden

An 1886 law that set a low capital requirement to stimulate the founding of shareholder-owned banks together with the promise of profits from the booming growth of industry produced a proliferation of banks, which peaked at eighty-four in 1908. A rash of bank failures in the preceding year, however, with millions lost in deposits and stock, led to concern that the creation of so many small banks could be more damaging to society than useful to industry. Moreover, banks with larger assets were required to finance Sweden's rapid industrialization and foreign trade and to counter fluctuations in the domestic economy through operations abroad. Nationwide banks were needed to meet the geographical expansion of industry and to smooth out cyclical and regional variations in credit demands. Thus, to foster a change to fewer but stronger banks, Parliament passed a law raising the equity requirement for new banks and requiring the founders of a bank to prove its value to society. These factors spurred the largest banks to embark on a program of mergers and acquisitions.

By 1917 the number of banks had been reduced by 30 percent. But like a little girl ironing clothes, as fast as one wrinkle was ironed out in the banking structure, another was ironed in. A legislative committee found that the number of branches had increased 70 percent since 1911, which "exceeded the boundaries of need and stimulated competition" and had a "bad influence" on banks' activities.[2] The opening of so many branches was alleged to be damaging to society because it led to higher costs and, since the commercial banks are securities traders, encouraged stock market speculation. Thus, the committee proposed that banks be required to obtain permission from the government before opening branches, although it recommended that "greatest caution" be used in refusing applications. Thus a burr was wedged under the saddle of bankers that would prove upsetting for more than sixty years. No other government policy so significantly infringed on the operations of Swedish bankers as this issue, which is so imbued with conflict between economic and social goals as to have become highly politicized at times.

The door was closed to another entry to markets when in 1918 the use of agents was banned in reaction to abuses by highly commissioned agents of some banks. That ban was followed by a law requiring government permission for the acquisition of a bank, with the acquiring bank ordered to seek the comments of all parties that would be affected by the takeover and to prove that it would not be damaging to society.

Partly as a result of the branching restrictions, the number of bank offices decreased about 23 percent in the first half of the 1920s. But their influence was dwarfed by a far stronger force: the worst banking crisis in Sweden's history. The 1921 depression forced banks to cut the size of their branch networks, and additional reductions occurred as weaker banks were compelled to merge with stronger ones. Between 1910 and 1930 the number of banks declined from 80 to 30 as the result of 74 mergers and acquisitions. The number of offices grew from 625 in 1910 to 1,410 in 1920 before declining to 1,045 by 1930. For three decades the number of offices remained quite constant, but the number of banks gradually declined to 16. The number of savings banks, too, decreased through mergers from a peak of 495 in 1926 to 447 by 1955. By then, the country's banking system essentially had assumed the structure it has today.

Structure of the U.S. Depository Institutions

Commercial Banks

The most significant difference between the commercial banks in the United States and those in Sweden is their vast number. In 1982 it was over one thousand times greater: 14,565 compared to 14. Based on population, if the United States had the same proportion of commercial banks, there would be 388. The overabundance of banks is the result of the dual chartering system, based on jealously guarded states' rights, and of protective legislation that restricts branching, based on the political clout of the well-organized small banks, which make up a substantial majority. About 70 percent of the banks have assets of less than $50 million and account for less than 12 percent of total assets.

Yet, paradoxically, there is more concentration in the industry than is generally realized. One percent of the banking organizations—banks and bank holding companies—account for over 50 percent of banking assets. Sometimes described as a substitute for branch banking, the holding company structure has facilitated expansion across state lines for banking companies, including the two largest, Citicorp and BankAmerica, which offer banking services through subsidiaries in almost all states. BankAmerica, with over 1,000 branches, is one of only ten banking companies with more than 250 branches. Of those, five are in California, which is one of twenty-one states that permit statewide branching. Eighteen states place limitations on branching, and eleven prohibit it.

Mutual Savings Banks

Modeled after the philanthropic eighteenth-century European savings banks promoted by Jeremy Bentham, the first mutual savings banks in the United States were founded in 1816, four years before the first Swedish one. The U.S. thrifts differ in that their profits can either be reinvested or distributed to depositors, while the Swedish units lack the second option. The first mutuals fulfilled an unmet need because, since the commercial banks then were interested only in business customers, the average citizen had nowhere to stash savings except under the mattress or in a strongbox buried behind the rutabagas in the garden. Although chartered only in eighteen states, primarily in the Northeast, the thrifts enjoyed great growth and by 1900 had nearly 46 percent of all savings.[3] But although there was consolidation after their number peaked at 678 in 1907 and their market share declined, they survived the Great Depression without suffering structural instability.

Never as committed to housing as the S&Ls, after World War II they diversified more extensively and boldly moved into payment services in 1971 by offering the first NOW (negotiable order of withdrawal) accounts, followed by preauthorized bill payment and POS services, credit and debit cards, and insurance. Their pioneering commitment to electronic technology was manifest when in 1975 the mutual savings banks had almost 90 percent of their offices on-line while only 45 percent of S&Ls and 14 percent of commercial banks did.[4] However, as their earnings were eroded by severe disintermediation when unregulated rates soared above theirs and the cost of funds rose disproportionately to income from their long-term assets, the ranks of the mutual savings banks were decimated by insolvencies and involuntary mergers. Although DIDMCA in 1980 permitted them to provide a broader range of services and increased flexibility in portfolio management, the relief came too late to prevent further consolidation during the phase-in of deregulation. At the end of 1982 the total assets of the 386 mutual savings banks constituted 6 percent of those of all depository institutions.

Savings and Loan Associations

While the S&Ls have about four times the assets of the mutual savings banks, they have shared the same perilous predicament in recent years, with many forced to merge with stronger S&Ls or be acquired by commercial banks, often on an interstate basis. Congress approved aid for the industry in late 1982; yet in the following year there were ninety-five failures and mergers arranged by the authorities. Another $72 million was needed from the FSLIC in the first half of 1984 to bolster the capital position of ninety-four thrifts.[5]

Usually called building societies when first formed in the 1830s, the need for the S&Ls originated in the fact that until 1916 the commercial banks were not permitted to make real estate loans, and after that, the loans were limited to half the appraised value of the property. Hence, the first S&Ls were cooperatives that accumulated the savings of members until each could obtain a construction loan for a home and were dissolved when all the loans had been paid off. By the turn of the century, there were 5,356, and they were operating in every state. By then they were taking deposits from and making loans to nonmembers, hiring professionals as managers, and evolving into corporate entities. Since they can be federally or state chartered, the number of S&Ls proliferated in the free-wheeling chartering climate of the first decades of the century, and by 1927 reached a historic peak of 12,804. By the end of 1935, however, only 10,266 S&Ls were left.

The survivors and the newly founded ones on the booming West Coast enjoyed dramatic growth during the postwar years. Not only did the government's ceiling on commercial bank interest rates give them a competitive edge in attracting savings funds, but because of their specialized role in housing, they also were tax-exempt until 1951. Thus, the thrifts' share of all financial institutions' assets grew to 33 percent while the commercial banks' share fell from 86 to 67 percent between 1945 and 1965.[6] That marked the end of their golden years as the era of high interest rates began in 1966, and by 1982 the commercial banks' share was up to 69 percent.

Credit Unions

Although most of the 20,000 credit unions in the United States are small, because there are more of them than all the banks and other thrifts together, when their growth rate zoomed to 18 percent during the 1970s, it startled the somnambulant bankers who previously had dismissed them as elephants do flies. When the behemoths took a good look at the little cooperatives, they found them tax-exempt, operating free of interest rate limits and branching restrictions, offering insured interest-bearing checking-type as well as savings accounts in convenient locations, and paying out profits as dividends. They enjoyed low operating costs, with usually only the treasurer a paid employee, since the sponsors provided free office space, clerical help, and payroll plans for savings and loan payments. Moreover, they were third-largest in consumer loans, with low default rates due to the information advantage inherent in the common bond requirement for membership. Although the common interest may be a church, social group, or labor union, about 85 percent are job-related, and four of the top five whose assets exceeded $300 million in 1981 are government employee groups. Green with envy, the bankers went running to the government, demanding an end to the unfair competition.

Actually they need not have feared, for the usual combination of poor management and government "help" soon served to get the credit unions into trouble much like the other depository institutions. Until 1971 their decisions were influenced by the fact that they were self-insured; but then the government stepped in with its insurance. As they experienced for the first time the giddy confidence engendered by state support, the groups assumed greater portfolio risks, and some invested in computers and spiffier surroundings. Thus, capital and liquidity declined, the number of involuntary liquidations ballooned from 1 in 1971 to 200 in 1980, and the industry went from the fastest-growing type of depository institution to the second-slowest by 1979.[7] In addition to losing deposits to money market funds, the credit unions also have suffered from some of the government's efforts to help the other thrifts with money market certificates and deregulation, which is smudging some of their previous unique advantages.

Branching in the United States: Pre-EFTS

One way to evaluate the convenience of payments services to consumers in different countries is to compare the number of people served by each branch. Although it is impossible to make precise comparisons because of the differences in size, opening hours, and quality of service in branches in different countries, the data from a 1981 survey reveal differences so striking as to transcend qualitative variances.[8] In Sweden, for example, the number of people served by each branch is 1,511; in the United States, it is 2,083—almost 38 percent higher. Compared to the major European nations, Australia, Canada, and Japan, the only country that seems to provide worse branch banking service for its citizens is Italy, whose backward system garners booby prizes for efficiency in banking. There is one striking similarity between the banking systems in Italy and the United States: both are highly fragmented, with geographic limitations on branching, although a few Italian banks operate nationwide. In Germany and France, on the other hand, there are about twice as many branches per person as in the United States. Nor can the deficiency in the United States be ascribed to size, for Canada provides better coverage in spite of its vast land areas. The data seem to confirm what most Americans have been complaining about for years: they are compelled to stand in line too long at bank offices for the simple reason that there are not enough for the population in spite of a glut of banks.

Inasmuch as convenience always emerges as the most important factor influencing customers' choice of a bank, the paucity of branches in the United States cannot be attributed to consumer choice. On the contrary, although the issue has generated internecine warfare in the industry for over a century, the public has seldom been involved in the policy debates, in part, perhaps, because for so many years the bankers' general air of arrogance and power in granting loans kept the public quietly submissive. In fact, the main reason for branching restrictions is to keep out, or at least reduce, competition. The large majority of small banks has succeeded over the years in lobbying state and federal legislators to protect their market areas by arguing that if legal barriers did not keep them out, a few big (and probably eastern) banks would move in and take over all banking and, who knows, perhaps the whole country. Appealing to Americans' basic distrust of bigness, they contend that the restrictions preserve competition. As one antitrust authority has put it, "In essence, a host of limited and petty monopolies is the price we must pay to avoid one giant monopoly."[9]

Federal restrictions on branching are rooted in a more fundamental policy issue: the dual banking system, which in turn is rooted in states' rights. In order to maintain a balance of power between both types of banks, national banks have been permitted to maintain branches only within the boundaries of the state in which their headquarters are located, subject to the same restrictions that apply to state banks. While that is a matter of some concern to state banking authorities whose positions are at stake and to politicians whose campaign coffers are enriched by state bankers, it hardly matters to bank customers who are interested in easier access to their funds and banking services.

The growth of unit banking in the United States occurred also as a reaction to the unscrupulous behavior of banks' agents in the days of wildcat banking. Their offices, like those of Swedish banks at the same time, were located as far away as possible from the head office to delay the redemption of bank notes, which angered the note holders. The Swedish government dealt with the problem of abuses by agents by forbidding banks to use them; Americans expressed their anger about the practice by denying the banks the branches that they wanted.

In the wake of the worldwide 1907 financial panic, which revealed the need for major reform of the United States banking structure as well as Sweden's, Woodrow Wilson in an address to the American Bankers Association (ABA) in the following year proposed a system of branch banking for the nation. While it is unlikely that more than a handful of the small bankers who made up the majority of his listeners would have voted for the Democrat in 1912 anyway, he could hardly have chosen a message more likely to alienate those diehard advocates of preserving the status quo: power, prestige, and profits to each on his own little piece of turf. However, the notion of a nationwide branching system so inflamed the imagination of one banker in the audience that after the convention, he investigated the Canadian system to which Wilson had referred and used it as a model in developing the first banking organization to span the United States. He was Amadeo P. Giannini, founder of the Bank of America and the greatest entrepreneur U.S. banking has produced.

In establishing stringent controls over the industry, the California Bank Act of 1909 imposed a requirement similar to that which Sweden would adopt a few years later when it stipulated that before a branch office could be opened, the Superintendent of Banking had to determine that it would be to the public advantage and convenience. It is significant that the California legislature created the first statewide branch banking system because the superintendent had the power to withhold permission for offices. If the official proved balky in granting permission, however, expansion-minded bankers such as Giannini got around the rule by buying a bank in the desired locality.

In addition to denouncing the bill to create the Federal Reserve as "socialistic, confiscatory, unjust, un-American and generally wretched," many members of the ABA feared the branch banking feature of the system as well.[10] Moreover, the act created an anomaly in that it permitted national banks to set up branches in foreign countries. Giannini pointed out the incongruity: "It is difficult to understand why branches of American banks are permitted to be established and operated in foreign countries but denied the right of establishment in other American states."[11]

The perceived policy difference was revealed again in 1919 with the Edge Act, which permitted banks to conduct international business across state lines as a means of enabling them to compete better with foreign banks. Meanwhile, the 1916 ABA convention passed a resolution against branch banking, which by then was permitted in twelve states, while nine banned it on grounds that local bankers best understood the borrowing needs of their community.

In an early manifestation of what would become as ritualistic for some bankers as the intermittent exodus from cities to mountaintops of religious cults in expectation of the imminent coming of the end of the world, many bankers in the 1920s anticipated an early relaxation of branching restrictions. But rather than just being wishful thinking, their belief was based on suggestions in the annual reports of the Federal Reserve Board for the years 1915 to 1919—while Wilson was in the White House—that the national bank branching provision be made more liberal. The viewpoint was shared as well by the Comptroller of the Currency who recommended that they be authorized to establish branches within certain limits. This emboldened several banks to form holding companies so that they could acquire ready-made branch systems, a device Giannini used successfully in building his banking empire.

But with a new administration in power in 1923, the small bankers, who indeed saw the end of their world in branching, formed the U.S. Association Opposed to Branch Banking and succeeded in convincing the new Comptroller of the Currency that branch banking spelled doom for the federal banking bureaucracy as well as for them. Thus the comptroller declared that unless branch banking was curbed, it would mean the destruction of the national banks and of the Federal Reserve System, which would be replaced by a privately controlled reserve system. His prediction shook up the Fed to the extent that its board decreed that no branches could be opened by state member banks without its consent and that none could be located outside the cities in which their home offices were established.

By 1925, although thirty states prohibited branching, eleven permitted it statewide and nine permitted it on a limited basis, yet national banks still were restricted to only one office, regardless of state laws. Nevertheless branching was gradually spreading. In 1900 only 87 of 12,427 commercial banks had branches totaling 119; by 1925, when there were 27,223 banks, 720 had branches totaling 2,525. During the decade, pressure for relaxation of the branching laws increased as the number of bank failures rose because the operators of banks in trouble wanted to have the option of merging and becoming a branch rather than fail. Hence, the McFadden Act was proposed to enable national banks to merge with and make branches of banks in trouble in states where branching was permitted. Although the bill was passed in 1927, emotions ran so high over the issue that during debate on the floor of the U.S. Senate, two senators got into a fist fight over it.

Largely as a result of the act, of the roughly 4,500 banks that ceased operations between 1928 and 1930, an estimated 2,000 mergers enabled banks to continue operating in states that permitted branching, while an unknown number were doomed to liquidation in unit banking states. But while the two sides argued at the time about whether branching exacerbated or ameliorated banks' problems, the record later supported the latter position. Of the 3,876 banks that failed between 1921 and 1926, none were banks with branch systems, and of the 1,345 that failed in 1930, only 8 were banks with branch networks in California. In response to the cataclysmic banking failures of the early 1930s, the number of states permitting branch banking doubled between 1933 and 1936 from 9 to 18, even though the ABA in 1934 called for a ban on all forms of branching, a position it held for nineteen years. But as competition from the thrifts increased and business account balances decreased, more banks turned to branching as a form of nonprice competition. Hence, during the 1950s the number of branches roughly doubled, and by 1960 only 18 states still prohibited branch banking.

Chain Banking, Securities Affiliates, and Holding Companies

Because most U.S. banks are too small to achieve the economies of scale possible with larger size and yet have found expansion impossible because of the regulatory environment, experiments in group banking began in the nineteenth century. So-called chain banking, in which there was common ownership of banks but each remained a separate corporation, existed in North Dakota as early as 1887 and flourished in Chicago around the turn of the century as a way around Illinois' rigid antibranching laws. Although chain banking did not expand the resources of the individual units for making loans as a branch system does, it facilitated certain economies through standardization and broadened the base of managerial expertise.

One chain in the South, where branching also had been widespread prior to the 1864 ban on it, had the largest number of units in the country: 125 regional banks plus a few in New York and New Jersey by 1911. But when the Florida land boom ended in 1926, the chain failed, along with about one-fourth of the state's banks. Banking chains proliferated throughout the upper

Midwest in the first two and a half decades of the century. Gradually, though, as larger numbers of investors became aware of the profits inherent in multiple-unit banking, the holding company form became more widely adopted because of the greater opportunities it provided for not only the acquisition of other banks but also the creation of affiliates for nonbanking as well as banking activities.

Because state banks had been underwriting and distributing securities since the end of the nineteenth century, national banks began forming state-chartered affiliates to handle those activities for them after the Comptroller of the Currency prohibited them from doing so in 1908. However, the fact that the government used them to underwrite and sell its vast volume of securities in World War I was sanguinely viewed by the banks as implicit approval for private investment banking activity afterward, an assumption confirmed by the McFadden Act, which in 1927 authorized them to underwrite securities. The direct result of this government green light as the market boomed was that between 1927 and 1930, the banks and their securities affiliates more than doubled their share of bond underwriting from 22 to 45 percent and were participating in nearly two-thirds of all new stock and bond issues when the market collapsed in October 1929.

With millions of dollars in savings lost and unemployment soaring as businesses went bankrupt, the public vented its anger on the banks, especially the big New York money center banks. Congressional hearings revealed that the banks had absorbed securities of questionable quality through their trust departments to help their affiliates and had sold them millions of dollars' worth of speculative loans that were paid out of new stock issues, while the affiliates in turn operated with larger amounts of borrowed funds than independent firms and sustained losses by receiving doubtful assets and by supporting the parent banks' stock. Although only the Bank of the United States was found to have failed as a result of the relationship with its securities affiliate, the hearings resulted in the most restrictive law to emerge from the depression: the Glass-Steagall Act, which completely changed the nature of U.S. banking by separating commercial banking from investment banking. At the time, however, the banks that had survived the bloodbath were so eager to get out of the market that they began divesting their securities affiliates, which had peaked at 182 in 1930, even before the law went into effect.

The use of holding companies to acquire control of other banks was first demonstrated on a large scale by National City Bank (forerunner of Citibank), which by 1911 had amassed what the Justice Department regarded as the most concentrated holding of bank stock in the nation with interests in sixteen banks, many in New York City. The acquisitions ended when the Solicitor General issued an opinion that national banks could not hold stock in other national banks through affiliates.

Meanwhile, A.P. Giannini was expanding his branch banking network beyond San Francisco, assisted by the formation of holding companies beginning in 1917. He used one holding company to acquire banks in northern California, another to buy banks in New York and Italy in 1919, and yet another when he finally succeeded in crossing the Tehachapi range—California's Mason-Dixon line—to penetrate the closely guarded Los Angeles market. By 1926 his holdings included, in addition to those banks, stock in 67 other domestic banks and 59 banks in 16 foreign countries, plus railroads, insurance, farm loan, securities, and real estate companies. In 1928, after failing in his attempt to buy Manufacturers Trust, he bought Bank of America on Wall Street and merged his other two New York banks into it to create a large East Coast headquarters for his ultimate goal of a transcontinental bank. Later that year he formed Transamerica Corporation to bring all his holdings together as he prepared for expansion beyond the 442 offices in California and 34 in New York the firm had. His dreams were impelled neither by megalomania nor avarice; already a successful businessman in 1904 when he founded his bank for "the little fellow," he never received more than a dollar a year in salary after he resigned as president in 1924 to work on major policies. Rather, his evangelistic fervor for branch banking was based on the efficiencies of scale and consumer benefits he saw in it.

Nevertheless, Giannini's nationwide plans scared other bankers, some of whom formed their own holding companies in self-defense against him and other "outside interests," that old bugaboo of small bankers. Group banking grew during the 1920s also as a result of the general consolidation movement in business in which 7,000 manufacturing firms merged and the chain movement swept retailing, eliminating millions of mom-and-pop stores and thereby reducing banks' deposits. As the auto changed the life-styles of the nation, the urban movement began, and those who remained in the country started banking as well as shopping in the cities. The ensuing impact on small banks, combined with an agricultural depression that had begun in 1921, enabled speculators to form holding companies made up of country banks they could buy at prices below book value. As a result of these factors, by 1931 there were 97 bank holding companies, each comprised of two or more banks, operating nearly 1,000 banks.

Bank Holding Companies during and after the Crash

Federal Reserve Board data indicate that during 1930–1931, the rate of failure for group banks was only 20 percent compared to 50 percent for unit banks. However, group banking was bitterly denounced in Congress by opponents who charged that it hurt competition, put the control of vast resources in one place, and inflicted more damage on the public in the event of failure than did unit banks. Hence, the Banking Act of 1933 directed the Fed to regulate holding companies. Ironically, though, when a chain of thirteen banks that had provided most of the banking services for the citizens of Nevada failed in 1932, resulting in the closing of its banks for eleven months, the bank examiners and governor asked Transamerica to take over. After the legislature in an emergency session enacted laws to permit branch banking, Transamerica purchased controlling interest, created a branch system, and reopened the banks. However, the number of bank holding companies declined to fifty-two by 1936 due to failures, less need for them as state branching restrictions were relaxed, and the difficulty in raising capital.

In 1930 Giannini had announced that with a Bank of America on each coast and Oregon's largest bank acquired, Transamerica would begin branch banking in every state. But as bread lines lengthened, Transamerica's profits plummeted, and its board announced abandonment of the project due to economic conditions and the unlikelihood of Congress' changing the law to permit interstate banking in 1931. It proposed, moreover, dismemberment of the empire Giannini had created. Although he was seriously ill in Europe, when the news reached Giannini, he immediately made plans to return from retirement and wrest control from the men to whom he had delegated it only a year earlier. In a bizarre twist of events, when the board was reconstituted to fight Giannini, it included two directors from the firm that was the U.S. banker for Ivar Kreuger, the Swedish "match king," and some newspapers erroneously reported that Transamerica had invested in what they described as his successful enterprise. In fact, shortly after the new directors joined the board, Kreuger sailed for New York in a last desperate effort to raise funds for his collapsing operation and went to the Bank of America on his arrival for a loan. But since Transamerica was in the process of selling the bank to National City Bank, he was directed there instead. After the sixty-two-year-old Giannini won the proxy contest for Transamerica in 1932, Kreuger left New York on his last voyage; he committed suicide when he reached Paris. The New York firm that had financed him lost $8 million, and Giannini always believed that Bank of America had had a close call with the Swede.

When, during the depression, the House Committee on Banking and Currency had asked Giannini how it could strengthen the structure of the banking industry, he had urged legislation permitting banks to do business across state lines like railroads and telephone companies and recommended nationwide branch banking. But his words fell on deaf ears. When the Bank of America in 1945 passed Chase National of New York in deposits and assets to become the largest bank in the world, it was in large measure due to his skill in skirting banking laws over the years. Smarting from their lack of control over the wily San Franciscan, during the 1940s the Federal Reserve Board and other bank supervisory agencies sought a way to harness him.

By 1948, Transamerica owned a controlling interest in forty-seven banks in five western states, and although it had voluntarily reduced its holdings in Bank of America substantially by then, the Fed instituted proceedings against the company on charges of violation of Section 7 of the Clayton Act, alleging that through its acquisitions it constituted a potential monopoly with the power to lessen competition. After two years of hearings, the Federal Reserve Board found Transamerica in violation of the antitrust law by a three to two vote, even though the banks it controlled had less than a 7 percent market share. Although the board ordered the company to divest itself of all bank stocks except those of the Bank of America, Transamerica did the opposite by completing the plan it had begun fifteen years earlier by selling its remaining shares in the Bank of America. In 1953, however, the U.S. Court of Appeals reversed the board's ruling, and the Supreme Court refused to set aside the court's ruling when the board appealed. In the end Giannini prevailed, although he was not there to hear the decision; he had died in 1949 a few weeks after his seventy-ninth birthday.

By 1950 the number of bank holding companies had declined to only 28 whose banks' deposits made up about 12 percent of all commercial bank deposits. But bank merger activity picked up again in that decade, stirring up the fears of small banks who demanded protection. When it became evident that Congress would succumb to the pressure by passing restrictive legislation, Transamerica went shopping. During the year prior to enactment of the Bank Holding Company Act of 1956, which prohibited subsequent interstate acquisition of banks, the company purchased control of twenty more banks throughout the eleven western states. While Transamerica had the largest interstate network, eleven other holding companies had banking subsidiaries that they, too, were allowed to retain under a grandfather clause in the law. Since the act prohibited a bank holding company from owning controlling interest in nonbanking companies and Transamerica preferred to retain those businesses, the firm divested itself of its banks in 1958. They became affiliates of a new bank holding company called Firstamerica Corporation (later called Western Bancorporation and now First Interstate Bancorp).

Designed to protect the markets of individual banks as branching restrictions did, in passing the Bank Holding Company Act, Congress made yet another attempt to preserve the mom-and-pop banking operations of the nation, although it cost consumers banking benefits similar to those they were already enjoying in large-scale retail store operations.

Alternative Approaches to Structural Policymaking

By trying to hold back the hands of time in responding to pressure from a special interest group, Congress provided another example of its usual ad hoc approach to policymaking concerning financial institutions. It was following no articulated set of objectives for what the structure of the industry should be to best fulfill national economic, social, and business needs; rather it was intended to preserve the status quo from an intraindustry perspective. Its action supported the populist goal of favoring small banks over large, yet it considered no means of achieving that end other than by limiting larger institutions. Moreover, its advocacy of small banks was not consistent; in the depression it had condemned many to failure when it subordinated federal law to state branching regulations. And rather than work with the industry to seek a socially desirable way for the banks to achieve economies of scale without having to use legal loopholes, it arbitrarily resorted to imposing more controls.

For its part, the reaction of the private sector constituted what was by then a patterned response of dodging laws that limited growth and competition. Its origins could be traced to the smorgasbord of regulatory environments laid out for Americans wishing to open a financial institution. First, there is the panoply of fifty different state legal and regulatory milieus. Then there is the Comptroller of the Currency, who supervises national banks. The FDIC oversees state-chartered commercial banks that are not members of the Federal Reserve System and insured mutual savings banks. The Board of Governors of the Federal Reserve System supervises state-chartered member banks, plus the holding companies and Edge Act banks. The Federal Home Loan Bank Board (FHLBB) oversees the federally-chartered S&Ls and state-chartered associations that are insured by the FSLIC or that are members of the Federal Home Loan Bank System. Finally, there is the National Credit Union Administration, whose name describes its function. The range of choices in selecting the most desirable set of operating rules is further extended if one is willing to wait until after the next election, when new officials probably will be appointed to run the agencies.

There are, of course, other approaches to creating public policy for the structure of financial institutions, an issue that took on special meaning as the age of computerization began in banking in the 1960s.

The All-in-One Regulatory Agency

Unlike their U.S. counterparts, Swedish bankers can choose only food from a smorgasbord; for regulation, they get the Bank Inspection Board, like it or not. The agency supervises all types of banks, their subsidiaries, finance companies, stockbrokerages, the stock exchange, the Securities Register Center, and the Credit Information Center—and does it with a staff of only sixty. To monitor the internal operations of the banks continually, the agency appoints special auditors, with one assigned full time to each major bank. Its operations do not cost Swedish citizens a krona; they are covered by fees charged to the supervised institutions. With a policy of strict political neutrality, its director, who served for ten years as a judge before assuming his position in 1971, has served under both Social Democratic and conservative governments. Its board of directors, which makes major decisions, is made up of three members of Parliament, two economic experts, and three bank inspectors, plus the agency's director and assistant director.

The caliber of staff benefits from the fact that in Sweden, as in most European nations, government employment for generations has attracted the best university graduates because it has high social status. Strict standards of integrity are ensured by law, and officials whose actions reveal improper use of authority are personally held accountable for damages, with penalties that include removal from office. For that reason, they are encouraged to search out painstakingly the implications of proposed actions. Patience, careful research, and consultation are not only intellectual traits of the Swedes; they also are mechanisms for self-preservation. In addition, the supervisors are supervised. The Swedish equivalent of the General Accounting Office audits the effectiveness of the agency periodically.

Although Swedish bankers characterize the bank inspectorate as "a kind of superior board of managers" and chant a litany of complaints about being overregulated, they have not been reluctant to accept help from the state when they have encountered difficulties.[12] The government gave massive infusions of money to the banks during the 1920s and 1930s, and in more recent years state subsidies to Swedish industries have kept banks' losses on outstanding loans to a fraction of what they otherwise would have been.

✳ The Strategic Planning Approach

The Swedish government regularly studies the state of the financial services' industry, sets goals as to the structure it considers best for existing conditions, adopts strategies to accomplish them, monitors their effectiveness, and does not hesitate to change course in response to new circumstances. But since policymaking always reflects values, to understand its approach it is necessary to identify those subjective elements.

The high barrier to entry that the inspectorate has erected through its rigid interpretation of the requirement that the founders of a bank must prove that it will be beneficial to the public gives established banks protection from new competitors. But the idea of letting the market solely determine the number of banks that will survive—as was true in the United States until the Continental Illinois debacle—has not been socially and economically acceptable in Sweden. The bank board believes that because of the major role of commercial banks in the nation's economic life and the high degree of industry concentration, a failure would create losses too widespread to be tolerable. Moreover, since the near collapse of the international banking system in the wake of the Banco Ambrosiano scandal, the agency's director has worked closely with his counterparts in other countries to tighten the integrity of the system by ensuring the stability of the multinational banks. Therefore, with solvency the prime objective, a certain degree of deficiency in competition appears to them not only inevitable but also desirable to a certain extent. The quid pro quo for this measure of protection is that the government has greater control over banks than over other businesses.

Another basic value is apparent in the protection given to the primarily small savings banks because of their size and special role in encouraging the socially desirable goal of thrift. One rule adhered to firmly in Sweden—and also in Germany although the thrifts have the biggest share of the retail market there—is that each must restrict its operations to a given geographic area, resulting in very little competition between them. To strengthen the competitive power of the thrifts, legislative changes in 1955 permitted them to offer a wider range of services, including checking accounts, thereby smudging the differences between them and the commercial banks.

Additional structural transformations were inherent in the official encouragement of mergers of smaller savings banks to make them stronger competitors. The results of the policy are apparent in the dramatic reduction in the number of thrifts by almost two-thirds since 1940. The merging of savings banks has become a trend throughout Europe in recent years, with a merger of all the Dutch thrifts planned and the British trustee savings banks consolidating into only four banks under the umbrella of a holding company.

The antitrust aspect of mergers, which has hampered such activity in the United States, was flatly rejected for years as inappropriate for Swedish banks by the inspectorate, which concurred in 1953 when the banks asked to be exempted from monopoly law. Hence, because the agency has the prime responsibility for seeing that the banks observe all laws, including those relating to competition, the Antitrust Ombudsman was not consulted in either of the major bank mergers in the 1970s, even though each resulted in the largest bank in the country. Since the creation of PK Bank was dictated mainly by political considerations, the ombudsman's opinion would not have mattered one way or the other; however, the government's argument at the time that another large bank was needed is consistent with his philosophy. He contends that in a small country, large size with resulting large market share can be allowed because competition is international, and to compete in world markets requires large-scale resources. Nevertheless, he subsequently succeeded in getting a law passed that states that acquisitions involving or resulting in market-dominating firms, including banks, are to be investigated by his office.

Because Swedish authorities continually watch developments in other countries, their policymaking was influenced by a major restructuring of the banking industry on the Continent. It began with the Debre reforms of 1966 in France, which lifted restrictions on branching, permitted banks to expand their scope of activities, and removed interest rate restrictions on loans. The Germans, who had ended all branching restrictions in 1958, eliminated all interest rate controls, and other nations enacted regulatory changes to equalize the operations of competing institutions. Hence, when Sweden in 1968 eliminated structural differentiation by permitting all banks to offer the same services, it was part of a deregulatory movement in Europe in the late 1960s and early 1970s.

While conceding that there are difficulties in deciding what structure is optimal, in order to preserve a balance between a few large banks and a large number of smaller ones, the inspectorate in the past negotiated agreements with the big banks that they would not buy any of the remaining provincial banks. But over time, the agency found that the smaller banks actually would benefit the most from mergers because otherwise the needs of their customers would grow beyond their capacity to meet them. Hence, it permitted the pact to expire.

To uphold their advocacy of large, nationwide banks, Swedish policymakers have effectively resolved two prickly issues—raised by politicians there and by small bankers and populists in the United States—that generated controversy for years. In response to concern that the evolution of fewer and larger banks could result in the neglect of local interests, every branch office is required to have local management, and municipal government authorities are entitled to appoint two members to local bank boards. They have dealt with the charge that large banks would constitute a concentration of power that could be dangerous to society by appointing government representatives to sit on the corporate and regional boards of all commercial banks and by creating PK Bank as a countervailing power to the large privately-owned banks.

Tangling with Branching

The flexibility that characterizes Swedish policymaking was evinced by the requirement of official approval for new offices, as opposed to the rigid U.S. bans based on location. Nonetheless, one-third of the requests were being rejected, leading some banks to merge to extend their networks, when a government study pointed out that the 1918 warning that caution should be used in denying requests was not being observed. That resulted in a relaxation of controls in 1955, which permitted a 38 percent expansion of branches to accommodate the urbanization process, the building of new suburbs, and the increasing demand for services as the number of deposit accounts doubled in the 1960s. Even so, the old problem of some being more equal than others surfaced in the favoritism shown to the state-owned bank and smaller banks while the inspectorate rejected about half of the commercial banks' applications. This drove the incisive Ph.D. who headed Sweden's largest bank to express Giannini-type exasperation with the idea that branching networks should be suppressed by regulation: "It has never been made clear why the consumer of bank services does not have as great a right to convenient service in the form of an accessible network of shops as the consumer of goods."[13]

Ironically, the number of new branches opened peaked in 1968, when the new laws gave banks the right to open offices, with the proviso that they first submit their plans to an advisory committee made up of banking, union, and inspectorate representatives. Although instructed to create a banking structure that would be satisfactory from a societal viewpoint, the group was given no criteria. Hence, in time it became evident that what had seemed like a good idea in theory was doomed to fail in reality. When the advisory group's rejection of commercial bank applications grew to 63 percent, the bankers reacted in an uncharacteristically rebellious way: in effect, they told the advisory group to stuff it and went ahead and opened the branch offices they wanted. Provoked to anger by this unprecedented display of independence, the Social Democratic government in 1974 declared the committee decisions legally binding, even though the inspectorate said there was no need for controls since the number of new offices was declining. After that, things got worse. As partisan interests began to overshadow objectivity and bad decisions were overturned on appeal to the government, the committee's work lost much of the calm and consensual style that customarily distinguishes Swedish decision making.

But in time the traditional style prevailed when yet another report proposed change, and the government in 1980 recommended an end to all controls. The statement by the center-coalition government that had ended the Social Democrats' forty-four years of control in 1976 reflected values that differed markedly from those of the SDP: "It is unlikely that banks any more than other businesses would conduct operations which are unprofitable. From a competitive standpoint . . . official establishment controls should be avoided as much as possible. Thereby one also avoids unnecessary bureaucracy."[14] The proposal called for the banks to report planned new facilities to the inspectorate and to obtain the views of the communities before opening or closing offices.

Copies of the document then were submitted for comment to all parties likely to be affected by the change in a centuries-old Swedish policymaking procedure known as *remiss*. In this consultative process for all major policy bills, the responses are reviewed and changes made before submitting the final proposal and explanatory text to Parliament. The procedure provides an opportunity for affected parties to influence policy and also generates valuable information for the government. By communicating the intensity of emotions stimulated by a proposal, it also helps determine what, if any, concessions should be made to appease those with differing viewpoints.

For example, in his response to the proposal, the Consumer Ombudsman expressed concern about the closing of branches in small towns where population was declining and complained that the existing committee lacked a consumer advocate. In its *remiss* reply, the inspectorate said it had always believed that the control should reside with it and huffed that *it* had represented consumer concerns on the committee, just as it always did. The Riksbank noted that the increase in costs of opening new branches, not regulation, had slowed their growth. The Swedish Bankers Association produced statistics indicating that the growth of branching had corresponded to the banks' expansion into retail banking in the 1960s, in spite of the controls in effect then, and had been based on marketing rationale. On the other hand, disapproval of the proposal was expressed in its *remiss* reply by the savings banks' association, which had been doing so well with the committee that it had no reason to want change. In some years, savings banks had had two or three times as many branch applications approved as had commercial banks, and in some years they had had no applications rejected. But the state-owned bank and the cooperative banks approved, and the change was implemented in 1981.

Thus, after more than sixty-two years, Swedish banks could open new branches without regulatory interference. But if it was a victory, it was a hollow one. By then, in an era of rising costs, with the populace well-banked and electronic technology changing the basic nature of delivery systems, it was a nonissue. The number of commercial banks' offices had been declining since 1971 and the number of savings banks' offices since 1969. In the first full year of freedom, while twenty-two new offices were opened, sixty-five were closed. But while Sweden had lagged considerably behind other European countries in deregulating branching and had bungled some of its efforts, it was still ahead of U.S. policymakers.

Where Machines Are Not Considered Branches

Delivery systems constitute the essential interface between financial institutions and their customers, the points at which payment transfers are initiated, information conveyed, and services offered. Thus, because it is this key link that is most affected by electronic technology, public policies affecting this area can critically affect the development of EFTS.

Because the money machines in Sweden are only CDs, comparisons to full-service branches would be unwarranted; however, the fact that Swedish banks opened some 100 service offices for cashing checks and handling salary payments in the late 1950s indicates a perceived value in meeting consumer needs through less than full-service facilities. Hence, it is more appropriate to view the units as sub-branches or service facilities, which are used extensively in Sweden and other nations, especially those with branching restrictions, such as Greece, Italy, and Japan. In those countries remote banking services are provided at factories and stores; from temporary facilities on a seasonal basis at university campuses, amusement parks, and resorts; by buses and boats in Sweden; and in Greece by mobile branches that operate like the canteen trucks in the United States that dispense coffee and doughnuts outside workplaces.

In fact, an enterprising Florida banker offered just such a service in the 1960s with an armored car that had a customer window installed on one side. It would pull up at business sites so that employees could make deposits and withdrawals from their accounts, with the transactions actually processed back at the bank's main office. But the U.S. Supreme Court put the kibosh on that in 1969 when, relying on a 1927 definition of a branch office as any place that takes deposits, cashes checks, or lends money, it ruled that the vehicle constituted a branch and was therefore in violation of the Mc-Fadden Act.[15] It thereby established a precedent that has been relied on repeatedly up to the present in cases involving automated teller machines and, hence, has hindered the development of EFTS in the United States.

In addition to producing chuckles at international banking conferences where U.S. branching laws are referred to as amusing anachronisms in an electronic age, such interpretation is regarded as strange in Swedish legal circles, where it is considered wrong for a judge to apply an outdated restriction to a new situation. Yet in Sweden no permission from the government has ever been needed for a CD. This is because, like the service facilities, CDs do not take deposits, and Swedish law defines a bank office as a facility that takes deposits from the public.

As an alternative to tortured applications of antiquated laws, Congress could write new laws. Indeed, the judiciary contends that the resolution of the problem resides precisely there. That body, however, has chosen not to address the matter.

Down the Regulatory Road with Blinders

Ironically, while even leftist nations deregulated industry structure in the 1960s in recognition of changes wrought by the retail banking revolution, in the capitalistic United States, banks were fettered by tightened regulation. Seemingly oblivious of the impact of that major development, technological innovations, and growing inflation, the regulators proceeded like horses with blinders on.

The Beginning of the End

As U.S. banking operations were computerized in the 1960s, it was not the potential of that awesome technology but the introduction of Magnetic Ink

Character Recognition for processing checks by EDP that some industry observers myopically hailed as perhaps "the most significant event of the twentieth century in the field of banking operations."[16] Lulled into lethargy by years of regulatory protection from competition, it never occurred to most bankers that just as EDP technology made it easier for them to handle payment services—the main source of their deposits—it also enabled any firm with computer and telecommunications capabilities to do the same. In fact, it signified the end of their monopoly and of the industry structure that they assumed was set in concrete.

As to that structure, although there are only about one-third as many S&Ls now as in 1933 and two-thirds as many mutual savings banks, the number of commercial banks has remained remarkably stable since 1933, when there were 14,352. However, after 1,467 banks ceased operating independently to merge between 1952 and 1960, the Bank Merger Act of 1960 was passed at the behest of the smaller banks. In ruling on merger requests, competitive tests were heavily relied on after the Justice Department in 1963 successfully challenged a merger previously approved by the Comptroller of the Currency.[17] The court in that case found that banks did not have real competition from thrifts, even though they had lost 20 percent of their market share to them in the preceding two decades.

As restrictions were relaxed, the number of bank branches roughly doubled in both the 1960s and 1970s, so that by 1982 there were some 41,000. The annual growth rate of bank branches in the United States between 1964 and 1977 was twice as great as that in other developed nations, according to a survey by the Organization for Economic Cooperation and Development (OECD).[18] Moreover, that growth rate was 1.67 times greater than the banks' annual growth rate of volume of business, which was only half the average of other nations' banks. The pattern of development for the S&Ls differed in that while the number of S&L offices increased by 76 percent between 1960 and 1974, the number of S&Ls declined by some 1,000. Although the annual growth rate of S&L branches was over three times greater than that of the OECD average, their volume of business grew faster than that of other nations' thrifts. However, the S&Ls' rate of branch expansion was nearly twice as great as the growth of their business, suggesting that for them as for the banks, much of the branch growth was a response to other than economic forces.

Like their Swedish counterparts, U.S. regulators criticized the banks' "failure [to adopt] more efficient marketing strategies than cash-dispensing, deposit-taking offices."[19] However, in the United States as in Sweden, the growth of branch networks constituted a form of nonprice competition that was facilitated by the fact that computerization made branch management easier to control. The banks needed to overcome their disadvantage of deposit rate ceilings, and the thrifts had to provide access to funds for holders of passbook savings accounts. Of special importance as the commercial banks entered retail banking, branches enabled both groups to follow the population to the suburbs.

The foundations of the U.S. financial industry were fatally undermined in 1966 when for the first time the ceilings on deposit interest were set below those on the open market and also were extended to the thrifts, a measure by which the government hoped to cool down the Vietnam war–fueled economy. However, to insulate the thrift institutions from commercial bank competition, the ceilings on passbook savings in the thrifts were set slightly higher than the rate the commercial banks could pay. While the ceilings inexorably would lead to both depositors and borrowers bypassing the regulated markets as inflation continued to mount, as bankers sought to circumvent them, the ceilings inspired an unprecedented wave of innovations.

One emerged in the late 1960s when a number of artful dodgers noticed that the Bank Holding Company Act applied only to firms with at least two banks; the result was the one-bank holding company (OBHC). Through them banks could engage in operations not permitted regulated firms. Thus, they provided the pleasures of forbidden fruit while generating additional revenues. Moreover, those activities met a need born of the computer age: to find more applications for the hardware to justify the costs, which always end up higher than planned. Thus, in the typical "monkey see, monkey do" pattern of banking, the number of OBHCs grew from 550 in 1965 to 1,352 by the end of 1970, after which the loophole was plugged.[20]

Nevertheless, between 1971 and 1977, the Fed approved some 4,000 applications for the holding companies to form or acquire firms to operate such computer-based businesses as computer leasing, data processing, mortgage banking, insurance, and card products. Although by 1982 there were 4,555 bank holding companies, which controlled 70 percent of all offices and 80 percent of deposits,[21] the chairman of the largest told a Senate committee in 1981: "A holding company is probably the clumsiest, most expensive way that exists to operate any business. We have only gone to [one] in order to comply with the law and gain some flexibility."[22]

Invasion of the Money Snatchers

The old regulatory barriers intended to insulate one type of financial firm from another crumbled in the 1970s as high interest rates provided the incentive and electronic technology the means to circumvent ill-conceived and ineffective regulations. Burdened with low-yield, long-term mortgages yet prohibited from offering short-term loans or checking accounts, when the thrifts suffered another wave of disintermediation just three years after getting their interest rate differential, the sheer drive to survive thrust them into EFT development. Perceiving in the technology a way to get into payment services through the back door, when they unveiled NOW accounts in the early 1970s it marked the end of the commercial banks' monopoly on payment systems and the beginning of the financial services revolution in the United States.

As people flocked to the thrifts to open NOW accounts, the bankers retreated behind the regulators and egged them into throwing statutes at their newly tough competitors. Although the bankers succeeded in having NOW accounts limited at the time to New England, innovators developed variations on the theme, so that by the end of 1974 checklike accounts were offered by thrifts and credit unions in twenty states. But while the bankers were busy trying to quash the NOWs in the East, another innovation popped up in Nebraska and knocked the industry for a loop. Inspired by the time-honored practice of cashing checks in stores, in 1974 an S&L installed electronic terminals in two Hinky Dinky supermarkets that enabled customers to make deposits and withdrawals from their savings accounts—a POS system—and that idea, too, was a success. In the same year a thrift launched a telephone bill-paying service, and S&Ls were authorized to set up statewide ATM networks. Yet when the banks were granted the same privilege, the small bankers challenged it in court and had the terminals legally, albeit absurdly, declared branches, thereby precluding competition in that area.

As the small banks battled with the big banks to prevent the development of EFTS and both engaged in combat with the thrifts, the "invisible hand" of the market became quite apparent as money market funds emerged to drain funds from them. Unhampered by regulations, the funds capitalized on the fact that the restrictions intended to protect the weakest institutions from failure had made the entire U.S. banking industry uniquely vulnerable to competition from the outside. With their computers already set to handle information exchange relating to financial assets, all it took to get into payment services was some advertising to announce their interest rates, an 800 telephone number, and a few more employees to handle the mail as the money poured in. From four funds with $100 million in assets at the end of 1973, they grew to 85 with over $80 billion by 1980.[23] To make bad matters worse, by purchasing billions of dollars of commercial paper, the money market funds enabled corporations to bypass the banks, thereby gravely eroding their loan business, too.

The real coup de grace was administered to the industry in 1977 when Merrill Lynch introduced its Cash Management Account, which attracted over 1 million affluent customers by providing access to funds held in money market or other investment accounts by check or Visa card and credit as well. With a huge asset base, a nationwide network of offices, and a loan portfolio that only thirty banks could match, the formidable intruder was already operating banks in London and Panama. The shaken banks and thrifts responded vigorously; they demanded that reserve requirements be imposed on the funds too. Perhaps out of a sense of guilt, the Fed did so in 1980—for a few months. Then a funny thing happened: the voice of the consumer was heard, and it said loud and clear, "Butt out." And the Fed did. For the first time in their lives, millions of small investors were enjoying the competitiveness of the investment market, and they were not about to give it up for the sake of the banks that had never paid market rates to anyone but large investors.

Following the imposition of interest rate ceilings in 1966, U.S. banks had rushed to open branches abroad where they were free of the ceilings as well as noninterest-bearing reserves and insurance assessments. Between 1965 and 1970, the assets of their overseas branches expanded from $9 billion to nearly $53 billion. But when they saw the number of foreign-owned banks in the United States grow from 30 in 1972 to some 100 with 300 offices in 1980, with assets increasing at three times the rate of domestic banks', they felt besieged from without as well as within. Moreover, the foreigners could branch nationwide and, because they were not subject to reserve requirements, could undercut domestic banks on loans so that by 1979 they were making 20 percent of all corporate loans. In addition, they could acquire banks while the domestic banks could not because of interstate, holding company, and antitrust laws. Crying "Foul!" the bankers demanded legislation and an investigation. The International Banking Act of 1978 remedied most of the inequities, and following its study of banks acquired by foreign firms, the Federal Reserve reported that there was no reason to fear a foreign takeover of the industry. It had found that the acquired banks were in fact a rather sorry lot: eighteen had been experiencing losses or, like Franklin National, were in receivership, and another six had a very low return on assets.

Banking by Loophole

Interstate banking is prohibited in the United States. Yet since the mid-1970s, the money center banks have set up coast-to-coast networks of loan production, leasing, and Edge Act offices that small bankers glumly view as Trojan horses whose doors will open, disgorging hundreds of pinstripe-suited dudes, when interstate banking is permitted. After California-based Bank of America ran an ad saying, "We love New York so much we have eleven hundred people here," a Big Apple banker observed, "You have to believe in the emperor's new clothes to say there isn't interstate banking in the United States."[24]

But while de facto interstate banking operations had for some years made a farce of the de jure ban on the practice, the acme of absurdity in banking regulation may have been attained when the Federal Reserve Board conceded the legality of use of a loophole in the law and thereby sanctioned the birth of a new type of bank designed to circumvent federal banking regulations. While the Fed was an unwilling midwife to the event, it had unwittingly sowed the seeds itself for the creation of what was to become, in anomalous financial argot, the "nonbank" bank. Under the Bank Holding Company Act (BHCA), the Fed has jurisdiction over the acquisition of banks, which in 1966 had been defined as institutions that take demand deposits. But in 1970, at the request of the Fed, Congress made the definition two-pronged by adding that the institution must also make commercial loans.

The potential impact of this definitional change on the separation of banking from commerce was not realized until 1980 when a nonbanking corporation was permitted to purchase a bank after divesting its commercial loan portfolio because it then no longer was a bank as defined in the BHCA. With the precedent established, other cross-industry acquisitions followed, as securities, insurance, and other nonbanking firms bought limited-service banks that either did not take demand deposits or did not make commercial loans. The first indication of the structural havoc that ultimately would result from the creation of the nonbank bank appeared in 1983 when the Fed ruled that the purchase of a limited-service Ohio bank by a Kentucky bank holding company (BHC) could not be prevented, even though it was aware that the applicant's reason for limiting the bank's activities was "to avoid bank status and the interstate banking prohibitions" in the BHCA.[25]

Within months, the Fed received an application from U.S. Trust, a New York BHC, to convert its Florida office into a consumer bank, one without commercial loans. When notice of the proposal was published, it set off a furor. It was blasted by the Conference of State Bank Supervisors, the State of Florida, the Florida Bankers Association, and every other group opposed to interstate banking. Simultaneously it set off a frenzy of activity by lawyers employed by other BHCs that wanted to do the same thing. In early 1984, Maryland's attorney general ruled that the acquisition of a state-chartered nonbank bank by a Delaware bank could not be prohibited because the loophole in coverage by the BHCA had "received federal regulatory approval. We must therefore conclude that this 'loophole' is currently the law."[26]

In March 1984 the Federal Reserve Board approved U.S. Trust's application because of the definitional constraint. It urged, however, that the loophole be plugged since its continued use had "potential for a significant, haphazard, and possibly dangerous alteration of the banking structure without Congressional action on the underlying policy issues."[27] Indeed it had; regulators were deluged by over 300 applications for nonbank banks. While legislation to close the loophole was passed by the Senate, it failed to clear the House, prompting the chairman of the Senate Banking Committee to call House members "a bunch of gutless politicians."[28] The Comptroller of the Currency gave preliminary approval to 108 applications but then stopped to prepare himself for a lawsuit filed against him by Florida bankers opposed to the nonbank banks. By late 1984, as much of the old federal regulatory structure sank slowly into the legalistic quagmire of the loophole, a banker complained, "It is a shame that we are forced to resort to Mickey Mouse exercises to achieve a legitimate economic purpose."[29]

Although the chairman of the Fed has said he does not want Sears in the banking business, bankers began to realize that they were competing with it and other major retailers, as well as securities and insurance firms, all of which have nationwide outlets. Thus, in another move to skirt the interstate banking ban, the banks began working together to develop interstate EFT systems so as to overcome their competititve disadvantage. With a speed that was dazzling after decades of foot dragging, both large and small banks turned to ATM networks as their main line of defense against their common enemies. By 1983 over half the commercial banks in the nation were participating in some 200 regional and 6 nationwide ATM networks and, all told, banking convenience had been enhanced by some 40,000 ATMs.[30]

Another structural phenomenon has been the emergence of regional banking systems as groups of states have passed reciprocal laws that permit regional mergers across state lines but prevent outsiders from buying institutions in the region. Based on the "infant industry" argument that the measures will give the banks time to become stronger through mergers before having to compete with the money center banks, by mid-1984 every state except California, New York, and Texas was part of one or more groups in varying stages of discussion and implementation. Although the Fed in 1984 approved three interstate bank mergers in New England, the Supreme Court in January 1985 announced that it would hear an appeal challenging the Fed's decision.

In yet another innovation in anticipation of interstate banking, some banks have made "stake-out" arrangements for desired partners in other states. An investment in the stock of the other institution is made, rather like pledging a troth with an engagement ring, with the understanding that the merger will be consummated when the law is changed.

Triage on the Battlefield

While schoolchildren, policymakers, and interest groups in the mid-1980s still referred to the three types of depository institutions in the United States as commercial banks, thrift institutions, and credit unions, a more realistic appraisal might be based on another triad of categories: the basket cases, the walking wounded, and the survivors. The Deregulation Committee created in 1980 to supervise the process of "restoring competitive equality" to the industry was assigned to a quixotic quest; there never was equality in the industry. It was an illusion maintained for years by an artificial support system of protective regulations that ultimately left many of the institutions incapable of surviving when exposed to the harsh realities of the external environment.

In the first two years following passage of the 1982 emergency assistance legislation for thrift institutions, which included permission for banks to cross state lines to acquire S&Ls that were in trouble, sixty-nine interstate mergers and purchases occurred. In spite of large capital infusions by government regulators, however, many thrifts, as well as commercial banks, turned to brokered money market funds to compensate for depositor funds lost to the unregulated market and to fuel growth. The practice led to the most costly thrift liquidation in history following the collapse in 1984 of a Texas S&L whose deposits had spiraled from $17.3 million in June 1982 to $308.9 million by February 1984, unaccompanied by increased net worth. Because all but $9.6 million of the deposits, which primarily were brokered funds from distant markets, were federally insured, the failure cost the FSLIC some $163 million. A subsequent congressional investigation revealed supervisory laxity by the regulators, whose defense was that their resources were stretched thin by demands arising from other failures. Perhaps so. In the first quarter of 1984, 40 percent of the nation's thrifts lost money. In August, American S&L, the largest in the country, suffered a liquidity crisis in which nearly $7 billion in deposits were withdrawn in three months.

The costliest bank failure in U.S. history occurred in 1982 with the closing of Penn Square Bank of Oklahoma City for allegedly unsound banking practices which resulted in losses of an estimated $1.5 billion. Because the bank had raised millions of dollars through money brokers in its last few weeks, the FDIC refused to cover some $200 million of the uninsured deposits of thrifts, credit unions, and other customers, thereby setting a precedent that was followed in some twenty cases thereafter. Dramatically demonstrating the fragility of the financial structure, its failure led within a year to the near collapse of Seafirst Bank, which required a $1.5 billion safety net before it was rescued by BankAmerica. The Seattle bank almost came a cropper because Penn Square not only made bad loans but also sold them, some to Seafirst.

But it took two years for the shock waves from the failure of the Oklahoma bank to rock the nation and the world as they did in July 1984 when the FDIC took over Continental Illinois, in large measure because of losses from its $1 billion in loans from Penn Square. In exchange for providing $4.5 billion from its insurance fund—an amount that dwarfed the bailouts of Lockheed, Chrysler, and New York City combined—the FDIC acquired 80 percent of the preferred stock of the nation's eighth largest banking company. Because of the bank's $42 billion in assets and worldwide banking relationships, plus more than $6 billion in deposits from 2,100 small banks, the government felt constrained to step in for fear of a domino effect. In May an emergency credit line of $7.5 billion from private banks and an FDIC guarantee of all depositors and creditors had been used, in vain, to try to stem a $9 billion run on the bank led by Japanese and European banks and investors. Because Continental must rely on volatile deposits by such big investors for 70 percent of its funds due to a state ban on branch offices that could gather more stable consumer deposits, the chairman of the FDIC blamed the bank's downfall in part on overregulation.[31]

With bank failures in 1984 exceeding those of any other year since 1939 and a record-breading 800 banks on the FDIC's problem list, the agency expected to pay out insurance losses of $2.6 billion, compared to losses that ranged from $30 million to $100 million per year before 1981. Controversy has erupted among bankers and the public over the 100 percent coverage given Continental Illinois' depositors while customers of failed small banks have received only about 60 percent of their uninsured funds. Further outrage followed the assurance by the Comptroller of the Currency that the eleven largest banks in the country are TBTF (too big to fail), thereby condemning the remainder to an uncertain future. By the autumn of 1984, only two bank holding companies were still rated AAA by Standard & Poor's Corp. Even more troublesome was the revelation in the midst of the American S&L crisis that the FSLIC could not cover even the $12 billion of insured deposits of the thrift's total $24 billion because the insurance fund had only $6.3 billion in it.

As a result of widespread news coverage of the industry's problems, the banks' one unique advantage in the past over unregulated institutions—public confidence—has been badly eroded. During the same week in which the FDIC ran an ad in the *Wall Street Journal* offering salaries of up to $75,000 for loan liquidators to work in Chicago on a portfolio of over $300 million, a poll revealed that one-third of Americans were less confident about the banking and financial system than they had been a few years ago.[32] Apparently as a result, the respondents opposed giving banks the authority to offer new services, such as insurance and real estate. Many, however, expressed a willingness to conduct their banking business with unregulated institutions by using the phone, mail, or ATMs.

Confidence in regulators seemed to be faring no better. While membership in the Federal Reserve System previously was regarded as a requisite to maintain an image of stability and security, between 1967 and 1979 over 400 banks left the system to avoid the requirement of noninterest-bearing reserves. After the Fed learned that member banks with two-thirds of the deposits in the system were planning to jump ship, the law was changed to require all depository institutions to maintain reserves. Moreover, a 1983 survey of members of the Association of Bank Holding Companies found they would prefer not to be regulated by the Fed anymore.[33]

With the shape of the U.S. financial services industry an increasingly amorphous mishmash of commercial banks, thrift institutions, credit unions, retailers, securities and insurance firms, plus nonbank banks, the 1980s seem destined to go down in history as the decade in which the old banking structure in the United States crumbled.

Notes

1. Interview with a high-level Swedish banking executive in November 1982.
2. Hans Bergström, "Affärsbankernas rätt att öppna avdelningskontor," *Ekonomisk revy* 9 (1959): 605.
3. Almarin Phillips, "Competitive Policy for Depository Financial Institutions," in *Promoting Competition in Regulated Markets,* ed. Almarin Philips (Washington, D.C.: Brookings Institution, 1975), p. 341.
4. Thomas F. Horan, "Outlook for EFT Technology," in Kent W. Colton and Kenneth L. Kraemer, eds., *Computers and Banking* (New York: Plenum, 1980), p. 22.
5. "The Problems Continental Illinois' Rescue Is Creating," *Business Week,* June 4, 1984, p. 109.
6. *The Report of the President's Commission on Financial Structure and Regulation* (Washington, D.C.: Government Printing Office, 1972), pp. 34–35.
7. Harold Black and Robert H. Dugger, "Credit Union Structure, Growth and Regulatory Problems," *Journal of Finance* 36, no. 2 (May 1981): 529–538.
8. Patrick Frazer and Dimitri Vittas, *The Retail Banking Revolution* (London: Michael Lafferty Publications, 1982), p. 37.
9. William F. Baxter, Paul H. Cootner, and Kenneth E. Scott, *Retail Banking in the Electronic Age* (Montclair, N.J.: Allanheld, Osmun, 1977), p. 179.
10. Roger T. Johnson, *Historical Beginnings . . . The Federal Reserve* (Boston: Federal Reserve Bank of Boston, 1982), p. 32.
11. Annual Report of the President to the Shareholders of the Bank of Italy, N.T.&S.A., January 10, 1928.
12. Ernfrid Browaldh, "The State and the Private Banking System," Supplement to Svenska Handelsbanken's *Index* (September 1946): 14.
13. Lars-Erik Thunholm, "Samordnad banklagstiftning," *Ekonomisk revy* 10 (1967): 563.
14. Proposition 1980/81:37, p. 4.
15. *First National Bank of Plant City, Florida* v. *Dickinson,* 396 U.S. 122 (1969).
16. Robert S. Aldom, Alan B. Purdy, Robert T. Schneider, and Harry W. Whittingham, Jr., *Automation in Banking* (New Brunswick, N.J.: Rutgers University Press, 1963), p. v.
17. *United States* v. *Philadelphia National Bank,* 374 U.S. 321 (1963).
18. J.R.S. Revell, *Costs and Margins in Banking: an International Survey* (Paris: OECD, 1980), p. 130.
19. George W. Mitchell, "Remarks," in Federal Reserve System, *Papers and Comments of the International Conference on Banking and Payment Systems,* Atlanta, April 2–4, 1980, p. 6.

20. Phillips, "Competitive Policy," p. 351.

21. Law & Business, Inc., *The State Banking Revolution and the Federal Response: New Frontiers of Financial Service Expansion* (Clifton, N.J.: Law & Business, Inc., 1984), p. 73.

22. Walter Wriston, former chairman of Citicorp, statement to Senate Committee on Banking, Housing and Urban Affairs, October 29, 1981.

23. Constance Dunham, "The Growth of Money Market Funds," *New England Economic Review* (September–October 1980): 33.

24. Walter Wriston, in comments to ABA convention, as quoted in "Sen. Proxmire Opposes Relaxing Restrictions on Interstate Banking," *Wall Street Journal*, October 16, 1980.

25. *Federal Reserve Bulletin* 69 (July 1983): 556–558.

26. Opinion No. 84-013 (March 2, 1984) (to be published at 69 *Opinions of the Attorney General* _____ (1984)).

27. *U.S. Trust Corp. Federal Reserve Bulletin* 70 _____ (1984).

28. Senator Jake Garn, quoted in "Comptroller of the Currency Approves Applications for 29 Limited-Service Banks," *Wall Street Journal*, November 2, 1984.

29. Fred C. Herriman of Chemical New York Corp., quoted in "Interstate Banking: The Big Gamble That Congress Will Make It Legal," *Business Week*, November 12, 1984, p. 143.

30. Steven D. Felgran, "Shared ATM Networks: Market Structure and Public Policy," *New England Economic Review* (January–February 1984): 26.

31. FDIC Chairman William M. Isaac, cited by "The Problems Continental Illinois' Rescue Is Creating," p. 112.

32. Survey conducted by the *American Banker* cited by "Less Confidence in Banks Cited by One-Third in Poll," *Wall Street Journal*, October 22, 1984.

33. Survey cited by "Volcker Defends Regulatory Role for Fed," *American Banker*, October 11, 1983.

4
Changing Competitive Forces

Effort to Compete on Equal Terms in Sweden

To stimulate competition, Sweden in 1968 amended its laws to permit all types of banks to offer the same services. Previously the groups had had specific functions, with the commercial banks providing short-term loans to business, the savings banks channeling household savings to home construction and local governments, and the cooperative banks providing loans to the agricultural sector. While the change was intended to help both groups of smaller banks, impetus for it came primarily from the savings banks, for which it represented the culmination of ten years of effort and over seventy-five years of aspiration. They had first sought permission to offer checking accounts at the turn of the century. Their timing, however, left something to be desired, coming as it did in the wake of revelations of a series of embezzlements in the banks. Hence, they failed then, as they did on four later occasions.

They did prevail in the battle for deposits between the wars, beginning with the banking crisis of the 1920s when nervous depositors pulled their funds out of the toppling commercial banks. Between 1925 and 1940, while commercial banks' deposits went up only 24 percent, theirs rose 44 percent.[1] They had an advantage over the shareholder-owned banks in that they did not have to pay dividends. But that was no help in their fight for deposits with the ubiquitous postal banks, which had an edge with their larger office network and more convenient hours. At the cost of both the commercial and savings banks, the combined market share of the Postal Bank and giro rose from 5.7 percent in 1930 to 17.4 percent in 1950, after which it stabilized.[2]

In the 1950s the competitive picture was drastically altered when the commercial banks for the first time came into head-on conflict with the savings banks in seeking deposits from the household sector. This gave the latter new bargaining power with the authorities in their quest for the holy grail of checking accounts. In the ensuing debates about lowering the barriers between sectors, overtones of protectionism punctuated the polemic, with the commercial banks arguing that industrial development required the funneling of savings through them because the thrifts' lending was mainly limited to housing. Moreover, the proliferation of free services that accompanied the new competitive efforts was viewed with alarm. It had, for example, become possible for a customer of a bank in one location to make passbook withdrawals in a bank of the same type in another place, a service compelled by competition from the Postal Bank. The hot breath of competition from the Postal Giro was plaguing the commercial banks even more. Although they had more than half the transaction deposits in the country in 1954, they had lost over 28 percent of the market since 1938 to the giro, whose share had burgeoned from 17.4 percent to 45.6 percent.[3] By then the Minister of Finance was recommending a study of the potential effects of uniform laws for all types of banks, and the 1955 banking law amendments finally authorized the thrifts to offer checking accounts.

It appeared, however, that the metaphorical elephant had labored to give birth to a mouse: the thrifts' customers did not share the executives' fervor for the accounts. In 1960, only 0.1 percent of their deposits were in checking accounts, with the bulk still in passbook savings where people could see balances that were calculated by bankers, not customers, and where the money on deposit earned interest.[4] Moving ever further from their initial purpose, by 1959 the savings banks were promoting shopping loans and were pursuing salary accounts. Due to their customers' aversion to checks, they offered direct deposit into savings accounts from which withdrawals could be made in any savings bank office by showing proof of account. The significance of those accounts in the makeup of their deposits is reflected in the change of turnover time. While in 1950 the average length of time money was deposited was about four years, by 1975 it had dropped to six months.[5]

In addition to the announced rationale for the 1968 change, certain political implications were inherent in the policy revision in Sweden. First, the savings banks have long enjoyed a close relationship with the nation's dominant blue-collar trade union and the SDP. Second, timing had an effect in that the policy was developed during the politically turbulent 1960s, when the radical Left was demanding nationalization of the commercial banks. Hence, the SDP majority in Parliament had a special interest in empowering the thrifts to compete more strongly with the commercial banks. Third, an idea emerged in the government during the 1960s that competition in banking should be based on different value systems. This concept divided the industry into the state-owned, private, and savings institutions. The oddity is that while the state-owned commercial bank is under great pressure to produce profits, the savings banks are described by their leaders as having a more ideological concept and are not primarily profit oriented.

In the fifteen years since passage of the legislation intended to strengthen the weaker competitors, the market share of the savings banks has gradually decreased while those of the cooperative and commercial banks have increased. At the beginning of 1983, the commercial banks had some 61 percent of deposits; the savings banks, 31 percent; and the cooperatives, some 7 percent.

Competing through Blocs

In recent years competition among the Swedish financial institutions has intensified markedly. Hence, a key question is how the small banks have been able to compete effectively with some very large banks and what role product offerings made possible by the policy change have played in their competitive endeavors. Since competition there, as in many European countries, occurs more between blocs of banks than between individual banks, the answer to the question lies within the groups.

Cooperative Banks

Because the cooperatives combine a form of ownership near and dear to the hearts of Swedes with a touch of the country from their past and offer a full range of banking services as well, they have become the fastest-growing bloc since dropping "agricultural" from their name in 1974. They have, moreover, a reputation for trustworthiness rooted in the fact that because members have been legally responsible for operations, personal integrity has ensured soundness. Their customers can deposit all funds into an all-in-one account that earns interest and provides checks, a Bankomat card, and transfers through Bank Giro. This simplifies bookkeeping and encourages use of the CDs for withdrawals. In addition, through subsidiaries and agreements with other firms, they offer financing, leasing, administrative and computer services, real estate transactions, and mutual stock funds.

As individual units with severely limited resources, the small banks obviously could not offer these services. But through their central organization they receive administrative, coordinating, and control services and have research, marketing, training, and computer services provided. Their association provides an expertise equivalent to that of a large bank, while their jointly owned central bank provides the facilities of a commercial bank. Moreover, memberships in Bankomat Center, Bank Giro, and Köpkort enable them to offer the most sophisticated retail banking products in Sweden. The unifying element in their services is electronic technology, demonstrating that in a shared EFT system, an account with a small, local bank provides virtually as much convenience as one with a large bank operating nationwide. On the other hand, the influx into cooperative banks of new customers who often have small balances and make small transactions could not have been handled without fully automated systems.

Savings Banks

Swedish savings banks differ from their U.S. counterparts in that, with each limited to a specific area, there is little competition between them. Hence, their bloc has been strengthened through cooperative endeavors going back to the turn of the century when their central association was formed. Today the association provides group management, develops policies, handles government relations, and operates subsidiary service units. Since each savings bank is an independent unit, however, the bloc does not have the homogeneity that characterizes the cooperatives. The savings banks differ greatly in size, with fifteen holding over half the assets of all, and considerably in philosophy. Although the association seeks to standardize the level of services, it can do no more than recommend in seeking to achieve a balance between those who cling to the traditions of a small town style and those who run modern operations.

The association provides staff training and assistance with administration, marketing, law, taxes, and operations. Its subsidiaries include architectural, purchasing, accounting, real estate, advertising, and investment companies, plus SPADAB. Through their central bank, the thrifts also own mortgage, municipal loan, and industrial financing firms and participate in an international banking venture. Most savings banks also belong to regional associations that focus on marketing and training.

Since the pressure for automation is strongly correlated to ever-increasing employee costs in labor-intensive industries, the savings banks felt these even more acutely than the commercial banks. This is because, although a large number of individuals have accounts with them, the average balances are very small compared to those in other banks. Thus, in Sweden as in the United States, the thrifts were leaders in introducing electronic methods. The Swedish savings banks differed, however, in going on to develop products on a systemwide basis for marketing by all the savings banks in their nation. Here they also parted company with the cooperatives, whose EFT services were developed by the commercial banks.

It is not all herring and aquavit, however. SPADAB has been the target of biting criticism for setting up subsidiaries that incurred large losses, resulting in higher prices for computer services than otherwise would have been the case, according to some disgruntled savings bankers.

Commercial Banks

The work of the Swedish Bankers Association, which promotes the common interests of the private commercial banks, differs from the others because its members compete with each other. Hence, it serves as a forum for research and cooperation, deals with the press and government, and ensures that its smaller member banks share the benefits of jointly developed systems and products so that they can compete effectively in the market. It has coordinated the formation of committees of experts from the banks that have made such major contributions to Swedish financial services as the standardization of payment system formats, paperless clearing system, uniform identification card for cashing checks, Bank Giro, Bankomat CD network, Credit Information Center, Securities Register Center, and national wage payment center for the building trades. For many years the association coordinated another activity that had a major effect on competition in banking: cartel agreements.

Cartel Agreements in Sweden

There was nothing secret about the agreements that set the prices of bank services; the Bank Inspection Board kept copies of them on file. Nor was this a quaint custom in the old days; the agreements endured until 1975. Moreover, it was the Riksbank that initiated them in 1933 when it negotiated an agreement between the commercial and savings banks establishing minimum interest rates on deposits. Subsequently the interest rate structure for deposits became the product of three-way agreements among the savings, postal, and commercial banks. The procedure was encouraged by the Riksbank, which, when it planned to change its discount rate, would meet with representatives of the bank groups and urge them to set new interest rates. Over time, those agreements were supplemented with more extensive schedules, which evolved into thick tariff books. These described the routines for standardized services for which minimum fees were listed and included other agreements, such as the 1963 one between the commercial and savings banks' associations setting opening hours from 9 A.M. to 6 P.M.

The bankers regarded the fixed prices as a "practical necessity" and pointed to their narrow margins as proof that the practice did not raise costs for the public.[6] However, when Parliament was considering the proposed deregulation of sectors in the late 1960s, it was pointed out that the intended stimulus to competition from the change could be counteracted by the agreements. This prompted the Antitrust Ombudsman to start monitoring the banks more closely and resulted in his filing an objection to a 1972 agreement between all the banks about interest on salary accounts. He beat a retreat, though, when he learned the Riksbank had approved the pact.

Undaunted, two years later he notified the bankers' association that its agreements were in violation of the Restrictive Trade Practices Act because they were closely followed, contributed to rising charges, and covered services that accounted for about one-fourth of the total revenues of the commercial banks. Thus, in one fell swoop, the doughty ombudsman earned himself a place in Swedish banking history, albeit at the cost of alienating the banks, their associations, the Riksbank, and the Bank Inspection Board, with the last named perhaps as aghast at his thrust into its fiefdom as by the substance of his charges. Although the association argued that the fees were set at or below actual costs and that the cooperation benefited customers by creating uniform standards of service, the ombudsman remained unmoved. In the Swedish style, the conflict was resolved behind closed doors so that in 1975 the banks' association simply announced to its members that the tariffs were being discontinued.

The Bank Inspection Board still has a cartel register in a file cabinet out in a hallway, but it looks a bit dusty. Whereas in 1971 there were some seventy agreements in it, now there are only about thirty, limited to competitively neutral areas. The ombudsman is notified once a year about its contents.

Banking Cartels in the United States

Lest the preceding account evoke a chorus of "tut-tuts" from free enterprise purists ready to cite differences in values between Europeans and Americans toward cartels, it should be pointed out that the deposit market in the United States was cartelized before the Swedish one and remained so until 1980, and the Swedish public has opposed such practices, which Americans have countenanced. The power of that opposition is revealed in a Swedish bankers' association memo from 1967, which warned that the impending release of a report describing the agreements governing interest rates on deposits would provoke sharp criticism.[7] To counter the anticipated reaction, it proposed issuing a press release to announce that the tariffs were being changed from binding to recommendations.

In the early decades of the century, U.S. bankers openly engaged in collusive activities, assuming that they were not subject to antitrust law because they did not engage in interstate commerce. Years before the Swedish bankers started doing it in the 1940s, clearinghouse associations in the United States set interest rates on loans as well as on deposits, opening hours, and service charges, while bankers in small towns determined them in discussions with their competitors. Then in the 1930s, when the government cartelized the deposit market along institutional lines, it also took over the task of fixing prices for interest rates. But while the Swedish interest rate agreements ended in 1975 with no evidence of their having inflicted any harm on the public or industry, the U.S. ceilings are not scheduled to end until 1986. They have cost consumers billions of dollars, including an estimated $5.2 billion in the 1968–1970 period alone, and have inflicted even graver damage on the industry by fostering disintermediation.[8]

Whether set by government or industry, the basis for all agreements restricting competition is the avoidance of risk. Hence, it was to achieve goals of safety and soundness that the government in the deflationary 1930s sought to shield the three classes of financial institutions from direct competition by restricting each to certain kinds of business. The commercial banks had checking accounts and could lend to business but could operate only in one state; the thrifts had higher interest rates but no demand deposits; and the securities dealers could cross state lines but could not take deposits. In effect, the Glass-Steagall Act impeded product extension, and the McFadden Act limited geographic market extension.

Free of interest rate ceilings in the 1950s and early 1960s, the S&Ls enjoyed dramatic growth after they started promoting the fact that they paid about 1.5 percent more for savings than the commercial banks, though that still was below the market rate. Although there is no evidence that the benefits of the low-cost funds provided to the thrifts to promote housing ever were passed on to borrowers, the profits they generated for the S&Ls in their halcyon days permitted such lavish amenities that punsters ascribed their many marble mausoleums to an edifice complex.

Cracks in the Regulated Cartel

Until the late 1950s, the commercial banks watched the thrifts with detachment. But as corporate treasurers became more sophisticated in cash management and turned to money market instruments instead of bank deposits, the growth rate of demand deposits slowed to less than a third that of savings and time deposits. To meet the demand for loans, the banks for the first time began competing directly with the thrifts for those individual accounts. By 1965 their old bulwark of demand deposits had fallen from 53.6 percent of assets in 1955 to 37.2 percent; however, the banks' share of savings and time deposits in the 1960s grew from 40.6 to 47.2 percent, primarily at the cost of the mutual savings banks.[9] To overcome the advantage the thrifts had in the interest rate differential given them in 1966 when the ceilings were extended to them, banks in states where it was permitted substituted convenience by extending networks of branches out into the suburbs. To offset the limitations on explicit interest, both types of institutions displayed great ingenuity in devising forms of implicit interest. One was the offering of premiums, which, in the late 1960s and early 1970s, gave the S&Ls' offices the ambience of department stores, with displays of dishes, appliances, pots, pans, and teddy bears that customers could obtain by opening or adding to accounts. Another was the banks' promotion of free checking accounts and their transfers of business balances between time and demand accounts to earn interest.

In spite of the innovations, by 1975 the banks' demand deposits had dwindled to 23.3 percent of assets. On the other hand, their share of the time/savings funds in depository institutions had grown to 51.3 percent. In the preceding decade, the share of the credit unions had also grown, from 2.8 to 3.7 percent, while that of the S&Ls fell from 35.6 to 32.3 percent, and the mutual savings banks' dropped even more, from 16.8 to 12.7 percent. Hence, the differential did not achieve its purpose of protecting the thrifts from commercial bank competition. Moreover, because the ceilings were kept below the market rates of interest in a period of sharply rising inflation and interest rates, they provided the rationale for the disastrous disintermediation of the 1970s and early 1980s.

Mass Money Migration

In 1966 and 1969–1970 large depositors who could afford the large minimum denominations moved their funds to unregulated financial instruments. But as inflation rose to 6.2 percent in 1973 and then to 11 percent in 1974, rendering the 5.0 to 5.25 percent regulated rates extremely negative, small depositors, too, began to shift funds from banks and thrifts to the open market for the first time in U.S. history. The vehicle that granted access to the market for the masses was an innovation made possible by the computer, the money market mutual fund, which was created in 1972.[10] With a minimum deposit of only $1,000 to $5,000 required by most funds, no sales charge, and a market rate of return provided on savings along with checking privileges, liquidity, and direct access to other types of investments, the funds attracted a phenomenal 10 percent of consumer savings over the course of some ten years. Because corporations were denied access to savings accounts until 1975 and then were restricted to a maximum of $150,000 in them, they, too, found the funds attractive.

Merrill Lynch was siphoning off more funds through its comprehensive Cash Management Account, which soon was followed by similar products from other brokerage firms, when the depository institutions in 1978 finally were authorized to issue money market certificates. Although the certificates enabled them to recapture $75 billion, over $150 billion remained in the funds, thereby demolishing the carefully nurtured tenet of bankers and regulators that, given the choice, the public would always prefer the safety of insured funds. The lure of interest rates more than 10 percent higher than those paid by the regulated institutions in a time of double-digit inflation produced an explosive growth of the funds in which their assets grew tenfold between early 1978 and 1980. In the competition for resources, the interest banks paid at market rates rose 330 percent between 1976 and 1981, thereby narrowing the spread between their rates paid on liabilities and return on assets from 2.95 to 1.40.[11] Nevertheless, by 1981 the banks controlled only 37 percent of the nation's financial assets compared to 57 percent in 1946; and between 1979 and 1982 the percentage of consumer and business short-term assets held by banks in checking and savings deposits was reduced by 50 percent.[12]

The commercial banks' share of time/savings deposits was down by 1982 to about where it had been in 1960, at roughly 41 percent, and that of the mutual savings banks was down to 10 percent from 21.3 percent. While the S&Ls' share was down only about 1 percent, the credit unions had managed to increase their share from 2.8 to over 4 percent. Overall the main difference was that by then, the money market funds had nearly 11 percent of the pie. And, of course, there was the untidy carnage of all the institutions that had failed.

In the intervening years, developments in electronic technology had eradicated earlier barriers to entry into payment services by eliminating labor-intensive account work and facilitating the mobility of funds so that costly offices were no longer needed. Hence, when regulators failed to respond to the inflationary pressures that transformed interest rate ceilings from a protective shield against intraindustry competition into a crippling deadweight against outside forces, the unregulated money market funds encountered no obstacles. They smoothly circumvented the outdated geographic barriers of the McFadden Act and Douglas Amendment and made a farce of the Glass-Steagall Act with its 1930s' focus on barring banks from the investment business. The result was a total breakdown of the product and market segmentation that the regulators had imposed on the industry. In a mind-boggling tragicomedy, the banking regulators in effect consigned more than 10 percent of the richest store of retail funds in the world to businesses over which they have no control and in the process created one of the largest "banks" in the country—Merrill Lynch—which also is beyond their control.

New Competitors

The upheaval of the U.S. banking industry as nondepository institutions attained a major market share of financial services has been an unprecedented phenomenon among developed nations. It is, moreover, ironic that an event that could occur only in a market so highly regulated as to render the industry defenseless against encroachment would take place in the bastion of the free enterprise system. But in addition to being hampered by regulations, most of which it wanted, the banking industry also was vulnerable because its unregulated competitors were more innovative, more technologically-oriented, and far more aggressive in marketing retail services.

For some forty years, the blanket of protection stifled competition and innovation in banking and discouraged the best and the brightest from entering the field. With liability management regulated, banking meant asset management. It required people who made slow, safe decisions, and the ones who made it to the top came from the commercial lending side. When competitors appeared on the scene, they complained to the regulators, who usually dispatched them in short order. Thus, marketing played second fiddle to loan production; those who could not make it in lending often were eased into it as part of the lifetime employment policy. It was an orderly world in which tradition, not change, was regarded as most desirable. It was about as secure as working in the post office and not much more challenging.

Hence, when EFT emerged with its potential to change the products, the market, and the players, as well as the speed of value transfers, banking to a good extent lacked the human resources to manage the transition from a service to a technological business. Incapable of dealing with the unwanted change, bankers lapsed into inertia, unaware that because the technology also heralded the obsolescence of the old regulatory barriers, they could no longer afford the luxury of procrastination. Unable to perceive the payments mechanism as an information system, they failed to see that those systems no longer could remain their exclusive domain. Because top managers lacked knowledge of marketing and had hired few experts in the field, they did not understand that banking's old line of products was at the end of its life cycle, with its demise hastened by inflation, technology, and a new breed of more creative, unregulated competitors.

In view of the fact that financial services in the United States are estimated to represent potentially a $4.5 trillion a year industry, the only surprising thing about the onslaught by nondepository firms is that it did not come sooner.[13] Certainly that potential attracted such smokestack industry firms as American Can, Armco, Deere, and National Steel, which have acquired financial services firms for diversification to help them through difficult times. An acquisition that was approved because it was the only bid for a Boston thrift with major problems has proved profitable for a New England oil and gas company because of countercyclical trends. When interest rates rise, the profits of financial services firms tend to decline while those of energy companies tend to rise, and vice versa. Similarly, money market funds were introduced as a means of raising and stabilizing profits for mutual funds and brokerage firms after they took a drubbing in a steep decline in the stock market. Retailers with large customer card bases, credit operations, and computerized systems see synergy in payment services as a low-cost complement to a package of other services. The unregulated firms also can offer a wider range of services, and while most are not federally insured, neither are they burdened with portfolios full of long-term, low-interest home mortgages or nonperforming loans to Third World nations.

Retailers Enter Retail Banking

The chairman of Sears, Roebuck, the nation's largest retail chain, knocked the socks off a lot of bankers in 1981 when he announced that the firm planned to become the leading purveyor of consumer financial services. Although a few technologically-attuned industry executives, who urged faster implementation of EFTs, had warned for years of the threat posed by the retailing giant, many chief executive officers whose entire career had been spent behind regulatory moats never could believe it until they saw it in the morning paper. Ironically, it was the banking industry itself that had created the Frankenstein monster when early in the century its disdain for handling retail credit forced retailers, oil companies, auto manufacturers, and travel companies to set up their own financial operations. Lacking the astuteness of European financial institution executives who always have handled credit for retailers as a means of preserving their hold on financial services, the myopic thinking had earlier come back to haunt bankers. After deciding that they did want consumer credit through their own card operations—half a century after the retailers and oil companies introduced credit cards—the bankers were frustrated by the major retailers' adamant opposition to accepting their cards.

Today it is estimated that retailers supply some 20 percent of the roughly $450 billion of total consumer credit in the United States.[14] The assets of General Motors Acceptance Corporation (GMAC) exceed those of the nation's five largest mutual savings banks combined by over 50 percent and approximate those of the four largest S&Ls combined. Although all financing business suffered in the late 1970s and early 1980s as interest rates exceeded usury ceilings, the retailers' credit operations continued to generate a commodity with inestimable value because market dominance may well depend on it: information. Their computerized data on the buying and payment habits of millions of consumers, along with their demographic characteristics, constitute an awesome competitive edge over the banks in the selling of financial products.

With the most extensive consumer credit data base of all, a card base larger than Visa's, a powerful IBM system linking more than 800 stores nationwide, and over half its net earnings from financial services since 1977, Sears' plans to expand that side of its business and move into EFTS should not have been surprising. Within one month of enunciating its new goal, the firm set about acquiring the largest real estate broker in the United States and the fifth-largest stockbrokerage. Since then Sears has developed a personal financial planning service, which it is offering along with securities, money market funds, mortgages, and insurance in Financial Network Centers in its stores. With generations of experience in home sales through its catalogs, which produce almost one-fourth of its merchandise revenues, the sagacious retailer also has experimented with videotex and teleshopping to sell merchandise and real estate and has bought half of a television translators' company because it views interactive television as the ideal vehicle to integrate its financial and merchandise businesses. Capitalizing on the transaction processing power in its computer and telecommunications systems, Sears in 1983 began processing retail remittances for customers of a big bank and handling credit card sales for a major oil company. Those ventures were followed in 1984 by a test of a telephone bill payment service as part of a plan to provide bill-processing services for other organizations.

This rapid wave of expansive innovations through Sears' deep pocket strategy has served as a lightning rod for complaints of inequity from apprehensive depository institution executives who point to Sears' freedom from reserve and capital requirements, geographic restrictions, and other regulatory constraints on flexibility in competitive activities. After the FHLBB in 1984 reversed an earlier ruling and said the retailer must divest its S&L or have its stockbrokerage stop underwriting stock offerings for thrifts, Sears sued the board. The firm charged that the board had bowed to pressure from smaller S&Ls that want protection. The board's chairman, formerly an officer of a thrift that competes with Sears' S&L, has warned of the danger of large, diversified financial services companies.

No less than other bargain hunters, traditionally low-paid financial institutions' employees have long enjoyed the discount prices offered by the nation's second-largest retailer, K mart. But when certificates of deposit and money market funds showed up among the cameras and blouses from Taiwan in Florida stores and were bombastically advertised as paying higher rates than the depository institutions offered, the industry hauled the retailer into court. Undeterred by this display of somewhat blemished southern hospitality, after the judge ruled the offerings legal, K mart announced plans to expand its financial services and insurance centers into more southern and midwestern states in 1985.

Hoping to avoid the crossfire, J.C. Penney sidled into financial services under cover of the dust as the melee raged over Sears and K mart. Like Sears, it already had a large insurance company, an extensive card base, and a nationwide POS network through its electronic cash registers. To complement those, it bought a consumer bank, which cannot make commercial loans. Unlike most banks, which fail to do strategic planning and seldom coordinate anything but the office Christmas party, Penney's also has a Manager of Banking Coordination and Strategic Development who knows something that many banks do not know: which products are profitable and which are not. He is there because Penney's analyses indicate that financial services are more profitable than retail sales.

While the second-largest supermarket chain has announced plans to sell money market mutual fund shares and life insurance policies, Boston-area shoppers already can buy insurance and get their income tax prepared at one supermarket. Even in Iowa, a department store owned by an insurance corporation sells insurance, money market funds, and other financial services.

As the old, established order disappeared before their very eyes, America's beleaguered bankers were reminded of the tag line of old-time comedian Jimmy Durante: "Everybody wants to get into the act."

Financial Supermarkets

For over a century, U.S. banking regulators perpetuated a system comprised of a multiplicity of small, specialized institutions, which were the equivalent of the old butcher's, baker's and produce shops. But just as many of those gave way to supermarkets after their customers discovered the better prices and convenience of one-stop shopping, the altered patterns of behavior of banking customers portend a similar trend. The rampant inflation of the late 1970s heightened their sensitivity to interest rates, and the advertising of new types of high-yielding accounts and sophisticated bundles of services sharpened their awareness of new investment opportunities, so that for the first time even customers with modest accounts began shopping for financial products.

They never had to leave home to do so either; toll-free telephone lines provided access to courteous representatives who knowledgeably answered questions and promptly sent information about accounts. Opening one was done by filling out a simple form at home and popping it in the mail along with a check or wiring the funds from a bank. After that, assets could be transferred by telephone at no cost between funds, including money market, government securities' and tax-free bond funds—many with check-writing privileges—and equity funds of varying degrees of risk. One mutual funds firm offers an all-purpose money market account with unlimited check writing, prestige credit card, discounts on brokerage commissions, bill-paying automatically or by telephone, direct deposit of pay, margin borrowing, ATMs, and comprehensive monthly statements showing all activities. Through the acquisition of consumer banks, brokerages and funds operators have further expanded their product lines; one offers home mortgages by mail, promising fast processing time and "no time-consuming visits to bank offices."

If the free-market competition generated by the emergence of the unregulated supermarkets set the bankers' teeth to grinding, the merger of American Express and Shearson Loeb Rhoades in 1981 jolted them into an uproar. It was bad enough that it linked the money market accounts of a brokerage with a worldwide consumer banking empire that includes not only travelers' services but also international banking, insurance, cable television, over 12 million cardholders, and one of the strongest electronic-processing capabilities for financial transactions in the nation. What enraged the industry was the fact that until then, this powerful new competitor had been regarded as a partner for whom the banks served as agents in distributing travelers' checks and cards that enabled holders to draw on bank lines of credit. After the Independent Bankers Association failed in its efforts to block the merger, Shearson/American Express rubbed salt in the bankers' wounds by acquiring a bank in Boston through a legal loophole. For American Express, the merger was part of a strategy adopted when its previously high profits from float on travelers' checks declined as a result of competition and high interest rates in the late 1970s. Thus, as it pursued a new goal of becoming a financial services superpower, its share of profits from banking grew from 9.4 percent in 1979 to 21 percent in 1983.[15]

Hard hit also by the collision of high interest rates and usury ceilings plus the nearly 60 percent increase in personal bankruptcies between 1979 and 1981, the consumer finance companies also have expanded their line of services by acquiring S&Ls and consumer banks.[16] Augmenting a nationwide network of loan offices, one company grants immediate cash loans to customers with preapproved lines of credit through ATMs. Prudential Insurance joined the ranks of financial services supermarkets by diversifying into securities through the acquisition of Bache and then into banking through purchase of a bank. Conversely, the large bank holding companies, through their operations of mortgage and consumer finance subsidiaries and, more recently, of discount brokerage firms, qualify, too, as supermarkets.

By virtue of its wide distribution network and broad range of products, which include real estate, mortgage, and insurance, as well as securities and its pioneering Cash Management Accounts, Merrill Lynch constitutes the prototype of the new innovative, aggressive, and diversified financial services institution that has revolutionized the old banking industry in the United States.

Competing with the Government in Sweden

Postal Bank and Kreditbank

Although Swedish banks never have encountered the bizarre competition U.S. banks have in recent years, they have been competing with their government's financial institutions for a century. To reassure the private savings banks that the Postal Bank was meant to be only a complement to them, Parliament imposed lower interest rates and deposit maximums on it when it was created. Nevertheless, by 1924 it was the country's largest thrift institution, and by 1960 it had almost one-fourth of all savings banks' deposits.[17] But while the private thrifts envied the Postal Bank its huge network of offices, longer hours, Saturday opening, and government guarantee, by the 1960s Postal Bank officials longed for greater freedom in their operations. There was an ongoing conflict between values in which marketing judgments clashed with political interests. On the one hand, they were constrained by political forces from using deposit interest as a competitive weapon to attract assets, and on the other the demand for prudence imposed by the state guarantee precluded the higher returns that greater assumption of risk would have generated. Even after the 1968 legislation permitted all other financial institutions to compete on equal terms, they were compelled to refer such profitable activities as lending, foreign trade, and securities transactions to the state-owned commercial Kreditbank.

In its 1973 comments on the proposed merger of the bank with Kreditbank, the Bank Inspection Board revealed that in the preceding year the Postal Bank had produced only a 0.36 percent return on assets, compared to the private banks' average of 1.22 percent. The board maintained that the bank could not continue as it was and that "a radical alteration" of the bank's situation was inevitable sooner or later.[18] In fact, it came in the following year, with its shotgun wedding to Kreditbank.

The 1945 banking committee that laid the groundwork for the creation of Kreditbank proposed that the bank ought not to be treated any differently from other commercial banks. It specifically stated that it should not have advantages in competing with other banks but should compete on like terms. A harbinger of things to come appeared when the Finance Minister branded the concept of competing "on like terms" as too vague to be practicable, and the committee's majority in 1949 more openly abandoned the principle when it agreed that, on the contrary, the state's work preferably ought to be done by the new bank. Since the principal reason for creating the bank was political anyway, well-reasoned philosophy was no more to stand in the way than time-honored policymaking practices. Thus, the proposal was passed by the committee with no public statement and no *remiss* circulated for comment. When asked about this breach of tradition, the official replied that he thought it would be better to get the comments of affected parties after the government made its decision.

During the next two decades, Kreditbank enjoyed significant growth, with its share of deposits from the public increasing from 6.8 percent in 1951 to 11.8 percent in 1960 and 13.1 percent in 1968.[19] Contributing to its growth were the facts that state authorities and state-owned businesses were requested to use the bank and that the public sector grew considerably in the period. By the end of the 1960s, the bank's network of offices covered most of the country, a growth aided by the favoritism given its requests for new branches by the bank inspectorate. The new bank also benefited when shortly after its formation, the Riksbank imposed credit restrictions. Since large deposits were flowing in then from numerous government entities, it became highly liquid at the same time other banks were turning away customers. Hence, Kreditbank quickly acquired a large number of new business customers.

When talk about a merger of the two state-owned banks began in 1968, the Postal Bank had 13 billion kronor in deposits and Kreditbank had 5 billion kronor, which together made up about one-fifth of all the bank deposits in Sweden.[20] The potential impact on the competitive environment loomed even larger in 1973 when their combined total assets represented nearly 30 percent of the nation's entire commercial banking sector.[21] The sheer magnitude of the Postal Bank's operations was awe-inspiring. Its office network of some 5,600 service locations dwarfed by some 38 percent the total number of offices of all the commercial, savings, and cooperative banks combined. It had almost 7 million accounts, compared to 6 million for all the other banks together. Its costs were similarly staggering: in 1972 they represented 88.5 percent of operating income, compared to the 59.6 percent average of all the other banks. It was the Postal Giro, however, that accounted for three-fourths of those costs. No problem; the giro was left behind in the Post Office.

The Largest Bank in Scandinavia: PK Bank

Like most births, that of Post-och Kreditbank (PK Bank) was marked by cries—of anguish from the commercial and savings banks. To them it spelled an early end to the whole idea of competing on equal terms. Not only was the new bank the largest in all of Scandinavia, but it also would enjoy a monopoly on the state's commercial banking business. It would get the largest branch network in the nation with the post offices—and without any aggravation from the Committee for Establishing Bank Offices. Through those offices, moreover, it would have longer service hours and Saturday openings to boot. It would benefit from the float on all those big government deposits. It would become the market leader in salary accounts with the two strong systems it was inheriting. And as if all that were not enough, it would probably steal away their best business customers since it was awash in a sea of liquidity at a time when they had been forced to close their loan windows because of another credit crunch.

From the inside, though, things looked different. Some executives were pessimistic about the bank's chances for success because it was undercapitalized. Said one "It's always difficult for a state-owned bank to have to go to its shareholders. Within Parliament it's easy to make points by saying, 'Look at PK—they're after more money again.'"[22] The computer systems were like a "good news, bad news" joke: both banks had been well-equipped, but with totally different systems. And after the government allowed banks to borrow funds abroad to finance business loans, PK lost its initial advantage in the credit market. There were structural problems, too, with top-heavy administration for the new bank; and since it got big so fast, it has to recruit from the outside, which is difficult in a small country. Another difficulty was gaining acceptance. One PK officer recalls, "At first, they'd just smile when we called on them. Then they'd say, 'No, it's a political bank; the government's really running it.'"[23]

In 1977 the Savings Banks Association successfully challenged the monopoly of the bank and the Postal Giro in getting all the deposits of state employees' salaries. In his decision the Finance Minister cited the 1968 law, which says the banking system must be built on free competition. Hence, he ruled that if a governmental unit found a bank that offered service on better terms, it should use it. Initial fears that the relationship between the bank and Post Office would contravene the principle that the latter must provide similar treatment to all were assuaged to a large extent by agreements in 1977 by which post offices permit withdrawals on all banks' passbooks and cash checks up to a specified maximum.

PK regards the post offices as branches for household savings and domestic bill paying and uses its 130 branches mainly for corporate business. The expected joint operations of the two never became a reality until the fall of 1982 when some post offices assumed a more branchlike character by making small loans on their own with PK funds. Unlike the Postal Bank, PK also pays full postage and the market price for advertising in post offices. Collaboration with the Post Office, however, plays a critical role in the bank's deposits. Accounts opened at post offices and deposits of the Post Office Administration itself together have accounted for as much as 65 percent of the bank's average deposits.[24]

To reduce the crushing workload imposed by the volume of transactions resulting from its one-third share of Sweden's salary accounts, the bank in 1982 launched a concerted effort to encourage greater use of CDs for withdrawals. As a result, while PK customers in 1981 made over half a million withdrawals per month, in the first six months of 1982 the volume was increased to about 1.3 million.[25] With a highly sophisticated computer system today, the bank also used technology as part of its marketing strategy. A marketing officer flatly states, "Our products now are computer systems."[26]

The private bankers characterize PK as a strong competitor that has successfully taken on not only the savings but also the commercial banks, from the provincial ones to the largest. Nevertheless, by 1983 it had fallen behind S-E Bank and Svenska Handelsbank, which have been expanding internationally. In what struck private sector bankers as an ironic twist, the French government in 1982 nationalized a bank that is 20 percent owned by PK Bank. An official of the Swedish bank reported that after some negotiations, it came out "all right."[27]

Competing with a National Institution: The Postal Giro

The Swedish Postal Giro has spent more than half a century convincing people to come down to the post office to pay their bills. As a result, practically every business, organization, governmental unit, and half a million individuals have a Postal Giro account. Another 1.5 million who receive their salaries and pensions through a giro-linked account at PK Bank can use the giro to transfer funds free of charge throughout Sweden and Europe. At its Stockholm headquarters, the service handles a daily average of 1.5 million transactions, which increases to over 3 million at the end of the month. As an official described it, "We're a traffic enterprise, like a train station."[28]

Its early development was bolstered by a ready acceptance by business and cushioned by a monopoly on government payments. People who had previously known no other way of making payments than with cash or an occasional money order because they were intimidated by banks found the bills that came preprinted on giro forms easy to pay at the post office, where they felt comfortable. And when their giro was hailed internationally, all Swedes basked in the reflected glory. In 1956 an English banker wrote, "It would be a complacent man who, after studying the efficient operation of the Swedish Postal Giro and the Swedish banks' customer transfer service, would argue that the British methods and costs of handling payments by cheque could not be improved."[29] Indeed, the vast popularity of the service had stimulated the formation of another giro system: Bank Giro.

The idea of competing with a national institution, and a state-owned one at that, is not for the faint of heart, and since bankers by nature tend to be risk-adverse, it took a while. In 1942 a bank giro was proposed to the bankers' association, although not for the first time; one had been suggested in 1928, just three years after the Postal Giro had begun operations. Its proponent acknowledged that at first he had feared it was impossible to compete because they had the post offices and he did not think the bankers could "produce anything equivalent."[30] But the banks faced two competitive threats: they were losing corporate business to the giro, and they believed it was hampering development of checking account activity. By effecting transfers between checking accounts in different banks, the system would streamline corporate-to-corporate transfers, enhance the utility of checking accounts, and keep funds within the banking system. Five years later, the bankers named a committee to look into it, and two years later they voted to put the service into effect in 1950.

Because the two services compile statistics differently, it is impossible to compare them by volume; however, while starting from a smaller base, the growth rate of the Bank Giro has been higher. Between 1975 and 1981, Postal Giro transactions increased only 13.6 percent while those of the Bank Giro went up 55 percent.[31]

In its endless quest for greater efficiency, the government in 1969 ordered a study of the feasibility of merging the two giro systems. But because the two operations differ fundamentally in their missions, organizationally and technologically, integration appeared unattainable. Hence, in 1977 the government asked a study group to investigate ways to achieve at least some commonality between them. After two years of analyzing and arguing, the two sides were still so far apart that agreement was impossible, which, if nothing else, put to rest the myth that Swedes can always achieve consensus.

Although Postal Giro officials took pride in the opening of their millionth account in 1981, that is one of the few cheery statistics in their recent annual reports. In 1982–1983, in-payments were up only 0.3 percent over three years earlier, and out-payments had declined more than 10 percent in the preceding six years. The only real growth had occurred in giroing, that is, transfers between accounts, which had increased 60 percent over the preceding decade.

But that growth poses a problem. Giroing reduces the number of transactions in post offices because no cash is involved. That, of course, was the whole idea in creating the service back in 1925. But it took over half a century before enough people had accounts so that most payments could be transfers between them. Meanwhile, the giro had become a major client of the Post Office, which handled all the in- and out-payments for people without accounts. However, to justify the personnel and facilities for providing those services, a certain volume of work is required. Hence, there was concern about jobs and offices when, for the third year in a row, the volume of two of the three most important payment transaction groups for Post Office Counter Services declined. Moreover, PK Bank transactions, which constitute the third important group, were expected to fall after the bank installed 100 more CDs in 1984.

With CD withdrawals and direct deposits already displacing tasks by postal workers, the reluctance of the giro to promote its autogiro (direct debit) service is understandable. Although it has offered preauthorized bill paying since 1974, increased use of the EFTS would further reduce the volume of both counter transactions and mail. Since the number of first-class letters declined in 1982–1983, the Post Office may have trouble paying its required 12 percent return on investment to the Treasury if it loses more business. On the other hand, failing to compete with the fastest-growing service at Bank Giro at a time when its old products are past their peak could further erode the fortunes of the Postal Giro.

To the giro, EFTS present a challenge; to the Post Office, EFTS portend an inevitable decline in mail volume.

Rationales for EFT Services

Direct Debits and Credits in the United States

The French introduced direct debits in 1955, and in Germany, where preauthorized payments have been popular for decades, the central bank promoted the concept a century ago to overcome a problem in covering bank notes. Yet when the insurance industry in the United States wanted to offer preauthorized payments in the mid-1950s, bankers recoiled in horror from such a revolutionary innovation. A New York banker sounded like a consumer activist of the 1970s when he cited as the initial objections not only operational complexities but also the potential for increased forgery losses and a feeling that it was "fundamentally wrong for a depositor to lose control over his account."[32] In spite of lawsuits over the question of liability, as the fears proved to be unwarranted and the convenience and discount incentives won over customers, by 1970 over 150 companies were offering the service. Today, with the original paper-based system converted to EFT, the insurance industry leads in private sector use of the service, with one company handling 1 million EFT payments monthly.

Bank of America offered a direct debit/credit program in 1967 to large customers with computer equipment, but it was the small Wilmington Savings and Fund Society, which, after inventing NOW accounts in 1971, introduced the first operational, profitable EFTS for consumers in 1972. Its plan included preauthorized bill-paying and transfers; direct deposits of pay, pension, and Social Security payments; a credit/debit card; CDs to encourage the use of direct deposits; a POS system that paid cash bonuses to compensate for the lack of check float; free checking and check guarantee; and instant passbook loans. By 1974, its system was operating in the black and was handling over 10,000 automatic payments a month. The stimulus to further development provided by its success was bolstered by the finding of a banking task force that preauthorized payments offered the greatest potential improvement in efficiency of all EFT services. It was estimated that with more than 40 percent of the existing check volume potentially convertible to the payments, banks could lower their net costs by more than $2.5 billion annually.[33] But by then most bankers were waiting to see what the government was going to do about the new technology, so the Delaware activities remained "an interesting experiment" in their eyes. One of the thrift's officers said, "It has been exciting though admittedly a little lonely out here on the frontiers of tomorrow."[34]

In 1973 Congress passed legislation permitting the Treasury to use direct deposits for recurring payments to Social Security recipients, government retirees, and veterans. The program, which began in late 1974, has subsequently grown to encompass over one-third of those payments and constitutes the largest use of electronic transfers in the United States. Indeed, the volume of federal EFT payments in recent years has been double that of the private sector; only in 1983 did the latter finally exceed one-third of the total.[35] Moreover, to provide the infrastructure needed for EFT, the Federal Reserve System has heavily underwritten the development of thirty-two regional ACH centers which are linked through the Fed's wire network. The Fed operates all but the New York ACH, the world's largest, which is run by twelve banks. Each of the others is managed by a local ACH association made up of banks, thrifts, and credit unions. Additionally, in line with its stated goal of encouraging the shift from paper to electronic payments, the Fed has been subsidizing the price of ACH transactions.

Yet in spite of the subsidies, the expenditure of millions of dollars for development of the capability, and the success of the Treasury program, after ten years less than 1 percent of all U.S. payments are electronic. The main reason for this slow adoption of EFTS is that there has not been sufficient economic incentive for large payors to give up checks because of the structural flaw in the checking system in the United States: float. A Boston banker has coined a most apt definition of the anomaly: "the unintentional gain or loss of value caused by the inefficiencies of our present check system."[36] With checks, the payor gains and the receiver loses, but with EFT payments, the opposite is true. Hence, it is not consumers who have blocked EFTS, because they are the winners; it is the large check issuers, including the bankers who created the system. Banks that issue payrolls, dividends, and trust account payments have not used EFT because the float value of the checks they issue far exceeds the cost of issuing them. Although the Monetary Control Act of 1980 (MCA) ordered the Fed to charge for float, which in the first quarter of 1983 averaged $2.3 billion daily, it has delayed compliance.[37] Thus, like a child getting tangled in the arms and legs of its long johns, while the Fed has subsidized EFT through ACH support, it has undercut its acceptance by making check use profitable. The Treasury knows that its gain of about 15¢ in processing costs per payment is offset in part by reduction in float but believes EFT payments are necessary to prevent a possible breakdown of its system in the future. Secondary subsidization of checks, however, is being eliminated with the imposition of Fed charges for clearing and collection services and the banks' move to full pricing to cover those fees and the interest they must pay on NOW accounts to be competitive.

The conversion to EFT of such income payments as those from private pensions and stock dividends has been held up because the issuers are the banks' trust departments, which are not inclined to innovate and also are isolated from the mainstream of the banks' payment mechanisms. Furthermore, since most banks do not know the actual costs of preparing and processing the checks they issue, they have little reason to change. Basic apathy and inflexibility also play a role, with bankers reluctant to change their systems to accept payment from their own customers in any form other than checks. Moreover, fewer than 10 percent can originate ACH transactions.

First Money Machines in Sweden and the United States

Although First Pennsylvania Bank installed a CD in 1967 and Chemical Bank had the first automated teller machine (ATM) in the United States in 1969, the value of those units was limited in that customers of only one bank could use them and they served customers only in one area. They were rather like the first telephone: super if you wanted to call an assistant in the next room but only promising past that point. Hence, the Swedish savings banks' systemwide approach to CD development in 1967 might be considered a strategic coup—were it not for the fact they were thrust into it by happenstance.

By the mid-1960s the Swedish banks had succeeded in getting thousands of wage earners' funds on deposit. But once their money was in the bank, people wanted to get it out. As the hordes of new customers filled the lobbies to overflowing, the banks were forced to extend their hours. A countervailing force, however, was at work behind the scenes as the bank employees demanded shorter work weeks. The issue came to a head in 1966 when the Bank Employees Union persuaded Parliament to declare Saturdays bank holidays, thereby delighting some 25,000 workers and enraging 1 million salary account holders who were denied access to their funds on the biggest shopping day of the week. Although the banks had opposed the measure, they became the targets of scathing criticism from the public and media.

From a competitive standpoint, there were two major points: since the postal workers belong to different unions, they would continue to work on Saturday, and that would affect the savings banks more because the Postal Bank was a closer competitor. Moreover, few of their salary accounts provided checks because their primarily blue-collar customers had never liked them. But since checks were better than nothing if a person wanted to shop when the banks were closed, they also feared losing customers to the cooperative and commercial banks. In desperation the savings banks turned to CDs, though the technology at the time was rudimentary. They had an available technological foundation in SPADAB, and approval of the plan and the proposal to order the machines was facilitated by the thrifts' central association. Hence, their first machines were operational while the commercial bankers were still discussing them.

Commercial bankers felt no urgency about the matter since they were promoting checks as a substitute for cash anyway. Their operational as opposed to marketing approach to the technology at that time was revealed when the bankers' group received word that the first shipment of machines was on its way to Stockholm; they panicked and called a meeting to decide what to do with them. There was a collective sigh of relief when one banker came up with the solution: he had room in his basement to store them. Nevertheless, by 1974 the commercial banks had a nationwide network of 100 Bankomat machines.

Across the Atlantic, "experts" warned that only large institutions would be able to afford large EFT systems, although by then the Swedish savings banks' nationwide CD network had been operating for five years. While two groups of privately-owned banks in Sweden, of all places, had developed their own competing systems, some Americans postulated that due to the often-cited "lack of consumer demand," the critical mass required to make EFTS feasible would be unattainable without government subsidies.

But experiments continued. An Ohio bank in 1972 found that "robot tellers" in a branch could handle 80 percent of the services offered by a staffed branch at one-tenth the cost. The thrifts introduced ATMs to provide customers access to their new NOW accounts, and in 1973 some 3 percent of U.S. households used the units. To encourage wider adoption of EFTS, the FHLBB in the following year ruled that S&Ls could operate ATMs statewide. To enable commercial banks to compete, the Comptroller of the Currency went out on a limb by declaring the terminals exempt from the definition of a branch and permitting national banks to install ATMs nationwide. This unleashed the furies of all the protectionist banking interests who fell over each other in their rush to file lawsuits challenging the ruling. The litigious melee in 1975 resulted in a court decision that undercut the comptroller by declaring that ATMs were indeed branches and therefore subject to the ban on interstate banking. Moreover, the court ruled, they were subject to the same capital and surplus requirements as branches, even in states that did not consider them to be branches. The IBAA failed, however, in its attempt to have the thrifts' ATMs declared illegal. Hence, the internecine war raged on between the big banks and the small banks and between the banks and the thrifts, to the detriment of the consumer, if to the benefit of a lot of lawyers, and ultimately to the outside forces that were building up their electronic capability while the combatants bloodied each other.

The Bank of America announced in 1975 that it had proved through extensive studies that ATM programs were not practical since each transaction cost $1.25 versus 40¢ per human teller. In view of the fact that the California giant had the largest brick-and-mortar investment of any other bank in the world in its over 1,000 branches, skeptics wondered if managerial pride had been factored into the statistics, since First National Bank of Atlanta had found by then that transactions through its Tillie the Teller machines were cheaper than those with tellers. By the end of 1976 there were 5,303 units, owned by some 700 banks, 100 S&Ls, 45 MSBs, and 15 credit unions. Thirteen states by then had declared that ATMs legally were not branches, but in the others with branching bans, banks could not achieve the volume required to justify the cost of installing the machines.

The cost factor was not rosy over in Sweden either; a 1976 study revealed that the number of withdrawals per month per CD was about half that required to break even. But since they had been installed to provide service when the banks' offices were closed, that would have been acceptable, except for one thing: two-thirds of the withdrawals were made on weekdays between 9 A.M. and 6 P.M., when the offices were open. Much to the surprise of the bankers, there was a marketing potential in CDs they had failed to recognize.

Growing Popularity of Money Machines

When the Swedish savings banks got their on-line CDs from Texas in 1978, they mailed a million unsolicited cards to all their salary account customers and ran a heavy advertising campaign. The promotion was so successful that by 1981, 25 to 30 percent of all withdrawals were made from the CDs. In fact, the terminals became too popular. By underestimating the use of CDs, the thrifts' officials had ordered insufficient note capacity in the units, and when they asked employees to service the terminals on weekends when they usually run out of money, they encountered labor union and security problems they had not anticipated. Moreover, the system technically could not always handle the heavy volume. As a result, the machines' downtime averages 10 percent, with 4 percent of that due to the CDs being out of money. Moreover, since it is up to the individual banks to service their machines, the downtime in Stockholm considerably exceeds that average. Unlike small towns, where bankers are known personally and cannot afford to irritate their customers, big cities provide anonymity for bankers whose CDs are empty.

Reflecting a "free ride" effect from the thrifts' promotion, use of the commercial banks' CDs increased 25 percent from 1978 to 1979, thereby creating lines and excessive downtime from the pressure on the older system. By that time it also appeared that checks probably never would be popular for shopping. So bowing to the inevitable, the bankers decided that if people preferred cash, they would provide it as conveniently as possible. Hence, their second-generation network has over three times more units, higher reliability, and greater note capacity, which is further extended by the capability to dispense notes of different values. By late 1982, a number of them averaged more than 10,000 withdrawals a month, with the most heavily-used unit in a Stockholm department store providing over 18,200 withdrawals per month.

Marketing studies show that usage patterns over the years have remained constant. With the exception of CDs in shopping centers and the railroad station, they match living patterns, with the peaks during the lunch hour, after work, and late Saturday morning. By replacing counter transactions, the banks find they can recover investment costs through labor savings. Their experience indicates that the more machines there are, the more transactions there are. However, the number of transactions per teller has not decreased as much as the number of CD transactions has increased, suggesting that Swedes carry less cash in their pockets than before. Although bankers concede that CD services have altered competition in that those who cannot provide them will be hurt, no one expects the customer to pay for them. A Bankomat official explains, "The break-even point in Swedish banking is almost a social issue. Because employers 'force' people to use banks, consumers won't pay fees for transactions."[38]

Ten percent of Americans had used an ATM by 1977; yet ten years after the first ones were installed, there were only 13,800 ATMs in a vast nation with over 80,000 banking offices. Bankers contended that they hesitated to make a commitment to ATMs because of the "lack of consumer demand," an argument rendered specious by the fact that consumers had never demanded the car or telephone or television or computer either. But when those innovations were introduced, people chose them because they found them more convenient than existing alternatives. The real reason for the bankers' resistance to ATM service was the uncertainty as to how long the sizable amount of capital required would be tied up before sufficient returns could be produced to justify the investment. The Swedish bankers, by comparison, could predict a timely payback because of the economies of scale they enjoy in the number of transactions per terminal and the number of terminals in their shared systems. They also had lower costs due to joint development, buying through large orders, and using less expensive CDs. Since most of their customers have direct deposit of income and pay bills through giro systems, there is no need for ATMs, which also accept deposits and transfer funds. But with ATMs considered branches in the United States and cooperation discouraged by fear of antitrust law and protectionist lawsuits, the development of retail EFT services, as a banker stated in 1978, was "hamstrung . . . primarily by legislative problems."[39]

Then, between 1979 and 1981 the number of ATMs in the United States almost doubled, and between 1980 and 1982 the volume of transactions more than doubled from fewer than 1 billion to over 2 billion.[40] The first major spur to growth came in 1980 when the Comptroller of the Currency approved ATM sharing agreements with out-of-state banks, and small banks did not fight the ruling because they were included in the networks. The second came in 1981 when Sears announced its financial services' plans, and Visa and MasterCard prepared to expand into ATM networks. Determined not to lose control over debit cards as they had over credit cards and united finally against outside competitors, the banks rushed into shared ATM systems. Even Bank of America, which had four ATMs at the beginning of 1980, had nearly 1,000 by 1984. Nonetheless, by 1983 a Florida supermarket chain had set up its own ATM network and was charging banks a transaction fee each time a customer used one. Safeway Stores, which cash about 1 million checks a day at an annual cost of over $90 million, had also begun installing ATMs and were considering diversifying into other financial services.[41]

But just as the wheels of progress picked up speed, the government again threw a monkey wrench into the works. This time it was a judge in upstate New York who ruled that an ATM in a supermarket was a branch of the bank that used it and was therefore in violation of a state "home protection" law, even though the store owned the machine. The judge cited the dilemma he faced in trying to apply a 1927 law to computerized banking: "The application of a 50 year old statutory definition to the type of technology which could never have been dreamed of at the time the legislation was enacted is fraught with inconsistencies which are not easily reconcilable."[42]

Pursuit of the Perfect POS

Boldly leading the way into the "cashless society" envisioned at the time, the Bank of Delaware in 1966 introduced a POS system that used touch-tone telephones. Bank customers inserted a plastic card into a slot in customized phones in stores and pushed the buttons to access the bank's computer, which debited their account for the amount of the sale and credited the merchant's. But due to costs, the experiment ended in two years. By then the Hempstead Bank on Long Island was designing the first on-line terminal-based POS system, which it began testing in thirty-five retail outlets in 1971, after the ABA adopted the magnetic stripe as the machine-readable standard for cards, and used until 1979.

To learn if it could extend the use of its cards, BankAmericard in 1971 cosponsored a POS test with a bank in fifty retail outlets, which, like many later POS projects, authorized but did not effect a transfer of funds. Two years later the bank now known as Citibank launched the first large debit card program and on-line authorization system when it issued 1.7 million machine-readable debit and credit cards and installed thousands of terminals in retail locations and bank offices as part of its EFT strategy aimed not at cutting costs but at increasing market share and revenues. After finding in earlier tests that the cost of POS terminals was not offset by reduced losses, Chase Manhattan in 1975 installed the first on-line electronic cash register (ECR)-bank authorization link in the United States, which worked for one-tenth the cost of calls and half the cost of terminal authorization. A direct transfer test by a Los Angeles thrift in the mid-1970s involving 100 terminals in 21 supermarkets proved disastrous because units useful only for customers of one thrift with a small market share in one chain of stores with a small share could not possibly generate the volume of transactions necessary for success. All told, about 10,000 POS terminals were installed in the 1970s; yet by the end of the decade, fewer than 20 systems remained in operation, with about half transferring funds electronically.

Profits in POS have proved elusive. The additional convenience for customers is so minor that they would not pay more for a POS transfer than for a check. There could be no competitive advantage for financial institutions since they would have to share a system to obtain the volume needed and meet retailers' demands for one system. But by doing so, they could keep a retailer out of the payments business. The main beneficiaries are retailers who could displace the high costs of handling checks, speed up check-out time, and accelerate cash flow. Their alternatives are to pay fees to a shared net-work or set up their own systems. Not surprisingly, a number of large retailers, including the nation's second-largest supermarket chain, have chosen the latter. The Florida supermarket chain that charges banks an entry fee of $25,000 for access to its ATM system plus usage fees, began installing a POS system in 1984. But since the chain cashes more than 10 million checks a year, it will not charge either customers or financial institutions any fees for POS transactions.

Competing with the Government in the United States: The Fed Flap

It is ironic that in a comparison of the payment systems of one of the most socialistic democracies in the world with that of the apotheosis of capitalism, it is in the latter that the private sector has suffered inequities in competing with the government agency that also is its regulator. Moreover, in payments services the Federal Reserve System enjoys a market share of 50 percent of third-party check services, 80 percent of domestic wire transfers, and 90 percent of ACH volume; has the only nationwide network in the land; has the power of rulemaker to enhance its competitive position as vendor; and enjoys legal and structural immunity from bearing certain costs of doing business.

In the past, the Fed and the correspondent banks cooperated in providing payment services to smaller banks. But after Congress in 1980, to encourage competition, ordered the Fed to start pricing its services, the agency lost some 20 percent of its volume in the first year. Hence, argue the banks, to protect its market share, the Fed delayed implementation of full pricing, changed rules governing check and wire transfer services to its advantage, and thereby forced some private clearing banks to operate at a loss.

At the heart of the issue is a lack of policy as to the role of the central bank in the payments system. Bankers contend that either it should be only a processor of last resort or it should eliminate the conflict of interest inherent in being a regulator and a competitor. While reluctant to criticize the Fed for fear of reprisal, some say that with its focus on monetary policy, payments system policy is often set at staff level. Indeed, Fed officials concede that the present arrangement may not be the ideal way to fulfill their mandate of insuring the integrity, safety, and efficiency of the nation's payment mechanisms.

Of course, with checks losing ground to EFTS, the argument in time will be moot. But by then the payment system could have been taken over by NCR, AT&T, and other telecommunications specialists.

Notes

1. Lars-Erik Thunholm, *Svenskt kreditväsen*, 10th ed. (Stockholm: Rabén & Sjögren, 1969), p. 119.

2. Ernfrid Browaldh, "Kronkurrensen på den svenska kreditmarknaden," *Ekonomisk revy* (1955): 358.

3. Ibid., p. 362.

4. Åke Janson, "Något om sparbankerna och deras verksamhet," *Ekonomisk revy* 8 (1960): 604.

5. Sparbankernas Information, *Savings Banks in Sweden* (Stockholm: Sparfrämjandet, 1979), p. 9.

6. Browaldh, "Kronkurrensen," p. 370.

7. Per Eric Bolin, "PM angående fråga om slopande av bankernas ränteavtal," *Svenska Bankföreningen*, December 8, 1967.

8. David H. Pyle, "The Losses on Savings and Deposits from Interest Rate Regulation," *Bell Journal of Economics and Management Science* 5 (Autumn 1974): 614–622.

9. Data relating to market shares for time and savings deposits from Bank for International Settlements, *Payment Systems in Eleven Developed Countries* (Basel: BIS, 1980), pp. 273–274.

10. Data from Constance Dunham, "The Growth of Money Market Funds," *New England Economic Review* (September–October 1980): 20–34.

11. George W. Mitchell, "EFT Issues and Outlook: Technology, Innovation and Banking" (paper presented at the Conference on Contemporary Issues in Cash Management, Bank Administration Institute, New Orleans, September 7–10, 1982).

12. Robert I. Lipp, "How Do U.S. Banks Plan to Resist the New Forms of Competition?" in European Financial Marketing Association, *Texts of the Presentations*, EFMA Conference, Monte Carlo, March 21–24, 1982 (Paris: EFMA, 1982), p. 22.

13. Ibid.

14. Data from Patrick Frazer and Dimitri Vittas, *The Retail Banking Revolution* (London: Michael Lafferty Publications, 1982), pp. 269, 278–279; also Federal Reserve System research data, unpublished.

15. "The Golden Plan of American Express," *Business Week*, April 30, 1984, p. 119.

16. "Beneficial: Selling Spiegel to Prepare for a Future in Banking," *Business Week*, July 6, 1981, pp. 92–93.

17. Harry Karlsson, "Elektronisk betalningsförmedling och konsumentskyddet," Institutet för Rättsinformatik-rapport 1981:1, Stockholms Universitet, App. 1.

18. Bankinspektionen, "Yttrande över en inom finansdepartementet upprättad PM om samgående mellan Postbanken och Kreditbanken," March 12, 1973, p. 2–5.

19. Thunholm, *Svenskt Kreditväsen*, p. 58.

20. Ibid., p. 130.

21. Bankinspektionen, "Yttrande," pp. 1–2, and Sveriges officiella statistik (SOS) for this and following data in paragraph.

22. Interview with Swedish banking executive in November 1982.

23. Interview with high-level PK Bank official in December 1982.

24. PK Banken, *Annual Report 1981*, p. 9.

25. Ibid.; Post Office, *Annual Report 1981/1982*, p. 21.

26. Interview at PK Bank in November 1982.

27. Interview with high-level PK Bank official in December 1982.

28. Interview with Postal Giro executive in December 1982.

29. G. Clayton, "The Swedish Post Giro," *Bankers Magazine* (London) (September 1956): 229.

30. Svenska Bankföreningen, "Protokoll hållet vid Ordinarie Bankmötet" (1942).

31. Statistics from Post Office and Bank Giro annual reports.

32. George V. Banks, paper presented at ABA's Preauthorized Payments Workshop, New Orleans, January 25–26, 1968, quoted in Dennis W. Richardson, *Electric Money: Evolution of an Electronic Funds Transfer System* (Cambridge: MIT Press, 1970), p. 90.

33. Donald R. Hollis, "EFT Strategy Considerations for Multinational Banks," in EFMA, *Texts of the Presentations*, EFMA Conference, Amsterdam, June 12–15, 1977 (Paris: EFMA, 1977), p. 227.

34. Sidney A. DaCosta, "Research Behind EFTS," in Bank Marketing Association, *Research as a Management Tool* (Chicago: Bank Marketing Association, 1974), p. 66.

35. George C. White, "Commentary: Corporate Electronic Payment Alternatives," *Journal of Cash Management* (January–February 1984): 51.

36. Eugene M. Tangney, "EFTS Impact on Banking and the Consumer" (paper presented at the IBM Executive Banking Conference, Fort Lauderdale, September 26, 1978).

37. George C. White, "The Conflicting Roles of the Fed as a Regulator and a Competitor," *Journal of Cash Management* (April–May 1983): 46.

38. Interview at Bankomat Center in December 1982.

39. Tangney, "EFTS Impact."

40. Bureau of Justice Statistics, Special Report, "Electronic Fund Transfer and Crime," NCJ-92650 (February 1984), p. 3.

41. "Safeway Stores: Back to Price Wars for a Company That Played It Too Safe," *Business Week*, April 5, 1982, p. 109.

42. *Independent Bankers Assn. of New York State, Inc. v. Marine Midland Bank, N.A.*, 583 F. Supp. 1042 (1984). Marine Midland Bank, backed by the comptroller of the currency and the Federal Reserve Board, has asked a federal appeals court to reverse the controversial lower court decision.

5
Technological Cooperation

Environment for Cooperation

Cult of Individualism

The National Commission on Electronic Fund Transfers concluded that: "the economic incentives of the marketplace will induce institutions to share equipment and services to realize economies of scale, either through jointly-owned projects or common use of systems provided by others."[1] However persuasive the economic rationale may have been for sharing, for years it did not prevail in the United States, partly because it ran counter to one of the most deeply rooted and pervasive cultural values in the land: rugged individualism. For years, there was a resistance to EFTS among U.S. bankers based not only on fear of the new but also on the fear that technology spelled the end of a large measure of their independence.

Historically the balkanized system of a multitude of independent banks, sheltered from competition by regulatory barriers and spread across a sprawling continent, spawned highly autonomous banking operations that were unique in the world. They were bolstered by the fact that the technology and expertise required to handle the paper-based mechanism with checks were so rudimentary that bankers needed no one aside from their formalized relationships with correspondents or the Fed for settlement and clearing. Their relationships with bankers from other cities and states were primarily social. At their ritualistic conventions, they would solemnly tell each other how great things were back in their banks, drink together, show off their wives' new fur coats, and then go back to their own little kingdoms where they reigned supreme. They were reluctant to surrender any measure of their freedom, even within the "families" of holding companies, where bank presidents can be as rebellious and balky as teenagers.

The bankers' distaste for dependency relationships surfaced on a broader scale during the computerization of the industry in the 1960s when their relationships with computer people were less than friendly. Computer personnel thought bankers were naive and confused, and bankers resented the fact that they had to rely on them to handle the new technology, which was beyond their purview. The antagonism that grew over the years between the two groups was usually attributed to the inability of technicians to communicate in the same language as the bankers, who joked that the computer experts could speak "only in bits and bytes." But beneath the rationalization was a growing concern: many bankers perceived that the emerging importance of computers imperiled their autonomy and threatened to dispel the mystique surrounding the basically simple business that went on behind the carved doors that opened only to the wealthy and powerful.

But while the intrusion of the technicians had been irksome when they were handling backroom operations, when they got the computers to start spewing forth new retail products, they became true threats. The bankers were forced to work with and surrender part of their control to iconoclastic newcomers who talked the new math but had never made a commercial loan in their lives.

Beyond this forced sharing internally loomed a more ominous threat. A banker can shuffle around papers to his heart's content all by himself, but electronic banking compels banks to cooperate and coordinate because the networks and systems do not work unless institutions are linked together—and the more linkages, the better. In essence, the technology enforced linkages and dependencies to an extent never before necessary. To reap the benefits of the new technology required the surrender of some measure of individualism because members of a network cannot do everything their own way. And therein lay the rub: people have to learn how to cooperate and share, and that has never been a strong suit of Americans, much less American bankers who for decades had complacently gone it alone.

As if those cultural blocks to cooperation were not enough, there were others in the sheer number of banks and in the competitive zeal that had precluded their working even with other banks of the same type against their mutual competitors. Because of the greater national emphasis on free enterprise and market forces, there was yet another major obstacle to cooperation, or at least another good excuse for not cooperating: fear of the Department of Justice's Antitrust Division. Although spokesmen for the division frequently tell bankers' meetings that they are not opposed to all cooperative ventures, the uncertainty they inject into the environment with their periodic challenges and their failure to communicate clearly what is and is not permissible has been sufficient reason for as conservative a group as bankers to just throw in the towel and not try at all.

Spirit of Collaboration

In Sweden, as in most European countries, there has long been a spirit of cooperation among financial institutions, as well as more cooperation between them and the government than in the United States. But if the technological areas of all payment systems lie on a spectrum between complete cooperation on the left and complete competition on the right, the U.S. one until recently would have been about as far to the right as Sweden's was to the left. In Sweden it has been taken for granted that cooperation is the only sensible approach to technological development. The Bank Inspection Board has a mandate to see that the banks are sound and thus profitable. But because individual systems could not be profitable in such a small country, the agency encourages sharing. The only caveat it imposes is that consumers must have the option to choose among payment mechanisms, and that is possible because of the two CD and giro systems, plus the paper-based mechanisms. Nor does the Antitrust Ombudsman regard shared networks as a restraint of trade because the bankers share technology while competing at the service level. Hence, they have been able to pursue innovation free of uncertainty about possible government intervention.

Their cooperative efforts have constituted a response to inflationary pressures on operating costs, Riksbank policies that squeezed profit margins, and social welfare policies that have made the cost of capital lower than labor. Furthermore, the large transaction volumes generated by the spread of retail banking and the nationwide operations of all banks—the large ones through branch networks and the smaller ones through associations—stimulated the joint development of EFTS as a way to reduce the costs of their payment services. The cost crunch has been exacerbated by the fact that in their eagerness to get salary accounts, the bankers struck deals with the labor unions that included promises not to charge fees on those accounts. Government pressure, too, has severely constrained their ability to pass on rising costs to consumers. Blithely unaware of the dictum, "There's no such thing as a free lunch," the public there expects free payment services. The banks also have used technological cooperation as a means of evading regulatory constraints on all the other facets of their operations because with EFTS they have found a way to compete without regulation. Another impetus to cooperation has come from the government, which has a vested interest in minimizing the cost and maximizing the efficiency of payment services, not only for the public good but also because it is a major user of the services.

The bankers' collaborative efforts have been facilitated by behavioral patterns inculcated in childhood, when Swedes are taught the virtue of collective action and the desirability of working together rather than going it alone. This attitude tends to subdue self-assertiveness and produce adults who are comfortable working groups. Moreover, since in a small nation people work together throughout their careers, they know each other well enough so that the law of anticipated reactions smooths cooperative projects. The propensity to organize and work together long ago led to their banking associations becoming sources of operational and technical support. Thus, as the industry became first mechanized and then computerized, technological cooperation became a natural part of their way of operating. In their projects, the large Swedish banks also have revealed political perspicacity by including the smaller banks so as to forestall any possible charges of restrictive operations. Moreover, since their systems ensure equality by permitting all banks to participate, they have encountered no resistance to development by small, local banks that otherwise, as in the United States, might have protested the "invasion" of their communities by electronic services provided by large, out-of-town banks.

The argument that sharing and cooperating blunt the edge of competition and inhibit innovation has been disproved in Sweden, where competition has sharply intensified since the banks started sharing uniform delivery systems. While the 1968 legislation enabled all banks to compete on an equal basis, it was the joint development of EFT services that enabled the smaller banks to compete successfully.

Inasmuch as the pace of implementation of new technology is positively correlated to a low level of start-up and operating costs, and cooperation reduces these, technological coordination also helps explain Sweden's leading, and the United States's lagging, role in adopting electronic services. The high efficiency rating garnered by the Swedish system can be attributed in part to another spinoff from cooperation: the greater amount of managerial and technical expertise accruing from group efforts as opposed to those of individuals—the old "n plus 1 heads are better than n heads" theory.

The great advantage to consumers is that one bank card can be used nationwide to get cash, shop, or charge a purchase, regardless of where the account is maintained. The equal access principle also applies to the Bank Giro, which is available to any customer of any bank. As to the question of customer loyalty, when people receive service from offices or CDs other than their own bank's, Swedish bankers have found that what matters to customers above all is the level of efficiency. Indeed, the bankers believe they have attained a happy medium between cooperation and competition. Said one, "Here we started with a common system, just the opposite of the U.S. where you started with all those individual systems and now are trying to put them together."[2]

Basic R&D in EFTS: Counterintuitive Contrasts

Fostered by Fear and the Fed

Growing fear that the checking system was in danger of collapsing under the burden of burgeoning volumes prompted the Federal Reserve System and commercial banking groups in the 1960s to sponsor studies of the economic and technical feasibility of using electronic technology as an alternative to the paper-based mechanism. Because of the high visibility of the check payment system, there was concern that a breakdown could seriously undermine the confidence of the American public in the integrity of the entire banking system. After a research group predicted in 1970 that the checking system would survive for at least ten years, the pace of investigation quickened to ensure that effective EFT technology would be developed in that time frame.[3] By then, a major EFTS study funded by the Federal Reserve Bank of Atlanta was already underway at the Georgia Institute of Technology. In its six-volume report in 1972, the team of researchers recommended a phased approach to EFTS, beginning with the development of ACHs to handle direct deposits and bill payments, followed by a pilot POS project, and then a feasibility study of check truncation.

Pursuant to its proposals, the Special Committee on Paperless Entries (SCOPE) was formed by the major California banks with the assistance of the Federal Reserve Bank of San Francisco, which participated in the research and development of the software and assumed virtually all the operating costs, to create an automated clearinghouse. With check volume then growing at an annual rate of 8 percent, the participants anticipated that direct credits and debits could displace some 30 percent of the checks and in the process also reduce lobby traffic and bank operating expenses. But since the entire project was operations-oriented with never a thought given to the need to educate and sell the public on the advantages of the new services over the old, and most bankers remained unconvinced, response to the costly venture was insignificant. Even after the passage of a decade, transaction volume through the ACH, which includes three other states, totaled about 6 percent of the optimistic projection of what it would be for California alone.[4]

The leading role assumed by the Federal Reserve in developing EFT technology illustrated two major differences in the relationship between the banking industry and government in the United States as compared to that in Sweden. First, there was a counterintuitive role reversal in the total absence of government from the developmental work by the private sector in socialistic Sweden and the dominance by government in the capitalistic United States. This carried over to the new technology the respective roles of the private and public sectors, which earlier had been cast in the two nations during the development of the paper-based clearing infrastructure. In the United States, the Fed had taken over the prime responsibility for checkclearing to meet a need that the fragmented and localized banking system could not handle and then had to build a transportation system to handle the movement of checks because the Post Office's service was so slow that it would have created even higher levels of float than those that have plagued the present mechanism for years.

Thus, as EFTS evolved, the Fed originally envisaged that it would take over the new infrastructure for what was perceived to be "an" EFT system. It planned to install and operate a nationwide communications network through which interregional settlements between financial institutions could be made. This monopolistic approach was consistent with the "public utility" concept of EFTS, which compared an electronic system to telephone, water gas, or electricity services. Although those utilities differ from banking in that they provide just one service through a single network, many economists and bankers considered the analogy relevant in the early stages of EFTS development in the United States. It was, however, never regarded as such in Sweden. Although the view was antithetical to the basic tenets of the capitalistic and competitive system of the United States, when faced with a new and complex system that required large capital outlays, and accustomed to the security afforded by the blanket of government regulation that sheltered them from much risk taking, many bankers were ready and willing to turn EFTS over to Uncle Sam. One banker, who caustically attributed the reluctance of some of his colleagues to take on the challenges of the new technology to a lack of "intellectual capital," said their attitude was, "Look, we just can't handle this kind of thing. Why don't we all either give it to the Fed or, you know, hand it out to somebody else?"[5]

The second difference revealed by the Fed's involvement in EFTS development was that while the Swedish government's interventions in the industry have often resulted in greater equality among the banking sectors, the Fed's conflicting roles as a regulator and payments processor have created inequities for financial institutions that were not members of its system. In the SCOPE project, for example, nonmember commercial banks and all thrift institutions were excluded from participation in the ACH. In order to receive their customers' credits and debits, they had to have them transmitted through a correspondent bank that belonged to SCOPE. But while the Federal Reserve found the pass-through type of arrangement satisfactory because it preserved competitive relationships and limited the number of endpoints in the settlement system, thereby reducing its costs, the thrifts contentiously viewed it as a highly inequitable form of discrimination.

As a defensive tactic to protect its members from exclusion from the clearing networks owned by the commercial banks and the Fed, the National Association of Mutual Savings Banks created MINTS, the Mutual Institutions National Transfer System, a computerized network for the relay of administrative and payments messages similar to those of the Fed Wire and Bank Wire systems. It enabled customers of any member of the system to use the facilities of any other to make withdrawals, deposits, or third party payments. Inspired by the venture, credit unions soon set up the same sort of network. But the Kansas Credit Union League went even further in 1974 when it bought a commercial bank to gain access to any regional or nationwide electronic networks those institutions might establish. As new facilities were created, infighting broke out between the S&Ls and the commercial banks for access to ACHs, between independent banks and the Fed for control of the message switching system, and between regional clearinghouses and thrifts and their associations over switches. The outsiders by then were pronouncing the acronym for the Georgia Automated Clearing House Association "Gotcha," which described their feelings about the predicament in which they found themselves as electronic systems developed.

At the end of 1972, when it recognized that a number of regional and local EFT networks would be created, the Federal Reserve adopted a policy of monitoring them to ensure that security was maintained and that they had the capability to interface with "the national network."[6] In a series of EFT conferences in the mid-1970s, at which much the same coterie of EFT believers from banking, industry, and government gathered regularly to debate the issues, Antitrust lawyers argued that there was no reason for the Fed to play as dominant a part in EFT clearing as in paper clearing and urged the board to announce a policy of being a clearer only as the last resort. One prescient division attorney in 1974 dared to enunciate the rank heresy that electronic clearing did not even have to be confined to the financial industry because it might more profitably be handled by a data communications company with economies of scale so great from its broad range of services that the cost of the clearing function would fall well below the cost of a network dedicated exclusively to clearing funds.[7] But because the bank card systems then were so strong, many at the time believed that they were the most likely candidates to run the nation's electronic clearing system. The Master Charge company had reportedly authorized nearly half a million dollars to develop a national EFTS that would enable cardholders to get cash, make purchases, guarantee checks, and transfer funds between accounts, and BankAmericard announced in 1974 that it had committed $250,000 to develop specifications for a prototype retail system. The acceptability of those plans, however, later was thwarted by radically altered bankers' attitudes toward the companies.

Thus, it was not until after the winds of change had wrought grave destruction in the industry that cooperation among U.S. financial institutions became a widely accepted norm. In 1983 a leading banker articulated the philosophy it had taken the industry so long to learn: "To achieve the highest volume possible over the shortest period of time . . . the sharing of facilities among competitors as well as correspondent banks will probably become a common denominator in the industry . . . complete sharing by most institutions will become the rule."[8]

Sweden's SIBOL Project

The research venture that had the greatest impact on the development of EFT in Sweden began in 1969, just before the social and legal aspects of the technology became the topics of debate. Called SIBOL (Cooperation for an Integrated On-Line Payment System), a consortium representing all the banks sought to determine the feasibility of developing a common electronic payment system. Their goals differed from those of their U.S. counterparts in that they sought to attain long-term economic and technological efficiency without any government participation. Because the large banks and associations at the time were planning and installing CDs and on-line systems, one goal was to avoid the development of a number of parallel and possibly incompatible networks. Others were to reduce the costs of document handling by creating paperless transfers between bank accounts and to offset partly the continuing shortage of manpower in the nation. The goal was not a "cashless society"; they did not consider it possible or desirable to eliminate cash as an instrument of payment.

Because no previous effort had been made to document an integrated payment system in general terms and because of their inability to forecast the technical state of the art at the time of implementation, the group formulated a mathematical model of the system that could be manipulated to demonstrate the economic implications under various assumptions. The data communications work was done in cooperation with the Swedish Telecommunications Administration (STA), which backed the study because it needed research into uses for the public data network it was planning. All standards essential for the system were worked out, including the cards, transaction layouts, account numbers, interfaces, procedures, and codes. The comprehensive four-part report recommended that the standards be adopted even if the system itself was not accepted, suggested that the banks clear data by exchanging magnetic tapes, and proposed that bank representatives participate in planning STA's data network. Projecting debit cards in the long run as an effective alternative to checks and cash, it proposed using them instead of credit cards at POS.

But in addition to the wealth of details, what attracted worldwide recognition was the far-ranging scope of the four alternative designs of the system developed. They demonstrated how a debit card could access accounts via on-line teller, POS, CD, company, and even *home banking* terminals. The designs also included support systems such as the two giros, a credit card center, the Credit Information Center, the Stockholm Stock Exchange, a real estate data center, the Riksbank, and the National Bureau of Statistics. There were volume forecasts, economic analyses, security measures, and an analysis of the sensitivity of cost per message to changes in volumes.

Requests came in from all over the world for information about the system, and SIBOL designers were invited to address international conferences. But while they were heroes abroad, they became the targets of vitriolic attacks at home as the project became embroiled in a storm of controversy. Triggered by a national census in 1970, an intense public debate about privacy and computer-based information files soon focused on the nascent SIBOL system as a potential threat to the rights of individuals. As the attack quickly became politicized, a bill was introduced in Parliament calling for public control of the project. In response, designers created a new plan, eliminating those portions of the system related to privacy. But while project participants viewed it as a neutral support subsystem for the banks and basically a continuation of the cooperation that characterized the clearing operation between banks, the outcome of the pioneering project became apparent even before the final report was typed; it was put aside by banking executives with the diplomatically worded appraisal that "the time was not ripe for it."[9]

One of the SIBOL participants has enumerated three main reasons for the rejection of the system. The first was the privacy issue, which was resolved in 1973 with passage of the Data Act. The second was the banking community's traditional fear of government intervention, which was exacerbated at the time by the demands for nationalization of the banks by the same political elements who called for public control of SIBOL. The third was that while in 1969, when the project began, the Swedish economy had been strong, a sharp downturn in 1970–1971 resulted in cutbacks in bank operations and a more conservative outlook that predicated against development projects. The list is as interesting, however, for what it does not say, since none of the reasons cited were technological in nature but rather were sociopolitical.

But all was not lost. On the contrary, the report produced consensus among the banks to implement its recommendation of common data clearing with tapes. Its standardization measures have been adopted, and payments with debit cards have been initiated. But beyond those specifics, by documenting an integrated nationwide electronic payments system, SIBOL made the entire Swedish banking community more future-oriented in its thinking.

Efficiency through Cooperation in Sweden

Clearing System

The Swedish payments system is characterized by a high degree of universal banking, which means that the financial institutions provide reciprocal customer services. The commercial banks have been cashing checks for each others' customers since 1961, and since 1966 all banks have been doing it across sectors. They have been transferring salary deposits since 1962, and since 1980 banks of all types, with the exception of PK Bank, have permitted withdrawals on each others' passbook savings accounts. The Post Office, moreover, has granted withdrawals on passbooks since 1974 and has been cashing checks since 1977.

As a result, there is a significant amount of data interchange, which until 1975 was carried out by exchanging paper documents. The conversion to a paperless data clearing system, as proposed in the SIBOL report, was undertaken in 1974 through a joint project coordinated by the Swedish Bankers

Association. Since checks constituted about 80 percent of clearing materials, the initial efforts were focused on them. Although the banks at the time recorded each others' checks by computerized means, they had to remove the clearing checks manually so that they could be forwarded via the Riksbank to the banks on which drawn. As a starting point, the banks standardized their account numbers and clearing document layouts. Then, to end the paper shuffling, they agreed to truncate checks, meaning that all checks remain in the office where cashed, including the roughly one-third that are drawn on other banks, and are not returned to customers. The office that cashes the check microfilms and files it, and only information about the transaction in transferred. While the check or a copy of it can be furnished on request, experience has shown that such requests are made in only 1 out of 10,000 cases. Truncation is facilitated by the fact that most commercial as well as consumer bill payments are made through the giro systems rather than by check.

Tellers enter all check-cashing transactions on their terminals. The bank data center receiving them selects the clearing items and sends them to Bank Giro, which functions as a relay and forwards the data to the banks on which the checks are drawn. The financial institutions have agreed that clearing items should be delivered to the account holder's bank on the same day the corresponding amount is cleared at the Riksbank. Hence, before a bank transmits its clearing transactions into the data-clearing system, it calculates the total amount to be drawn on each bank. These totals are reported to the Riksbank, where the banks' clearing accounts are updated. Although financial institutions must have teller terminal systems encompassing the greater part of their office networks to participate in the system, today all except some thirty smaller savings banks qualify, and the Postal Giro joined in 1982.

Since the introduction of paperless check clearing, the system has been expanded to handle practically all types of clearing transactions, including salary transfers, money orders, passbook withdrawals, giro documents, and credit data. With all paper documents retained in the receiving offices, the Swedish banks have succeeded in stemming the flood of paper. Having accomplished that, they decided in 1983 to initiate a project to upgrade their data clearing system from tape-based to on-line. With a central computer at Bank Giro operating as a central switch for communication between the banks' data centers, the system is expected to start operating on a trial basis between the two largest banks in 1985.

Computerization and Joint Ventures

Although some 11 percent of the largest Swedish bank's operating costs are related to computing and automation, only the big commercial banks there have their own computers. The smaller ones either use service bureaus or have joined together to invest in a computer. For example, four provincial banks operate a data center and through their joint venture have developed common software packages for checking account systems. None of the savings banks owns its own data processing equipment; they lease it from a jointly-owned subsidiary company. Indeed, some small savings banks do not even use computerized procedures and are not linked to SPADAB, which processes about 90 percent of the savings banks' accounts. Yet while not possessing uniform capabilities, the financial institutions have found synergy in working together to develop some highly efficient nationwide projects.

A milestone in cooperative efforts was reached in 1969 when Sweden's largest union and the largest employers' group concluded an agreement by which the wages of all building trade workers in the country are directly deposited into the bank or postal accounts of their choice through a center formed by a consortium of all the banks and the Postal Giro. Through the fully automated system, which handles over 2 million wage deposits a year, union fees are automatically deducted from pay. It also disburses unemployment compensation, which in Sweden is paid by the unions. Prior to the establishment of the center, the workers had been paid in a highly erratic fashion.

A similar activity is carried out by the automated Securities Register Center, which sends out dividends on a preauthorized basis. Its operations are based on a 1971 law for simplified handling of stock shares to reduce the handling of paperwork, which previously had circulated between the stock exchange and shareholders. Half-owned by the state and half by the banks and other stockbrokers, the center also maintains the shareholders' register, handling changes in ownership and issuing new share certificates through data-based routines. Two-thirds of the stockbrokers in Sweden are banks, including the commercial banks, the savings and cooperative banks' central banks, and two large savings banks.

To avoid redundant operations, members of the three banking sectors in 1975 formed the Credit Information Center. It provides the banks with necessary information for evaluating the creditworthiness of individuals and corporations and provides individuals with the information furnished about them, as required by Swedish law.

The banks' heavy dependence on functioning EDP systems has led to mutual security studies, which have resulted in the drafting of comprehensive plans for handling the technological and organizational aspects of computer breakdowns. In addition to a mutual assistance agreement, most banks are participating in plans for the creation of a back-up data center, located outside Stockholm and operated by a separate company. The banks also have prepared a manual detailing precedures for the operations of their systems in the event of war.

To solve the bad check problem that undermined confidence in checks for so long, the banks in 1981 adopted a uniform format and common standards for identification cards. They bear a photo of the account holder, his or her signature, a magnetic stripe, a bar code for use at POS, and the personal identification number assigned by the government to each citizen. Security procedures in manufacturing the cards are controlled by a supervisory group within the Swedish Standards Institute. Another joint effort has resulted in an on-line system for verifying the legitimacy of all checks presented to tellers. Each day the Swedish Bankers Association issues a list of stolen checks to member banks, which is routed to their data centers. Every check presented is automatically compared against the information in the warning bulletin after the teller enters the data from the check into the terminal in the bank office.

Credit Cards: The Days of Crime and Woes

Although the use of checks continued to grow in the United States, credit cards were *the* bank products of the 1970s. By then the banks had merged their own cards into BankAmericard and Master Charge to gain broader customer recognition and achieve economies of scale. While the companies do not issue cards themselves, they entitle banks affiliated with them to use their trademark and provide services such as authorization and interchange systems. After the Federal Reserve declined to handle their transactions, two systems of clearing evolved, with Master Charge using regional associations and BankAmericard a national system. The companies also developed the descriptive billing format now widely used by thrifts and some banks for NOW accounts.

Because the cards eliminated the need for consumers to go to the bank to get a signature loan, they expanded the use of convenience credit so that by 1974 bank cards accounted for 32 percent of revolving credit, compared to the 60 percent held by the retailers.[10] In terms of volume, most card transactions in 1973 were made with oil company cards, but in terms of dollars, the volume of card transactions by retailers was twice as big as that of the oil and bank cards combined. Between 1973 and 1976, credit card accounts grew at an annual rate of about 30 percent, greatly exceeding that of both checks and cash, which were expanding at about 7 to 8 percent per year. By 1976, the 75 million bank credit cards accounted for 2 percent of transactions. However, J.C. Penney still had more cardholders than either Master Charge or BankAmericard.

As the size and operational efficiency of the bank credit card companies grew, only the very largest businesses could compete with them. The card companies undercut the profitability of smaller card operators and displaced thousands of in-house cards as merchants found it cheaper to turn their credit sales over to the banks. Those decisions soon were proved to be wise. Although by the mid-1970s some credit card operations were very large, the cost per transaction showed no sign of declining. More surprising, research indicated that each credit card averaged only one transaction per month, which seemed disproportionate to the extensive investment in card systems. For many years, the bank credit cards were known to be unprofitable, but this problem was attributed to the growth stage of the business. Then a 1978 study revealed that because the banks charged no fee for credit card use, although each transaction cost over 50¢, most bank credit card operations were barely breaking even or, at best, were only slightly profitable. Large retailers could afford to carry such a marginal operation because their cards produced extra sales and generated customer loyalty. But banks could ill afford to give away their card service since they were already subsidizing checking accounts to the tune of some $7.2 billion a year.

The government intervened in card operations with legislation in 1974 prohibiting the companies from banning discounts for cash sales in their contracts with retailers. Then the Department of Justice pressured the two big card companies to permit their member banks to issue both cards. By increasing competition for retail store acceptance, the so-called duality exacerbated an already declining proportion of income from merchant discounts.

By 1977, with Master Charge well-known and Visa promoting its name change from BankAmericard, about 39 percent of U.S. families had bank credit cards. But the strong image of the cards was acquired at the cost of the banks' own identity as homogenization of the business developed, with all banks in a community offering the same products. If that situation was less than optimal, at least it was banks offering the cards.

The plot thickened when Visa opened its doors to other businesses by permitting cards to be issued for nonbanks whose names were imprinted on the blue band. What was regarded as truly traitorous in the banking fraternity, however, was the fact that the first such card was issued in 1977 through an Ohio bank to Merrill Lynch, thereby enabling the brokerage firm to offer its Cash Management Account customers the same privilege as the banks from which it was about to drain billions of dollars and many of their best customers. As the bankers watched with growing outrage, the nonbank program grew to encompass thirty firms, including retailers, airlines, car rental companies, and even the American Automobile Association, all of which participated through member banks. The rumble of discontent erupted into open revolt in 1979 when Visa permitted J.C. Penney to issue cards directly without going through a bank and, on top of that, gave the company a lower merchant discount. As frosting on the cake, Visa provided the retailer with an electronic interface, so that transactions could be authorized through its electronic cash registers and enter the Visa network directly, with the sales drafts remaining in the stores. That did it. Enraged, the member banks put an end to letting outsiders issue Visa directly and had the names of nonbank participants moved to the back of the cards.

The dissension arose because while the card companies are owned and theoretically controlled by the banks that have franchises, like any other large company with many small shareholders, the real power is vested in the chief executives. Hence, as they aggressively built the companies into large international operations, the organizations took on a life of their own, with goals and strategies that more closely mirrored the values of their managers than those of the members. Visa's president explained, "Years ago, it was clear that Visa's efforts must be global and that institutions must surrender some degree of authority to an equitably-owned central organization."[11]

While the marketing-oriented chief executive saw the Penney's deal as a real coup and the nonbank program as a great way to expand the card base, the bankers, who were more concerned with Visa's service to them than with rank plastic growth, were deeply troubled by two aspects of the Visa plan. One related to safety and security. When issued under the control of regulated institutions, the card programs were protected the same as depositors' funds. But when provided by unregulated firms, the failure of a business could endanger the safety of the payment system, like the failure of a bank. The newcomers, moreover, had no experience in dealing with fraud and other payments-related crimes for which the banks had devised comprehensive deterrent measures. Another issue was competitive. By permitting banks to act as agents for securities firms, Visa enabled them to begin competing directly with banks by adding a payment mechanism to their range of financial services that banks could not offer. It gave nonbanks the best of both worlds: experienced operators to handle a payment service for them without the burden of reserves and other regulatory restraints—and at a time when many in the regulated industry were struggling for survival as the result of massive disintermediation.

Thus, while originally it was only European bankers who considered the big card companies as threats, by the late 1970s many Americans were beginning to share the doubts expressed by a German banker who believes in a decentralized approach to cooperative payment ventures: "We must ask ourselves . . . whether such titanic organizational entities as the worldwide credit card organizations . . . do not in effect tether the competitive marketplace so completely that our many and diverse banks will find themselves losing ground to a financial giant."[12]

The bankers in effect answered the question by collectively yawning when Visa, and later Master Charge, introduced debit cards. Due to the open membership policies of the card companies, there was no competitive advantage in issuing the cards. The evolution from cashiers examining cards to electronic terminals reading the data on magnetic stripes also meant that there no longer was a need for a big brand name. Moreover, because the debit card is more closely tied to the deposit side of their business in that it can access all of a customer's accounts, the bankers adamantly refused to lose their identity with it as they had with credit cards.

Retailers rebelled against paying commissions of 1.5 to 2.75 percent on every sale with the equivalent of a check, which, unlike a credit card, cannot produce sales to customers who need deferred payments. The discounts also made the cards, which are designed for POS use, unacceptable to supermarkets with their low profit margins. Angry because they were forced to take the new card in order to offer credit card sales, merchants cheered on a group of Seattle retailers who sued Visa over the package deal. But since the suit was settled out of court, no legal precedent was set. With primarily thrifts and credit unions issuing the cards, in 1982 there were only some 4 million Visa and MasterCard (the name Master Charge adopted in 1980) debit cards, compared to 120 million of their credit cards and 50 million bank debit cards. Since then, the number of bank debit cards has nearly doubled to 100 million.

With the volume of transactions stagnant in recent years and the number of cards having peaked in 1979, the bank credit card is in the mature stage of the product life cycle. Since a 4 to 5 point spread is needed to operate the services profitably, when the cost of money rose to 16 percent and higher in the late 1970s and early 1980s yet state usury laws limited the interest rate the banks could charge to between 12 and 18 percent, the red ink flowed. Matters were not helped by the fact that the number of cardholders who paid in the free period started rising in 1975, so that by 1980, half the Visa accounts were paid in full each month, meaning they operated at a loss to the bank. With 65 percent of banks' card income derived from interest on credit extended, 32 percent from merchant discounts, and less than 4 percent from fees in 1980, the head of Visa warned that without repricing, the industry could lose in excess of $500 million in 1981.[13] The reaction to the imposition of annual fees was fast: about 20 percent of all cardholders in 1981 cancelled at least one card.

Because the credit card systems are basically paper based, retailers often have to wait several days for their funds while receipts are processed. The systems' old leased lines also are more costly than the new data networks. Moreover, since only 5 percent of retailers who accept cards have direct electronic links, most must make telephone calls for authorizations above floor limits. Since this is troublesome, clerks often do not bother. That negligence has contributed to the buildup of the iceberg the titanic card companies have encountered: massive fraud and credit losses.

From 1975 to 1979, credit losses for the largest banks rose 19 percent as the result of fraudulent use of cards, including stolen cards, counterfeiting, and the sale of charge slips to retailers. As a result of the sharp rise in such losses, in addition to the cost of funds, Visa estimated operating losses in 1980 of some $1 billion. Bankers are highly reluctant to disclose data concerning fraud, but the Bureau of Justice Statistics has reported that losses per transaction by the major credit card companies went up 88 percent between 1979 and 1982. Government officials believe that the fraud losses result largely from counterfeiting techniques used by syndicated criminal enterprises working with corrupt merchants. Although the card crime crisis has prompted new federal legislation and a host of system changes, in 1982 Visa estimated fraud and credit losses alone of $1 billion, a figure that greatly exceeded loss figures reported in the news media.[14]

Although the banks, which by 1984 held 57 percent of revolving credit in the United States, found cards a cost-effective substitute for loan officers in making small consumer loans, many jumped ship as the losses mounted by returning to the practice of issuing only one credit card and by trying to convert as many customers as possible to the use of debit cards. In the rush for the lifeboats, the old cooperative spirit, which had led to the formation of the card companies, gave way to the pragmatic philosophy of every man for himself.

Cracks in the Swedish Cooperative Framework

Conundrum of Cards

In spite of the expenditure of vast sums of money and persistence that would put a terrier to shame, the promoters of credit cards have failed to impress the Swedes, who use them for only about 1 percent of store purchases. This minuscule use is rooted in negative attitudes toward their credit function. For years, school teachers inculcated in Swedish children the idea that saving was a sign of good moral qualities while borrowing revealed weak character. And when installment buying was introduced into the country with the increased sales of cars in the late 1920s, the practice was denounced on the floor of Parliament as a corrupting influence on society.

But when interest in a more convenient form of consumer credit grew in the late 1950s, merchants and banks formed some card companies. By the early 1960s all the major banks were running card systems, but none was making any money. They decided to cooperate and by merging their companies created Köpkort, a joint venture of all the commercial banks, which later were joined by the savings and cooperative banks. The new company struggled along until the mid-1970s when, after a large retailer successfully promoted sales with its own credit cards, some 150 to 200 in-house and finance company card schemes popped up.

Because of the new interest in cards, Köpkort members were deliberating whether to issue Visa cards when some savings bank officials made an end run and surreptitiously entered into independent negotiations with Visa.

Thus, even though the thrifts owned an 8.2 percent interest in Köpkort, in 1978 the largest savings bank became the first Swedish bank to offer Visa. When they recovered from their shock, Köpkort executives hurriedly negotiated a deal to issue MasterCard. But while the Visa defection had been by only one thrift, in 1979 the other members learned that thrift officials, in spite of their participation in the joint venture's activities, were "playing under the blanket," as they put it: they were planning to issue their own combined credit and debit card.

Enticed by the unprecedented growth of credit and high profits being made by the unregulated finance companies, the savings banks established their own card/finance company and launched a new credit/debit/CD card. But by then the government had extended to finance companies the same regulations imposed on banks, thereby subjecting them to the same oft-imposed credit restrictions. Another problem arose when retailers refused to pay the fees of 2 percent for credit and 1 percent for debit purchases the company sought, even though they were less than the average 3.5 percent fee paid to other card companies. So in order to get the card accepted in a large number of stores, the company gave in and signed up retailers so long as they had a savings bank account.

When a purchase is made with the card, the customer indicates on the sales voucher whether it is to be a debit or credit. If a debit, the funds are transferred within a day or two from the customer's account to the merchant's. For debit purchases below about $20, the same charge is made as for checks written below that amount to discourage its use for small purchases. For credit purchases, a direct debit of a fixed part of the expended credit plus interest is made monthly from the customer's account. But even with free debit use and the lowest interest rate in Sweden for credit, a card company executive has stated that both functions are being used less than expected due to people's attitudes about cards. Hence, the card company has sustained operating losses. The impact of political as well as economic and social factors has been felt by the venture: credit restrictions were imposed again by the government just before the card was introduced.

Although the commercial and cooperative banks had refused to offer a debit card at a loss, in late 1984 they decided to issue a credit/debit/CD card because with their card company participating in a POS field test aimed at developing a national system, the card was needed to activate the POS terminals.

The Galling Giro Breakaway

Established solely as a service facility for clearing payment orders, Bank Giro is jointly owned by the commercial banks and operated through a consortium agreement in which the savings and cooperative banks also participate. Thus, through a series of meetings beginning in 1981, bank and giro representatives created a new personal bill-paying service. The giro staff did a system design for handling the anticipated large volume of small payments and, after computing comprehensive cost analyses, the group came up with a fee schedule to make the effort worthwhile yet attractive to customers. But after participating in the planning sessions, the savings banks again went off on their own and secretly entered into negotiations with the Postal Giro. Those culminated in an agreement by which they offered their customers the same type of service but through the postal unit. Moreover, whereas the Bank Giro system was calculated to produce a small profit, the thrifts' plan was loss-producing; they offered it free of charge. Hence, the other banks were compelled to offer their service through Bank Giro free, too.

Stunned by what was regarded as a serious breach of the code that reflects communal judgments about appropriate conduct in cooperative ventures, a Bank Giro official asked a savings banks' association executive why they had taken such a deviant course of action. He replied that they had adopted a strategy of maintaining a separate image in their customers' eyes. Sic transit cooperation.

The Unconsummated Union

When the savings banks ventured into CD technology in 1967, their joint effort spread the costs of the capital-intensive project and lowered them through the large order of equipment. The scope of their cooperative efforts was greatly extended in 1969 when Nordisk Spardata was formed to coordinate the development of EDP and telecommunications technologies and new equipment among the savings banks' DP companies in all the Nordic countries. Through that organization, a teller terminal system was developed and nearly 11,000 terminals supplied. The group also designed and ordered 735 modular on-line CDs for Finland, Norway, and Sweden in 1976 at a cost per unit of some $10,000, which was about half the price that U.S. banks were paying then on an individual basis for machines. Moreover, as a result of that international coordination, the Swedish savings banks' CDs are linked to those in the other Nordic nations.

Following their lead, the postal, commercial, and cooperative banks in 1971 formed a consortium, Bankomat Center, to develop and operate their competing CD network, with the company's expenses to be paid by the banks in proportion to their customers' use of the CDs. Although reconciling the interests of so many different and competing banks was more difficult and time-consuming than the corresponding effort in the savings banks' organization, all participated in the planning of the systems to ensure that their requirements would be met. To meet the stringent demands for reliability in the on-line network, a redundant system was designed with two minicomputers in front of the computers for the banks, and each CD was assigned to a specific bank, which was responsible for supplying it with cash. Site selection was based on customer convenience plus the criterion that each unit had to pay for itself within seven years in the form of savings from an equivalent volume of teller transactions. But since the marginal cost of CD transactions is only about one-seventh that of an ATM's, that was not difficult to attain. The bankers could purchase and install their own CDs as well.

Initially, Bankomat Center provided mutual support for the banks as they entered the new era of electronic self-service for their customers. But over the years, the confidence born of experience gradually reduced their dependence on the center, and the banks bought their CDs from the company. In 1984 a new agreement was signed that ensured continuing cooperation but with greater independence, and the Bankomat operations were transferred to the Bank Giro Center. Bankomat Center now exists only as a small coordinating organization for the common marketing and security matters related to the CD network.

In the 1979 plans for the on-line Bankomat system, the final step was to be the integration of the savings banks' CDs into the system in 1980, based on an agreement between their association and Bankomat Center. Thus, in ordering the new units and planning their system, consideration was given to compatibility with the thrifts' network. But after innumerable postponements, Bankomat members by 1984 questioned whether the savings banks really intended ever to carry out the link-up of the systems.

In the United States: The Historic Breakthrough in Cooperation

Joining Hands Out on the Plains

The fear of faltering as they took their first tentative steps into EFTS led many U.S. bankers in the mid-1970s to reach out for the familiar protection of the government. As a director of the Bank Administration Institute said, "Headlong, fear-driven stampedes into fields which it doesn't understand has cost banking dearly in the near past—especially in credit card competition. I believe that this could happen again in EFTS."[15] Thus, while Federal Reserve System economists joined Antitrust Division lawyers in encouraging private sector initiative in developing newer and better clearing systems, some bankers revealed an atrophy of enterprise resulting from too many years of leaning on the Fed. At the conclusion of a POS credit card trial in 1972, said an Ohio banker, "We urged the Federal Reserve System to supply the common ground services for a switch and processing center. . . . [We] believe that the Fed must be a party to the funds transfer and settlement of balances between principals at point-of-sale."[16]

Indeed, the Fed had to keep fighting off the bankers' advances. In 1974 the Atlanta commercial banks asked the Federal Reserve bank in that city to fund and operate an experimental POS system, which included the transmittal of credit authorization information for bank credit cards, as well as for debit cards and checks. The Fed refused to handle the switching and processing operation, which would have opened another can of worms in that if it handled transactions with bank credit cards free of charge, it would have given them an unfair competitive advantage over sales involving cards issued by thrifts and credit unions.

Economists from academia also argued that the Federal Reserve would be the only appropriate organization to undertake the operation of what they envisioned to be a public utility like the telephone system. They contended that it would not be "socially desirable" to have more than one system and suggested that "the government will hopefully take steps to prevent such inefficiently competing systems from evolving."[17] Fortunately, things seldom turn out the way economists predict. One would be hard pressed, moreover, to think of many occasions on which the U.S. government has done something to prevent an undesirable situation from evolving. Recent history provides ample evidence, on the other hand, of the government quite consistently waiting until there is a crisis before much of anything gets done.

Because there seems to be an inverse relationship between the distance west of Washington where people are and their relative degree of dependence on the federal government, the folks out on the plains west of the Mississippi were less inclined to sit around and wait for the Fed to set up EFT arrangements. One of the first financial institutions in the nation to issue a debit card was a Nebraska savings and loan, which introduced it along with a preauthorized transfer service in 1968 and six years later made history by installing electronic terminals in the Hinky Dinky supermarkets. After it was cleared of charges of violating branching laws in suits brought by the state and the Independent Bankers Association, the S&L franchised the service to other thrifts in the state, thereby becoming a pioneer also in shared EFT networks. Emboldened by the success of the thrifts' network, two-thirds of the commercial banks in the state formed the Nebraska Electronic Terminal System, to consist of ATMs and POS terminals, with membership open to all banks but no other financial institutions, in accordance with the state's mandatory sharing statute. Although the Antitrust Division of the Department of Justice initially refused clearance, the Cornhuskers ultimately prevailed by restructuring the proposal so as to meet the objections of the government attorneys.

Meanwhile, another statewide EFT network had been developing just to the south in Kansas, a state whose banking laws, while restrictive in branching, are progressive in electronic services due to legislation passed in 1975, which permits terminals to be placed anywhere in the state so long as they are available to any bank willing to pay a fair share of the costs incurred in research, development, and operation, with the owner entitled to a reasonable profit on the investment. After an out-of-state co-op in 1975 began soliciting the correspondents of the largest bank in Kansas to join a proposed five-state network, the bank decided to form its own. Within fifteen months, an on-line network of ATMs, POS terminals, and check guarantee phones linking sixty banks and forty-five merchants had been set up that included terminals at the Boeing plant and a university. Retailers found they could process customers in one-third the time it took to write a check and were virtually eliminating a costly bad check problem. By the end of 1978, with some 1.5 million transactions running through the system annually, the bank was already planning to add utility and loan payments to the system.

Another shared statewide network that began operations in 1976 is the cooperatively-owned Iowa Transfer System (ITS), which outdoes even the Swedish Bankomat network by including banks, credit unions, and thrifts. Participating institutions, which now include just about all of them in the state, buy stock in the corporation, with the amount of stock based on the size of the bank's deposits. Like the Swedish CD networks, the members have an option of either setting up their own ATM machines as part of the network or just issuing ITS cards to their customers if they cannot afford to install machines. The system also closely resembles the Swedish system in that ITS operates a central clearinghouse for ATM usage fees, since the member institutions are charged on a per-transaction basis for their customers' use of the machines.

While the Iowa system has been highly successful, a proposal for an eight-state network of thirty-eight banks, which had planned to operate over 1,500 POS terminals and thirty-five ATMs on a shared basis, came a cropper in 1976 when Missouri legislators rejected a necessary enabling bill.

If conditions were not auspicious for that EFT venture to the east of Kansas and Nebraska, the outlook was rosier to the west in Colorado where in 1978 the man known as the "Father of Plastic Banking" activated a regional network that would evolve into the first nationwide banking system in the United States. Between 1967 and 1976 D. Dale Browning had developed a cooperative marketing program for credit cards through the Rocky Mountain BankCard system of Colorado National Bank, which included 530 banks in four states. An ardent advocate of the need to preserve a bank's individuality in the market, when Visa officials announced in 1976 that they planned to introduce a debit card, Browning decided to cut them off at the pass by creating his own card, named Plus, which was a combined ATM/check guarantee/charge card. Within two years the Plus network was geographically the largest of the nation's shared electronic banking systems, with 270 participating financial institutions in twelve states that extended from Kansas to California.

The door to expansion was opened in July 1980 when the Comptroller of the Currency issued an opinion excluding ATMs not owned or rented by a national bank from the definition of a branch; a bank's customers could use terminals in other states as long as such use was compensated for by transaction fees and did not give national banks a competitive advantage over state banks. By equating ATM sharing to correspondent services, the legal groundwork was laid for interstate ATM networks and transcontinental financial services for the first time in the nation's history.

Toward Transcontinental Togetherness

If the comptroller's opinion greased the wheels, the signal that sent the locomotive of shared interstate networks roaring down the tracks was the announcement in 1981 by Visa and MasterCard that they intended to set up nationwide ATM hookups. The two companies had the inside track on developing such nets since they had national brand names and cardholder bases. They also were fortunate in having distribution systems consisting of thousands of member banks; they were unfortunate in that most of those bankers were mad as hell at the card companies.

To prevent Visa and MasterCard from molding ATM interchanges in the imperfect shape of their credit card systems and to retain control of the payment system in the face of mounting competition from nonbanks, two national joint ventures comprised of many of the country's largest banks soon were created, one made up primarily of Visa members and the other of MasterCard members. The lead was taken by Browning, who immediately began formulating plans to resolve the operational, legal, and security ramifications of the massive undertaking. By the end of the year, the banker's efforts resulted in the incorporation of the Plus system by twenty-six banks, including Bank of America and Chase Manhattan Bank. The system promulgates a philosophy of encouraging both intersystem and intrasystem competition while allowing members maximum latitude to develop and preserve product differentiation. Equity between large and small institutions is ensured by permitting members without ATMs to participate if they agree to share subsequently acquired machines.

A major milestone in banking history was attained in July 1983 when Browning announced on the *Today Show* the creation of the first nationwide banking system in the United States, achieving with electronic technology what A.P. Giannini had been unable to attain with brick-and-mortar offices half a century earlier. Four hours later, an official of the Bank of America—

appropriately—withdrew $50 from his San Francisco account at an ATM at Chase Manhattan Bank; in Denver the occasion was marked by the withdrawal from an ATM of funds from a Nevada bank. The service, however, is incomplete in that it still is not possible to deposit money into an account through the out-of-state ATMs because of banking law. By early 1984 the system included 34 proprietary banks and 1,155 sponsored member institutions operating 2,500 ATMs in 47 states to serve 18 million customers.

The second of the national systems to come on-line was the Cirrus network, which was jointly organized by the head of the 300-member MPACT system in Texas and a top executive of First Interstate Bancorp, whose 665 on-line ATMs in eleven states constitute the largest such net of any single banking organization. Soon they acquired as partners other major banks, including Mellon Bank and Manufacturers Hanover Trust Co. After identifying the markets in which they wanted representation, they signed up proprietary banks in each and then gave them the right to license other institutions as associates. The principal and associate members have a direct connection to the network switch, which allows faster transaction processing. They, in turn, may sign up correspondent members to share their link to the switch. Since correspondents negotiate their fees with the banks that license them, smaller banks can participate in the system at a reasonable cost. The Cirrus network by 1984 was providing ATM service in 43 states to nearly 20 million customers of 700 banks through some 5,000 terminals.

Another national network is The Exchange, which links 2,200 ATMs in 34 states, although its operations are concentrated in the Northwest, Florida, and Illinois. It is jointly owned by Automated Data Processing, Inc. (ADP) and The Exchange regional network.

The Nationet system is different in that it consists of a group of twelve regional networks that agreed in early 1983 to begin sharing their terminals. Since its switch does not perform any authorization functions or allow the direct connection of terminals to it, all members must operate in an on-line mode and agree to share all off-premise terminals. Much like the Swedish systems, Nationet believes in equal access to all and provides a neutral infrastructure that permits member institutions to offer nationwide services regardless of their size. By late 1983 the system spanned 27 states, with over 4,000 ATMs owned by the largest number of financial institutions of any network by far: 3,300.

Regional systems, too, have thrived since 1980, with the largest in Michigan linking over 1,330 ATMs in late 1983 and a six-state net based in Texas linking over 1,000. As the number of shared terminals increased 45 percent from mid-1982 to mid-1983, even direct competitors started sharing in sparsely populated areas where the need for economies of scale outweighed marketing considerations. The Publix supermarket chain that aced the Florida banks with its own ATM system drove competitors into each other's arms in 1983 when virtually all of the state's financial institutions belatedly formed a huge network in self-defense.

But while 20 to 25 percent of ATM transactions were made at network machines in 1984, in Illinois development still was thwarted by obfuscatory unit banking laws, and Chicago handily retained its title as the nation's most backward retail banking market. After finally getting their machines linked, Chicago bankers in 1984 remained unable to agree on the terms of sharing, fearful perhaps that some bank might get more than 3 percent of the retail market. But if there was naught but ill winds that blew in the Windy City for consumers of financial services, relief was just a shop away. With retailers installing ATMs and POS terminals and linking bank networks to their electronic cash registers for check authorization, deposits, and withdrawals, by the time the bankers get their act together, the retailers well may have taken over the payments system in the nation's second largest financial center.

As ATM use boomed, the synergistic impact of one EFTS on another was manifest in a renewed interest in POS, with a dozen trials underway in 1982. While the largest was in Denver, where 4,800 terminals were set up in 500 stores, one of the longest-running direct debit tests was begun in 1981 by ITS. It has proved so successful that the same hardware and software were adopted by Florida's Publix supermarket for their POS service. The shared ATM nets have augmented POS acceptance by getting a critical mass of cards in people's hands, familiarizing them with terminal transactions, and setting up the switches, the computerized systems that route electronic transactions among interconnected banks and thrifts. With their net interest margins less healthy than in past years, the banks now are more interested also because direct debits reduce operating costs. However, local cooperation is mandated at POS because just as merchants accept checks from any bank, they insist on access to all with electronic debits. As the Florida phenomenon has shown, if the financial institutions cannot work together, an outsider will step in and do it for them. It's not all that hard anymore.

Need for Cooperation in POS

"The World's First" That Wasn't

While U.S. thrifts were pioneers in POS development because it provided a way around regulatory constraints, the Swedish savings banks also tested POS early—but for another reason. In 1978 they had a card base of some 500,000 as a result of the mass mailing used to introduce their on-line CDs; so they embarked on a POS project because it provided another application for their card.

Analyses of the numerous POS experiments indicate that an on-line system is appropriate for retail outlets that generate a large volume of sales while simpler, less expensive off-line systems are better suited for smaller shops with lower volume. The SIBOL study had projected the need for terminals in a large number of stores and had warned that because of the uneven time distribution of retail sales, it was unrealistic to use a real-time system. Nonetheless, that is just the type of on-line system the savings banks chose. Then they selected for their test nineteen stores and eleven gas stations in a sparsely populated county called Blekinge. Not only was volume lacking there, but the people use cash for 97 percent of their purchases because, a project leader said later, "They're not used to plastic and don't like new things."[18] Those factors, however, were subordinated to the fact that a Swedish oil company had already chosen Blekinge as a test market for its own on-line debit card system linked to self-service gas pumps, which the banks wanted to use, too.

The project team then found that there was "no suitable" equipment available; so they sent out specifications and found two companies that guaranteed installation on time. They imposed tight deadlines on the Nordic manufacturers, neither of which had ever made such equipment before, because they were afraid that if word got out about the test, their competition might beat them to the market with a similar system. A project leader explained, "If you are the first, you are dictating the terms and the other banks have to join the system on your conditions."[19] Since state-of-the-art custom-designed equipment tends to be pricey, it was not an inexpensive venture. In addition to the hardware, there were line costs, the setting up of a separate system, marketing costs, and the man-hours of people from the four thrifts in the area, the association, SPADAB, three other subsidiaries, and the thrifts' central bank—all of which requires a strong commitment from an executive board. When asked how approval was obtained for all this, project leaders said, "Everyone was enthused because we told them we'd be first in the world with such a system"[20] When asked if they had researched the topic first, they replied that they had read everything about POS they could find, and a delegation had flown to the United States in 1978 to visit some POS projects. Although about ten direct debit systems were then running, the project leaders said the ones they saw were only authorization services.

Apparently no Swedish newspaper checked the veracity of the claim since all referred to "the world's first." Even the National Board for Consumer Policies, which is supposed to prevent the duping of consumers, ran a three-page photo-story about the test in the January 1980 issue of its magazine, in which it reiterated the spurious claim several times. The reporter, who had joined the jaunt to the United States, wrote, "It's the first time in the world a person can pay in cash with the help of a card and terminal."[21] Yet even within Sweden, Esso for several months by then had been operating a card system with terminals in self-service gas pumps that debited customers' bank accounts. A picture caption in the article said, "Only a sketch in the USA, but already a reality in Blekinge."[22] That was wrong on both counts: it had been a reality in the United States since 1971, and, due to hardware and technical delays, the Blekinge test had not begun when the magazine came out.

That story was only part of the promotional program, which included brochures appealing to national pride by saying that Swedes were the first in the world to test the debit card. The campaign also reached back to one of the original themes used by the Postal Giro: fear of crime. Even the four-color brochures touted the advantages of the system in reducing the risk of robbery. To do that, of course, the system would have had to displace most of the cash the stores usually took in.

After all the hoopla, "reality in Blekinge" became a nightmare to everyone involved. The system kept going down, and there was no backup; the machines were unwieldy to use, frequently broke down, and sometimes gave the wrong balance. Those problems resulted in people waiting in line and becoming irritated because it took longer than paying with cash. When the machines malfunctioned, it took days to get them serviced, so after store personnel encountered problems with the units, many simply stopped using them. Due to the problems, one store dropped out of the test, leaving eighteen. The local press contributed to negative attitudes toward the test by confusing debit cards with the unpopular credit cards. But after a while it did not seem to matter, for practically no one used the system.

Meanwhile, back in Stockholm, government officials who had been exposed to the publicity about the imminent coming of the "cashless society" were beginning to worry about the implications of it for society and whether there should be more control over the new system and who should exercise it. As the Swedish predilection for investigating manifested itself, a steady stream of government officials and bankers started drifting into the hitherto sleepy area. Confusing EFTS with POS and compounding ignorance with puffery, one government-subsidized researcher of computerization initiated a study of the project, which he described as "the first Swedish in-line [*sic*] EFTS pilot system."[23]

The visitors soon learned that waiting to see people use the system was about as rewarding as watching paint dry. The records of three stores involved in the test tell the story. In one, 0.6 percent of sales went through the system in February and 1.3 percent in August. In the second, use peaked at 2.6 percent in March and went down thereafter. In the third, it went up to 1.2 percent and then down to 0.8 percent. The highest rate of use was at the gas pumps, where some 6 percent of purchases were paid for with the savings banks' card.

The thrifts' association changed the project manager three times during the test. At one point, a manager jokingly called Stockholm to ask for reinforcements, saying that the only groups not attacking the project were the

Red Cross and the United Nations. Mercifully, they finally pulled the plug, and three and a half-inch headlines screamed, "The Cashless Society—A Fiasco!"[24] One story summarized it thus: "The savings banks' test with a payment card in Blekinge failed. . . . The technique functioned badly, the interest from the public was slight, and personnel thought it was troublesome. Now the equipment is gone, and those involved are blaming the failure on each other."[25] Its promoters had promised to make Sweden a world leader with a test that as designed and executed, never could have done so, even if it had been "the world's first." By putting competitive concerns above system integrity, the group rushed into the test with inadequate preparation and equipment that was not fully operational. Hence, they ended up with the worst of both possible worlds: the test was so limited in use because of the problems that they learned nothing new, and rather than enhance their reputation, they badly tarnished it.

The thrifts' association covered all costs, which were estimated to be about $2.5 million, although project leaders say that the official cost was never calculated. They admit, however, that their initial estimates were off by a factor of about 15. Hence, if nothing else, the test did confirm that profit is not the driving force for the savings banks in Sweden.

Yet in 1982 one of the test managers told an international conference, "The test was not a flop . . . everything turned out so well."[26] He said they had not continued it only because of security problems; yet those had been recognized by the team before the test began. He also stated that the risk for robbery had been reduced; but the displacement of cash would hardly confirm that. Unfortunately, it is difficult for foreign listeners to evaluate the validity of such representations.

Toward a Nationwide POS System

In contrast to the botch at Blekinge, since 1982 a group of Swedish executives has been carefully shaping plans for a POS system based on a wholly different philosophy of cooperation as opposed to competition and of meeting the needs of the market rather than expecting people to adapt to technology. The initial impetus for the effort came from STA, which organized representatives of the banking (including savings banks), retail, hotel and restaurant, travel agency, and card sectors whose businesses are most directly affected by such a system. Their goals are to stimulate planning, share knowledge, and lay the groundwork for a nationwide POS system. Rather than focus on the technology itself, the group first identified the problems that had to be solved for different interest groups and then evaluated the technical and economic considerations of possible solutions. This led to a framework for a flexible system that allows different levels of technique while eliminating highly manual routines.

A field test of a communications system for authorizing card purchases began in the fall of 1984 with the installation of over 400 terminals. To meet the individual needs of retailers, three classes of equipment are being used, ranging from a telephone to a sophisticated transaction terminal. STA is conducting the operational and economic analyses of the test, the costs of which are being shared by the participants through a consortium they have formed. Although initially the system will be capable of handling only 500 terminals, it is designed to accommodate at later stages up to 5,000 to 10,000 terminals.

In spite of the Swedes' well-nurtured cooperative traits, getting the card companies signed up for the project was described as extremely difficult because their competitive instincts tended to overcome their social mores. However, participants agreed that the evolution to POS is inevitable. Thus, since they are a peace-loving people, they wanted to avoid an uproar like the one that blocked the development of a technically brilliant but socially insensitive POS system in Denmark. Moreover, since they are a pragmatic people, the bankers have learned over the centuries how important it is to protect their turf. Hence, the message was not missed when in early 1981 Salzburg bankers launched a POS service to keep the funds transfer sector there from being taken over by retailers or credit card companies. As one Austrian banker warned, "If the banking institutions do not wish to suffer large losses in market share, then they must do something . . . [to] prevent nonbanking concerns from making inroads in this area."[27]

Notes

1. National Commission on Electronic Fund Transfers, *EFT in the United States: Policy Recommendations and the Public Interest* (Washington, D.C.: NCEFT, 1977a), p. 98.

2. Interview with high-level banking executive in December 1982.

3. Arthur D. Little, Inc., research study for the Monetary and Payment System Committee in 1970.

4. Data from George C. White, *White Paper* (March–April 1982), p. 8.

5. John S. Reed, "Discussion," in Federal Reserve Bank of Boston, *The Economics of a National Electronic Funds Transfer System,* Conference Series No. 13 (Boston: Federal Reserve Bank of Boston, 1974), p. 44.

6. *Federal Reserve Bulletin* (December 1972): 1010.

7. Concept from statement by Donald I. Baker, "Competition, Monopoly and Electronic Banking," in Federal Reserve Bank of Boston, *Economics,* p. 56.

8. Eugene M. Tangney, "The Future of Electronic Banking as Seen by the Futurist: Possible Options, Possible Strategies, Possible Tactics" (paper presented at Bank Marketing Association Electronic Banking Conference, Houston, March 2, 1983).

9. Harry Karlsson, "Elektronisk betalningsförmedling och konsumentskyddet," Institutet för Rättsinformatik-rapport 1981:1, Stockholms Universitet, p. 24.

10. Statistics from Allen H. Lipis, "Costs of the Current U.S. Payments System," *Magazine of Bank Adminstration* (October 1978): 27–31.

11. Dee W. Hock, "Remarks," in Federal Reserve System, *Papers and Comments of the International Conference on Banking and Payment Systems* (Washington, D.C.: FRS, 1980), p. 138.

12. Eckart van Hooven, quoted by S.R. Lloyd, "The New Battle for Europe," *Banker* (London) (November 1980): 18.

13. Hock, "Remarks," p. 141.

14. David Thibodeau, "Cardholders Attitudes towards Payment and Cash Availability Alternatives," In European Financial Marketing Association, *Texts of the Presentations*, EFMA Conference, Monte Carlo, March 21–24, 1982 (Paris: EFMA, 1982), p. 82.

15. Robert H. Long, "Discussion," in Federal Reserve Bank of Boston, *Economics*, p. 37.

16. John Fisher, "Discussion," in Federal Reserve Bank of Boston, *Economics*, p. 88.

17. Mark J. Flannery and Dwight M. Jaffee, *Economic Implications of an Electronic Monetary Transfer System* (Lexington, Mass.: D.C. Heath and Co., 1973), p. 74.

18. Interview with Blekinge project leader in November 1982.

19. Lars Söderström, "What Swedish Savings Banks Learned from Their POS Experiment" (paper presented at International Savings Banks Institute, Tenth International Automation Conference, Lyon, France, May 3–7, 1982).

20. Interviews with project leaders in November 1982.

21. Helena Stålnert, "Handla penninglöst—är det så vi ska ha det?" *Råd & Rön*, no. 1 (1980):11.

22. Ibid., p. 12.

23. Bo Hedberg, "Computers in the Retail Industry," in *Job Design and Automation in Sweden*, ed. Bo Göranzon (Stockholm: Center for Working Life, 1982), p. 54.

24. "Kontantlösa Samhället—ett Fiasko!" *Ny Teknik* (Stockholm), September 25, 1980, p. 1.

25. Ibid.

26. Söderström, "What Swedish Savings Banks Learned."

27. Helfried Plenk, "How Important Are POS Systems?—How Rapidly Will They Spread in Europe," *Savings Banks International*, no. 4 (1981): 10.

6
Privacy, Security, and Employment

Privacy: Anxiety about Abuses

In the mid-1980s, when Americans stand in line to use ATMs even when tellers are available without a wait, it is hard to believe that only a decade ago consumer advocates were predicting that people would never accept EFTS because of the dangers to personal privacy lurking within every computer. Like the nineteenth-century Luddites who tried to stop the industrial revolution with axes in English textile factories for fear of losing their jobs, some privacy prophets of doom reacted more emotionally than rationally to EFTS. Since the basic cause of all the hubbub was the discovery of the electron in 1897 by J.J. Thomson, the wry humor in a toast said to have been drunk by the research workers in his laboratory at dinner appeared prescient: "To the electron: may it never be of any use to anyone!"[1]

Like many of the greatest inventions, electronic data processing has a potential for good that is matched by its potential for harm. Because file keeping itself can be prejudicial to privacy, the ability of computers to facilitate the activity crystallized concerns about the new technology. Privacy first emerged as an issue in 1961, six years after the Bank of America had become the first bank in the world to install a large computer, when the president of a California computer firm expressed concern to a conference of technical writers about the increasing amount of information being collected about people. He speculated that it might culminate in all such data ultimately flowing into one giant computer center, thereby placing the privacy of all Americans at the mercy of the person with power over the computers.

Two years after the Bank of America automated all of its checking account transactions with thirty computer systems, the issue became popularized in a 1963 *Time* magazine story. In an effort to shake people out of their inertia about the government's growing accumulation of computerized data on citizens, the writer warned that it could lead to a "computerized Big Brotherhood."[2] The reference to Orwell's allegory about the dangers of an intrusive government was soon picked up by civil libertarians who adopted Orwell's and Huxley's anti-utopian novels as basic scripture in their holy war against the computerized invasion of privacy.

The first official recognition of public concern about the role of computers in the invasion of personal privacy came in 1965 when a congressional subcommittee added the topic to its agenda for investigation of government surveillance of the populace. It thus also became the first time that Congress became aware of the political power in the emotionalism of the issue. Politicians found they could easily make the ten o'clock TV news and generate headlines by scaring folks about "the magic of computers" and the potential for people standing "psychologically naked" in the eyes of federal agencies that would know everything about them.[3]

Meanwhile, oblivious to the focus of the hearings, a project for the creation of a National Data Center to serve as a statistical resource for the federal government was rolling along with its own momentum in the Washington bureaucracy. Hence, when its sponsors proudly announced their plans in 1966, they were startled to be met with brickbats rather than commendations. The emotions aroused by the controversy over the plans not only doomed the project but also later were to generate more heat than light on the implications of EFTS for privacy.

More fuel was thrown on the fire in 1968 by an article in *Look* magazine that depicted an airline's computerized flight reservation system as a hotbed of easily accessible information for surveillance of people's whereabouts and associations.[4] Although the allegations in the article were later proved false, they had already been incorporated into a major book on privacy by a university professor and then been repeated in reviews of his book in major newspapers and by Ralph Nader in a magazine article. Extrapolating from the assumption that the account of access to the airline's sytem was accurate, the law professor also warned of the "trail" left by use of travel and entertainment cards: "It may be an interesting one, especially if you happen to shop or dine at the same places as some Mafia capo or suspected subversive."[5] Although the researchers who later disproved the accuracy of the magazine story also refuted the "trail" surveillance theory, one of them had expressed fear, too, of the potential for invasion of privacy through credit card trails in an earlier book.[6]

In Sweden the impact of computers was first felt in the second half of the 1960s, a time of unrest marked by dissatisfaction with what many perceived as a trend toward a society dominated by technocracy and mass consumption. Initially, the demand for remedial measures was motivated not by revelations that abuse had actually occurred but rather by fear of abuses. But after a 1965 court ruling that the right of free access to public documents also applied to computer data bases, commercial exploitation did occur. In response to public complaints, the government in 1969 set up a commission to study the issue. But shortly after the group began its work, the normally phlegmatic populace exploded in outrage when the 1970 census asked people to divulge sensitive personal information for data bases. Feeling threatened from both the public and private sides, the public reacted so vehemently that Parliament temporarily blocked some government computer projects until protective measures could be adopted. One observer explained the mood of the time in this way: "If you were a Swede and saw how little privacy you had left, you'd be interested, too, in protecting it with a fair degree of viciousness."[7]

In fact, Swedes commit an unmatched amount of information to 500 government and 4,500 commercial data banks, and since 1947 every citizen has been assigned a personal identification number. In part it is needed to sort out the thousands of people with identical names, such as the fifty-some pages of Karlssons in the Stockholm telephone directory. More important, it is needed because the welfare state requires a huge amount of record keeping, partly to ensure that money goes to the right people.

For that reason, data protection originally also was a political issue in that the Social Democrats wanted statistical data to measure the effects of social programs and the conservative parties argued for data protection. Privacy issues proved attractive to opposition parties prior to the defeat of the Social Democrats in 1976, not least because of the media attention they garnered.

Due to its conservative leanings, industry supported the Data Act proposed by the commission in 1972. The computer industry, however, lobbied for the law because it feared a backlash effect without it. In fact, the only organized opposition to the act came from groups that believed that it should have imposed more stringent controls on the government.

World's First National Computer Privacy Law

Because Sweden has a tradition of freedom of information, its efforts to counterbalance the opposing values of openness and secrecy were closely followed from both sides of the Atlantic. Hence, when its Data Act was passed in 1973, it became not only the world's first national data bank control law but also a regulatory model for other nations. Since 1766, the right of free access to, and copies of, public records had enabled citizens to monitor the conduct of officials and provided information for policy debates. But application of the principle to computerized documents raised two problems. First, although the information about individuals had always been available to them under the law, computerization made it much easier for other public agencies and commercial firms to access it by transferring the data on magnetic tapes directly into their own computers' memories. Yet private citizens who lacked computer facilities could not use the information. To resolve the second problem, the commission proposed amending the law to require that printouts be provided to the public. To resolve the first, the group proposed the Data Act.

In creating the pioneering legislation, the commission faced some unusual difficulties. One was the lack of legal precedent and feedback from practice because the computer revolution created wholly new problems that defied classification into existing legal molds. Moreover, utilization of the technology permeated both the public and private sectors. Thus, the group endeavored to write a law with norms broad enough to encompass the various interests and values involved, specific enough to offer practical guidance in concrete situations, capable of growth and adaptation along with the technology, and responsive to political, social, and cultural forces. As the first administrator of the act said, "Technical innovations and devices like computers can seldom be judged from all aspects before they influence society. They are invented and set up and used . . . and plodding behind comes the law, more or less supported by public opinion."[8]

One immediate problem in drafting the law was defining privacy. Even though Swedish film star Greta Garbo revealed a pervasive cultural sentiment when she insisted, "I vant [*sic*] to be alone," the commission perceived privacy not as an absolute value meaning freedom from interference but as one value competing with others in a complex societal environment. Because there must be a certain amount of interchange of information for an advanced economy to operate, the group concluded that a person must be prepared to accept some infringement of privacy. Hence, the focus shifted from the right of preventing the collection of personal facts to an extension of control over the content, dissemination, and use of personal data.

To ensure flexibility and provide authority to impose controls, the commission chose an administrative approach and called for the creation of a Data Inspection Board (DIB) to license commercial data banks, supervise the operation of their systems, and serve as a data ombudsman for the public. A licensing system was chosen for two reasons. First, when reviewing an application for a license, it is possible to judge beforehand the risks it may pose to privacy. If they are considered great, the license can be denied or, as is usually the case, regulations can be issued for handling the file. The second reason is that it is less expensive to build into a computer system from the beginning the necessary measures to protect privacy than it is to add them afterward. Since an opinion by the agency that such controls are required sets a precedent for subsequent similar cases, it ensures equity by precluding any business from having a competitive advantage by offering less security and privacy. From the Swedish point of view, the disadvantages of relying only on the court system for protection of privacy are that nothing can be done until after an invasion of privacy and resulting damages have already occurred and that the addition of protection to systems after the fact is less efficient than building them in from the start.

The law states that no computerized file containing information about individuals may be established or maintained without a license issued by the DIB. Although government agencies are excepted, they must consult the board before setting up a data bank so that it cannot be done in secrecy. Those licensed to maintain such files are obliged by the act to: (1) inform a person upon request of the contents of material in the file relating to him or her; (2) supplement a file if the relevant information is incomplete; (3) correct inaccurate data; and (4) provide proper monetary compensation to a person who has been injured as the result of incorrect information in a file. Thus, the right of public inspection serves as a countervailing force to concern about the accuracy of data in personal files and its use. The act also defines a new criminal offense called data trespass, meaning unauthorized entry into a data system to obtain or attempt to alter or destroy data, which carries a penalty of up to two years in jail.

Experiences with the Data Act

Although the Data Act directs the DIB to inspect computer operations, the law states that it should not cause higher costs or greater inconvenience than is strictly necessary. Thus, in 90 to 95 percent of the cases, DIB staff members call ahead to make an appointment before inspecting a computer installation. Their rationale is based on the fact that if they arrive without advance notice, they may not be able to meet with anyone who can explain the system, which is necessary since it is impossible to be familiar with all of them. Moreover, they have found that after they announce an impending visit, the licensee starts putting things in order. One official explained, "We've seen very few situations where the work preliminary to our visit was not in the public interest."[9]

Since about 65 percent of computer files are used only for internal purposes and do not contain very sensitive information, the board has worked out simplified procedures that permit the cases to be handled without delay. Because, as is true of all organizations with large systems, the installation of a bank's EDP system is expensive, it is important for management to know during the design stage that it can proceed without later interference from the board. To provide that assurance, the DIB can issue an approval in principle in the beginning of or during the development period.

Inasmuch as Sweden is one of the most computerized countries in the world, the fact that the DIB had processed 37,000 applications for licenses by the end of 1982 might evoke an image of a vast bureaucracy. But since the board's director has resisted expansionist tendencies, the DIB operates with a staff of only thirty people on a budget of about $1 million annually. Moreover, since 1983 the agency has worked toward a goal of supporting its operations completely from license fees. To insulate implementation of the law from political pressures, the government has given the director a lifetime appointment and provided for a board that reflects differing viewpoints.

The right of every person about whom information is maintained in a computerized file to a report of the contents pertaining to him or her once a year without charge was one of the most controversial issues in the private sector when the act was passed. Yet the initial fears about the costs of the provision have proved unwarranted, with the vast majority of requests addressed to government agencies rather than businesses. A DIB official recalls that an executive of a large firm who was upset by the provision at first conceded four years later that during that period only one person had come to the company and asked to see his file. While the banks have been little affected by the obligation, the Credit Information Center operated by them has had a number of such requests each year, which it is well-equipped to handle.

In 1982, the agency received about 1,000 complaints. Most were resolved by a telephone call or letter to a record keeper, and about 300 were subjected to a more detailed investigation. Complaints not only come into the agency but also are made about it. In one case that attracted media attention in Stockholm, a credit card company wanted to obtain statistics on the use of its card in restaurants in order to develop customer profiles. Thus, it sought permission to learn how often cardholders ate out, where they went, how many guests they entertained, how much they spent, and so forth. The DIB told the firm it could do it, but only if it first obtained permission from each cardholder. That response so angered the company's manager that he complained to the press that the board was "bureaucratic."

The provisional character of the Data Act was apparent in the bill proposing it, which stated that in the event the control procedures became "unnecessarily burdensome or impeded development," the act would have to be amended.[10] Hence, at the end of 1976 a committee began reviewing the effectiveness of the measure. While the 1978 report concluded that it was functioning well, it recommended an amendment to prevent the linking of files, which occurs when information in one data bank is accessible to another data bank through use of common identifiers. Although, the committee said, it was primarily public agencies that were doing it to check the veracity of data submitted, credit information agencies also were accessing official files to check out statements from credit applicants.

Over the course of a decade, the Swedish approach has proved flexible enough both to safeguard the individual's right to privacy and satisfy the information requirements of the country. It has, moreover, avoided the danger that such legislation might raise obstacles to the utilization of new technology like the law that required a man with a red flag to walk along the train tracks in front of the first locomotives.

Credit Information Act

Along with the Data Act, Parliament passed the Credit Information Act to deal specifically with that issue. Although there is some overlapping between the two laws, the credit act places a three-year limit on material relating to creditworthiness and forbids filing details concerning payment defaults unless established by a court decision or involving a bankruptcy petition. The law requires that a written statement be provided free of charge to the subject each time a credit report is sent out, stating what was submitted and who requested it. In addition to the annual free report, everyone has the right to receive for a fee at any time information as to whether a file exists about him or her and, if so, a description of its contents. Besides requiring clarification of errors, if incorrect information is disseminated, the law requires that corrected reports be sent as soon as possible to every recipient of the erroneous data. The act also forbids the unauthorized disclosure of information by anyone who is or has been engaged in credit information activities.

Although the banks had decided in the 1960s to build a centralized center for the automated handling of credit information for all of them, construction was delayed until after passage of the law in 1973. By waiting until then, they were able to build in the administrative and operational capabilities necessary for both compliance with the law and efficiency. In practice, the management of the Credit Information Center has found that information permitted in files under the law is much the same as banks maintained before except that files now cannot contain judgments about people and other "soft" data. The most significant difference is that data are protected in a completely closed system from which withdrawals cannot occur without automatic recording of information detailing what was removed, by whom, and when.

In administering the act, DIB officials became involved in a minor skirmish with finance companies that did not want to consider marital spouses separately but wanted to obtain and use information on both in making credit decisions. After the Minister of Justice took the side of the firms, the staff of the DIB enlisted the support of the members of Parliament on their board, who converted it into a women's rights issue, which was politically unassailable. The agency's position prevailed.

Until recently, the DIB received twice as many complaints about credit information and debt recovery problems as about privacy. This led staffers to observe, tongue in cheek, that people apparently were more interested in their money than in their privacy.

Perils of Paranoia and a Patchwork Response

Following passage of the privacy acts in 1973, the Swedish people had been able to get back to business as usual. But in the United States, because no remedial action was taken, the privacy issue continued to fester. In addition to its substantive character, the issue had a symbolic value because many people assumed that computers inevitably would lead to new and larger files about individuals. The need to separate the legitimate aspects of the issue from the rhetoric became more difficult when alarmists interjected the broader issue of government surveillance. That element had not beclouded the more constructive response in Sweden, which, although it has the most comprehensive and best-referenced files about citizens of any country, runs little risk of becoming a police state.

Empirical evidence refuting the fears was presented in 1972 when a study for the National Academy of Sciences (NAS) reported that computer usage had not created any revolutionary new powers of data surveillance; that in most organizations the contents of records had not been increased in scope; and that where the individual's right to privacy had been respected in the past, it was with computerized systems too.[11]

Nevertheless, in the following year an academician conjectured, "One can readily imagine using the BankAmericard system for police stop-check procedures directed against political dissidents."[12] Although such speculation revealed a not-too-hidden agenda that would preclude the objectivity required for rational analysis, the Office of Telecommunications Policy awarded a grant to the professor to write a report about EFT, which was published at taxpayers' expense in 1975. Ignoring the NAS report, the Swedish Data Act, and the experience of European nations with the services, the writer rambled from one wild conclusion to another about perceived horrors:

> It's clear that any operational form of EFT would have to entail the transmission of a good deal of personal data. . . . EFT accounts would become an automated, bureaucratically recorded diary of every consumer's movements and activities, as well as his or her financial resources. . . . Such a system could serve to store data on a person's political reliability. . . . Inherent in the idea of EFT is the notion of a separate agency keeping charge of a person's financial resources. The question inevitably arises as to when such an agency should be authorized to debit the account without permission from the user.[13]

While the legitimate concerns of the public called for a clarification of the issues, the author fanned fear by warning that the direct deposit of Social Security payments could create a system in which "agents of the state would constantly monitor the use of the EFT network, ready to swoop down upon any user."[14] Revealing yet another preconception that vitiated the integrity of the report, the writer asserted, "Perhaps the one approach to development of EFT policy, clearly incompatible with the underlying assumptions of this report, is the laissez-faire philosophy of 'letting the market decide.'"[15]

In a later book, dedicated to the memory of George Orwell, the writer conceded that his report had become the "focus of annoyance" and quoted a distinguished group of academicians who had said of his paranoiac fantasies, "Only the government could create [such repression] . . . and whether or not it does so will hardly depend on whether EFTS is used for bill paying." [16]

The incorporation of EFT into the privacy debate arose from a misconception, a failure to separate intertwined issues, and a lack of knowledge of payment system practices. The misconception was that there would be one EFT system, like the national data center that had been proposed earlier, rather than a large number of competing systems. If the European experience with such systems had been studied in conjunction with the background of the larger, more fragmented, and highly competitive banking system in the United States, the perspective gained might readily have dispelled the notion. The intertwining of the surveillance issue with electronic value exchange called for separation; a different medium of information exchange in no way altered the existing responsibility of financial institutions to maintain standards of confidentiality toward customers' records. Nor was it a new situation. Banks had computerized customers' records more than a decade earlier without creating any new privacy problems. In fact, while anyone could poke into and read paper-based records without others knowing, computerized records provide greater security in that access is limited to only a few. Moreover, computer programs can facilitate the detection of unauthorized instrusion by recording what information has been sought and by whom.

Finally, the millions of checks Americans write each year create more privacy problems than EFT transactions and leave a significantly more accessible trail than do computerized transactions. Clerks and bartenders can see what people are paid, and a review of the month's transactions makes a person's life an open book. Nor is privacy regained when the checks are returned; microfilm copies, carefully indexed for easy reference, exist in various records. Since signatures are a matter of public record, getting a copy of one is a piece of cake. And anyone who believes that all signatures on checks are verified at banks before funds are transferred probably also spends Halloween in a field waiting for the Great Pumpkin. Certainly for any run-of-the-mill crook who cannot enjoy the economies of scale achieved by the Mob, it is easier to get phony checks made than plastic cards. Also, although there are limits on withdrawals from machines, there are no limits on the amounts for which checks can be written. Indeed, if the privacy alarmists had been around when checks were introduced, they could really have had a field day.

In addition to the hysterical and uninformed who incited fear about the dangers of EFT, there were professional scaremongers who preyed on people's fears of the unknown to sell books. One example appeared in 1981, years after the passage of U.S. privacy legislation and after the Swedish Data Act had been proving for seven years that privacy could be protected while people used EFTS. The writer warned of the dangers of fraud and crime with EFTS and resurrected the bogeymen of the 1970s: "[EFT will] open an individual's entire financial history to credit bureaus at the push of a button . . . [and] augment dissemination of personal information to third parties."[17] The first allegation contradicts the nation's foremost authority on computer crime who has stated that there is less fraud with automated systems than there was with paper-based ones.[18] The second is absurd because EFT provides no more information to credit bureaus than checks do, and the third represents another example of convoluting EFT with privacy rights. Ignoring the use of EFTS by small financial institutions in Europe and the United States for the preceding fifteen years, the Washington lawyer also raised the populist specter of "a handful of banking giants" dominating the industry because, he asserted, only large financial institutions would be able to afford the technology.[19]

But while that recital of fears was old hat, a journalist who sees telecommunications as casting some sorcerer's shadow across the land came out with some new scare stories about the potential of EFT in 1981. He warned that "extending EFT to the home increases the opportunity for sophisticated practitioners of computer fraud to tap into transactions and divert funds from your account to theirs. . . . The way could be cleared for 'legal' manipulation of your accounts by government agencies. . . . [It is] bound to promote consumer debt."[20] The last point disregards the fact that because on-line systems enforce limits on extensions of credit, they provide far more effective controls on spending than paper-based systems. Regarding the "sophisticated practitioners," even overlooking the security measures that make such interference extremely unlikely, it is inconceivable that criminals with such technological prowess would bother with the small potatoes of consumer accounts when they could be dipping into rich corporate accounts. As to surveillance, that bugaboo was reduced to proper perspective by the manager of a robot company at an international conference on privacy who observed, "I think it is very comforting that the flow of data . . . is increasing to such an extent that the amount of it would be too astronomical for the most ardent Big Brother that one can imagine to monitor."[21]

One puzzling aspect of the wave of anti-EFTS hysteria in the United States in the 1970s was the receptivity accorded such views by the banking community. The casual observer might have thought the bankers were masochists in the way they invited consumer advocates to abuse them orally at conferences and then nodded profoundly and clapped enthusiastically at the conclusions of their speeches. But there was one consumer advocate who correctly identified the underlying rationale for the seeming paradox. Although he was wrong when he echoed the American Civil Liberties Union's line about EFT making "the most intimate details" of a person's financial history available "at the touch of a button" and erred in predicting that most consumers would not choose EFTS, he was dead right when he reported that the industry itself did not want EFT because it would eliminate much of the float, "which is so profitable to the bankers."[22] In fact, the shrill voices of the consumer advocates provided the bankers with a socially acceptable excuse for what they did not want to do for economic reasons. The supreme irony of the situation was that the consumer advocates were arguing the wrong side of the issue: every economic study and all the experience with EFT services have clearly established that the greatest beneficiary of them is the consumer.

Consumer Protection with Agencies in Sweden

Because the benefits of EFTS were readily perceived in Sweden, consumer advocates sought only to ensure that the services were available to all. The high priority accorded consumerism there is attested to by the fact that two agencies are charged with protecting consumer interests in financial matters. A fundamental difference in perceptions emerges from the description of consumers' relations with banks by the two agencies, however. The director of the Bank Inspection Board (BIB) believes that while it was true in the old days that banks appeared big and powerful and customers small and dependent on the banks' benevolence, "today one can honestly say that the pendulum has swung to the other extreme."[23] The National Board for Consumer Policies argues that because the consumer is in a weak position in relation to private enterprise, consumer policy must in part "rely on compulsory legislation and other more direct interventions."[24] There also is a difference in perspectives. While the consumer office spent three years investigating the use of credit cards to learn if people needed protection from their own impulses, the bank board has devoted more attention to the problem of crimes against banks. The adversarial approach of the consumer group to the banks also differs markedly from that of the BIB, which prefers to work with them in a spirit of cooperation.

The consumer credit laws passed in the 1970s were not a reaction to specific problems, like the privacy laws, but rather reflected prevailing attitudes of distrust of business and disdain for consumption, which were easily translated into political issues by the Social Democratic government. Since the laws govern banks' and card companies' marketing, it placed supervision of those activities in the hands of the consumer agency. That, however, collided head-on with the work of the BIB, which has been deciding since 1906 what is best for bank customers as well as banks and believes that, because depositors are consumers too, it provides the best possible consumer protection by ensuring the soundness of the banks. Hence, to end the duplication of effort, after the coalition government unseated the Social Democrats, the government proposed moving consumer protection back to the BIB. The issue became something of a political football when, after the Social Democrats returned to power in 1982, they gave the authority back to the consumer agency.

Over the years, the BIB has found that about one-fourth of the complaints it receives about banks are valid, and of those, the banks settle about half to the satisfaction of the customer. In the remaining cases, the agency can only use persuasion since it has no punitive authority. If the customer and the bank cannot resolve the matter, they can go to court. That solution, though, is seldom resorted to. Because Swedes regard litigation as an acknowledgment of personal failure, the country has one of the lowest litigation rates in the world—half that of Japan.

Reality in Sweden has refuted the scare scenarios in the United States of how people would be at the mercy of technology in the EFT era. Between 1978 and 1982, when there were over 100 million withdrawals, the BIB received only some twenty to thirty complaints about CDs. More important, the records indicate that no one has ever proved that a customer lost money because of a malfunctioning machine. Nor has there been one complaint about an invasion of privacy from an EFT service. In addition to the protection of the Data and Credit Information acts, officials stress the significant consumer protection inherent in the Bank Secrecy Law, which has always guarded information about customers' relationships with banks and which in no way has been altered by EFT services.

Swedes cluck bemusedly when told that some Americans are afraid of possible dangers in automatic deposits of salary and other payments. People under the age of thirty-five there have never been paid any other way and consider it odd that Americans do not have the same convenience. In the same vein, they regard preauthorized payments as practical. As to the fearmongers' notion that consumers would lose control of their finances with EFTS, the Swedish banks send out frequent statements so that customers can quickly detect any erroneous or unauthorized debits posted to their accounts. If a bank errs in carrying out an electronic funds transfer or does not do it at the specified time, the customer can obtain legal recourse.

Further consumer protection is afforded by the Bookkeeping Law, which requires that an audit trail be created through verification of every transaction and that all account materials be saved for ten years. The law, which has been adapted for developments in EFT, also demands immediate correction of bookkeeping errors. Its procedures are relied on to reconstruct transactions when customers claim faulty EFT service or unauthorized transactions.

If a credit card is lost, payment responsibility for unauthorized use ends when the card issuer receives the report. Holders of CD cards similarly are responsible for reporting missing cards, but additionally they must report any suspicion that someone has unauthorized knowledge of the code required for its use. The banks warn people not to write the code on the card or on a note attached to it. But the practice persists, even though cardholders may be held responsible for damages on the basis of carelessness in handling the code.

Judicial Approach in the United States

Although EFT services do not increase the danger of invasion of privacy, because no coordinated policy framework had been developed for dealing with the issue of data banks relating to financial relationships prior to the widespread introduction of the payment mechanisms in the United States, the issue influenced public attitudes toward EFTS. Concern about computerized files also affected the SIBOL project in Sweden, although the nation already had EFT services. The approaches of the two countries to the legal resolution of the issue, however, were widely divergent. While the U.S. legislation is mind-numbingly detailed, the Swedish laws are models of brevity. The Data Act is nine pages long, and the credit act, seven pages. Moreover, while the U.S. approach to data protection is curative, the Swedish one is proscriptive. Only the United States relies on the judiciary for the enforcement of privacy protection statutes; all the other computerized nations have a supervisory agency, often combined with regulatory-inspection authority.

In 1971 an American legal scholar had proposed the creation of an agency to educate "the data worshipers, the privacy paranoids, and the general public" as to the need to reconcile society's data needs with concerns over privacy.[25] However, he considered a comprehensive approach unlikely because of Congress's reluctance to intercede in the operations of federal agencies and its unwillingness to regulate "an influential segment of American industry."[26] Even though an agency, he argued, would provide needed flexibility in dealing with the issue, he deemed it unfeasible in the United States where agencies had become unpopular due to politicized administrators, inadequate staffing, and bureaucratic tendencies. This was confirmed by a Harris poll in 1979 that found no widespread support for a privacy agency, with respondents stating that they did not believe that an agency could protect them.[27] Displaying an awareness of public attitudes, the administration rejected the Privacy Study Commission's proposal for an agency, saying the rights could be enforced through the courts.

A review of court decisions involving privacy does not, however, inspire much confidence in the judiciary. In 1974 the U.S. Supreme Court refused to acknowledge any basis for privacy expectations on the part of banks or their depositors.[28] With three justices dissenting, the Court upheld the Bank Secrecy Act, which, contrary to its name, required banks to collect and report customers' financial transactions to law enforcement agencies without the notification or consent of the customers. Justice William Douglas, however, argued that

> one's bank accounts are within the "expectations of privacy" category. For they mirror not only one's finances but his interests. . . . A checking account . . . may well record a citizen's activities, opinions, and beliefs as fully as transcripts of his telephone conversations.[29]

The Court showed its insensitivity to the issue again in 1976 when it ruled that because bank records are records of commercial transactions and belong to the bank, customers could not expect privacy in them.[30]

To overcome the presumption of that decision, Congress passed the Right to Financial Privacy Act in 1978, forbidding financial institutions to disclose customers' records to government officials except in response to written authorization from the customer or legal demand by the agency with notification of the customer. In its two-year study, the Privacy Protection Study Commission found that the Privacy Act of 1974 was neither strong enough nor specific enough to solve the existing problems. Yet while the commission had been directed to develop the outlines of a national information policy, its 800-page report was so detailed and fragmented as to bring little clarity to the confusion. Hence, privacy laws in the United States lack consensus on goals, deal with procedures rather than substance, and are difficult to enforce.

Not surprisingly, in a 1983 Harris poll, three-quarters of the public said they were "very" or "somewhat" concerned about threats to their personal privacy and accused both credit bureaus and the government of breaching their privacy.[31] Moreover, a large majority said they wanted tough new laws to protect personal privacy—like the Swedish ones.

The U.S. approach to consumer protection has led to such complexity that some question whether the laws actually help consumers or confuse them as well as business people. For example, the Electronic Fund Transfers Act of 1978, which does not apply to privacy, set disclosure requirements, error resolution procedures, and liability limits for lost or stolen cards. However, even the author of the enabling regulation has expressed concern that the disclosure statement required is so complex it may result in "information overload" for consumers.[32]

Taking account of the fact that in addition to the multitude of federal laws there is a staggering array of state laws governing EFT, privacy, and consumer protection, the U.S. legal approach to the issue could only be measured in terms of pounds of paper and thousands of government employees. Yet after ten years of piling law atop law, consumers, business, and government officials express dissatisfaction with the result. There would seem to be a lesson in the fact that the sixteen pages of law and thirty people that Sweden applied to the same issues in 1973 have been working just fine.

Security with EFTS in Sweden

Although scare headlines in the United States have predicted that massive amounts of funds would be swindled routinely if EFTS were implemented, the actual experience in Sweden over the course of two decades has proved them delusive. Of course, as we saw earlier in the Easter Holiday Caper, there has been crime involving EFTS. Just as the introduction of the first paper money was followed within a year by the first counterfeit money, so too has the new technology inspired innovations in crime. In two court cases in 1977 and 1978, when CDs were operating off-line, producers of counterfeit cards were convicted under forgery law after illegally obtaining money from machines. But the systems' integrity has been greatly enhanced with installation of the on-line machines.

The principal protection against unauthorized use of CD cards is a code that for Bankomats is computer-generated but is chosen by savings banks' customers. While the thrifts use the occasion when the customer keys in the code as a way to familiarize him or her with use of the machine, it poses a security problem. Because certain combinations are chosen by people over and over again, if a card is found or stolen, efforts to guess the code are far more likely to succeed with a personally selected code.[33] The code itself is stored neither in the magnetic stripe nor in the CD system, and the message containing it that is transmitted to obtain clearance for a transaction is encrypted so that it cannot be intercepted. Because of the importance of the code, it is an offense in Sweden to try to read it while a person is keying it into a machine. Moreover, a bank employee who opens an envelope containing a code is subject to prosecution. There also is a provision in the criminal code for the tapping of information on a line used for the transmission of EFT data; it constitutes data trespass.

As in the United States, the possibility of guessing a code is limited since the card is automatically retained or blocked in the CD after more than two unsuccessful tries. Withdrawal limits per transaction and week also serve to protect cardholders in case of theft or loss of a card. Additionally, blocking functions are programmed into the systems to prevent the use of a counterfeit card or one reported lost or stolen.

Computer Crime and Vulnerability

Since computer crime per se has not been a reportable crime, Swedish police have been able to compile only rough statistics on such occurrences. The data do, however, confirm a 1982 statement by the head of the BIB: "Crimes related to the use of computers have been committed, but as yet not in any spectacular way."[34] Out of 30 reported cases over an eight-year period, 11 involved banks and post offices. By comparison, during that time there were 741 robberies of banks and post offices and 102,722 cases of check fraud. The data do not identify the victims by amount, but over half of the computer crimes involved sums of $10,000 or less, and over one-fourth involved amounts smaller than $4,000. Two of the crimes involved amounts exceeding $100,000; one, an amount in the $80,000–100,000 range, and two, amounts in the $40,000–60,000 range. Eight cases, including such crimes as a bomb threat, sabotage, and property damage, were not financial in nature. In the cases involving banks and post offices, four crimes were committed with forged Postal Giro out-payment cards; two were transfers between accounts; four were overdrafts on the culprit's own account; and one was incorrect entry of data. None was related to EFTS. Only half the perpetrators of all the computer crimes were computer experts; half had previously been convicted of crimes; and two were under the age of fifteen.

At the request of Parliament, the Committee on the Vulnerability of Computer Systems was created in 1977 to lay plans for counteracting risks in connection with war and terrorism. In its report a year later, the group concluded that vulnerability was unacceptably high due to the concentration of large centralized systems and computer installations. The need for internal controls also was emphasized by the committee, which found examples of "dissatisfied, dishonourable or undependable staff members causing damage by, for example, destroying information in files."[35] More ominous was the finding that in the event of the use of nuclear weapons, even in a war not involving Sweden, an EMP (electromagnetic pulse) effect could destroy or damage computers and communications systems. High-altitude explosions in particular, the report warned, could have long-range effects, up to several thousand miles away. Yet while this could cripple any country with a heavy dependence on computerization and EFT, the group could find no other national investigation of the vulnerability inherent in dependence on the technology.

Battle against Plastic Rip-Offs

As opposed to the low probability–high loss problem of vulnerability, the high probability–low loss problem of fraud with plastic cards has imposed far greater demands on the efforts of bankers in recent years. At the less sophisticated end of the rip-off spectrum is the case of the traveler from the countryside who, while sitting on the john in the men's room at the English train station, had his trousers containing his money and credit card pulled off him from under the door. Since the ploy left the victim less disposed to chase the thief down the street than might otherwise have been the case, the perpetrator pulled the trick three more times before being apprehended. Barclaycard executives claim, though, that their authorization system is so fast that often a stolen card can be identified and the police notified in time to catch the user in the store, which then results in a reward for the clerk.

At the other end of the spectrum is the massive wave of credit card fraud in the United States involving organized crime, which is a greater problem than counterfeit currency and costs the nation's financial institutions far more than losses from bank robberies, which totaled $46.8 million in 1982. By comparison, in Sweden, where plastic crime has not reached such a high level of professionalism, bank robberies continue much as before, and blow-ups of night depositories have even increased in recent years.

It was reported in late 1979 that Massachusetts banks were losing over $3 million a year on card frauds, with one Boston bank alone suffering losses of $500,000 annually.[36] In 1981 one European bank reported the loss of over $10 million in credit card fraud. But the losses increased astronomically after organized crime moved into the lucrative rip-offs in the early 1980s. In early 1984 a storefront "sting" operation in New York City cracked what was termed the largest card counterfeiting ring in the country as it prepared to produce cards from California banks in anticipation of the Olympic Games. The counterfeit Visa cards and MasterCards the gang cranked out accounted for over $50 million in losses to financial institutions in 1983. Bearing the names of virtually every major New York City bank, each card was used for about $1,000 in charges until the actual customers discovered them on their bills at the end of the month. In what sounded like a playback of the Stockholm police's criticism of Swedish banks in the 1970s before they adopted a more stringent identification card system, U.S. law enforcement officials have warned that they may not help banks in the future with the problem unless they force retailers to demand identification from cardholders.

In an effort to thwart counterfeiting, Visa and MasterCard in 1983 began issuing cards that contain holograms (three-dimensional photographic images). To foil the copying of magnetic data from the back of a credit or debit card onto another strip of tape, Sweden has added electronically watermarked magnetic tape to its lengthy list of standards for cards. Even fake tape on a card, however, is not enough to activate an ATM because the Personal Identification Number (PIN) also must be keyed into the machine. But since one study has found that over half the Americans who have cards write their PINs on them, those in search of ill-gotten gains have it relatively easy.[37] As a replacement for the not-so-secret PINs, SRI has developed a signature verification technology by which a computer compares the pressures and directions made as a name is written over an electronic pad with the original pattern in its memory.

The French Solution: *La Carte à Mémoire*

The French have taken the lead in card technology by developing the first fraud-proof card. Called the memory or chip or smart card because of the integrated circuit chip imbedded in it, its advanced technology makes it formidable to counterfeit, and its unerasable memory cannot be altered. In fact, its circuits self-destruct if anyone tries to alter the stored data. Moreover, it also protects privacy because it bypasses the telecommunications network. While a magnetic stripe card is only a passive repository of information, the chip card can record transactions in its own memory, independent of a bank computer. Invented in the early 1970s by a Frenchman who soldered a microcircuit to a piece of plastic to create what he envisioned as an electronic wallet, development of the technology has been backed by the government as part of its strategy of building the microelectronics industry to create jobs and help the nation's economy.

The chip card is programmed with buying power by the bank up to an overall limit, which is drawn down each time it is used and with a per-transaction limit. When the card is inserted into a POS terminal, the transaction details are registered both on it and on the retailer's storage cartette. In the process, the customer can check on how much value remains in the card and the retailer on whether the customer has been blacklisted by the bank. While low- and medium-value transactions are internally processed by the machine, for amounts exceeding the guaranteed limit, the POS machine can call an authorization center using the telephone line. At the end of the day, the retailer can unplug the cartette and bring it to the bank or transmit its data by telephone for batch processing.

Before the French began testing the chip card for use as a combined credit/debit card at POS in three towns in late 1982, they had started using it in a home banking test. By using a videotex terminal with special electronic card interface, the cardholder could read the transactions and available credit balance recorded on the card with privacy ensured. This constituted a giant step forward from the security system for Europe's first full-scale home banking test launched in 1980 by Germany's Verbraucherbank, to which over 2,000 customers had subscribed by the end of 1981. The fact that that many people signed up says something for the German character since, in order to access the bank's computer, the customer must first enter his or her account number, a six-digit PIN, three ten-character codes, and, for each transaction, a specific code. Those hardy souls who make it through the security procedure are rewarded with access to all the services offered in branches except cash transactions.

In a third application of the card, the French in 1983 began testing two versions of it for use with pay telephones. One is a billing card that charges calls, and the other is a prepaid card whose microelectronic fuses are blown out as message units are used, like the holographic cards utilizing laser technology that the English use for pay telephones.

Although the chip card in 1984 cost about five times more than the magnetic card because it was not being mass-produced, its cost is offset by the fact that it does not need the vastly more costly computers and telecommunications required by the magnetic card. Moreover, because the chip card is intelligent and can perform many operations with a very simple terminal, the machines for its use are cheaper and more reliable than those for magnetic cards. In addition to its security and economic advantages, the memory card offers a consumer benefit that check-addicted Americans cherish as dearly as the French: it provides the same day or two of float that is customary with checks drawn on local banks and thus reduces the likelihood of an embarrassing authorization refusal.

Yet in spite of its advantages, the chip card has not been greeted with unalloyed joy. Some have attributed this reaction to the NIH (not invented here) syndrome, which probably has some validity since the French are not loved as much out of as in France. While the French say the purpose of the card is to reduce the volume of checks written for small amounts, Swedish bankers argue that the goal could be achieved at less cost by simply imposing a fee on such checks as they have done. Because the cards eliminate the need for leased lines that support on-line systems, the telephone companies that are still reeling from the breakup of AT&T could hardly be expected to embrace the cards. Certainly IBM and the other manufacturers that have committed huge amounts of money and years of manpower to developing POS systems that rely on their profitable mainframe installations are not beating the drums for the little wonders.

While the French government proudly promotes the chip cards, Uncle Sam would be shooting himself in the foot if he did so because they are ideally suited for displacing much of the cash currently used for some 280 billion transactions a year in the United States. Inasmuch as the $120 billion in coins and currency in the hands of the U.S. public and the $20 billion in the vaults of commercial banks represent an interest-free loan equal to about 5 percent of the Gross National Product at a time when the national deficit exceeds $200 billion, it would not be surprising to see the Secretary of the Treasury himself pitching the little buggers into the Potomac.

The argument that there is no need for the chip card in the United States because of the use of on-line systems is rendered inane by the horrifying losses incurred because the systems are so expensive that most retailers are not linked to them. And therein lies the reason for the opposition to the card in the U.S. banking community: the managerial pride and billions of dollars invested in on-line magnetic card systems. There is so much personal pride in decisions resulting in the expenditure of vast amounts of a firm's money that they later appear to have been writ in stone and handed down from a mountaintop, never to be altered. Large projects acquire recognition in an organization as "J.B.'s baby" or a certain team's crowning achievement, with which those involved are forever after identified. Fear, too, plays a role. The promoters of the on-line systems spent years selling their top management on the need for them and received approval for the commitment of funds from the board only a few years ago. Even big, otherwise brave men blanch at the idea of having to go back to the top brass and say, "Let's throw it out—something better has come along." They know what would be thrown out, and it is less likely to be the system than the bearer of such tidings.

While most European countries rely on the less costly off-line systems for transactions below a certain amount, the atomistic nature of the U.S. banking system led to the adoption of on-line systems to verify all transactions. Until the introduction of the chip card, off-line systems were quite vulnerable to overdraft frauds. However, with on-line machines, the average loss now is less than $100.[38] On the other hand, the high cost of on-line systems helped delay wide adoption of EFTS in the United States and also denied to U.S. bankers the profitability that the Europeans can achieve with far lower volumes of transactions.

In retrospect, it is ironic that when Americans debated the implications of EFT services before they were widely used, the focus of attention was on protecting consumers from the technology. By 1984 it was apparent that a more significant problem had been overlooked: how to protect the financial institutions from the rip-off artists out there in the public.

EFTS and Employment in Sweden

In seeking to anticipate the effects of EFTS, another area of concern in the United States was employment. But while a look at the Swedish experience is instructive, the issue must be viewed from the perspective of their culture. It has been said, for instance, that whenever you get more than half a dozen Swedes in one place, they form an organization. But by the time the Bank Employees Union was founded in 1887, there were some 800 people working in the commercial banks. At their first meeting, the number one topic on the agenda was crime: not from outside the banks but from within, and not by underpaid clerks but by management. Two Stockholm banks had been rocked by discoveries of extensive embezzlements, which forced one to close and left the second in a weakened condition. Thus, the employees were worried about job security and about getting pensions. Ten years earlier, one bank had set up a fund to benefit employees after twenty-five years' service at age fifty-five or sixty. That, however, was not as generous as it might appear, since the average life span in Sweden then was fifty years.

To read the memoirs of bank workers at the turn of the century is like slipping between the pages of a Dickens novel, with clerks slaving over ledgers on Christmas Eve because the books had to be closed at the end of the year. As late as World War I, when heavy work loads made it necessary for employees to work seven days a week, they would get no more for working weekends than dinner money at noon and sandwiches and beer at ten o'clock at night.

But by the 1920s the employees would have welcomed those work-related problems to the workless ones created by the depression, bank crashes, and mergers. As unemployment soared to 26.6 percent in 1921, those who had jobs in banks were forced to accept salary cuts, and, to save money, many dropped their union membership. During that decade, union officials saw a way to renew interest in membership by appealing to a cultural trait: the Swedes' insatiable desire to enjoy the long, warm summer days that compensate for their dark, dreary winters. Unbeknownst to them at the time, the concept also would have a greater impact on the future course of Swedish banking than any other issue the union would embrace. It began in the early 1920s when the union persuaded the banks in southern Sweden to close earlier on Saturday in summer, and by 1928 the practice had spread to Stockholm.

While for years the bankers were sluggish in adopting new machines because there was no lack of job seekers for their low-paying but high-status jobs, the depression of the 1930s changed that situation. Hard times forced them to introduce efficiency to reduce costs, and the birthrate, which by 1933 had declined 40 percent from its 1909 level, produced such severe labor shortages in the 1950s that the Postal Bank and Postal Giro at times were forced to restrict new business. The latter part of the 1950s was marked by discord between the employees' desire for shorter hours and the bankers' need to provide longer hours for their growing number of customers. Thus, when the workers demanded every Saturday off in summer, they encountered adamant opposition from the employers, who viewed it as unthinkable in view of the competition from the Postal Bank and Postal Giro, which offered Saturday service. It was a classic collision of values. As one banking official saw it, "If they get Saturdays off, the service hours must be lengthened one way or another."[39]

By 1966, they had succeeded in doing just that. Oddly, no one in the union at the time ever considered what the banks might do to try to compensate for the substantial blow to their competitive position. In hindsight, one bank employee conceded that it goes to prove the old adage that sometimes the worst thing that can happen is to get what you wished for.

But while the workers were taken aback by the introduction of the first CDs, in recent years they have been able to participate in decision making relating to the introduction of new services. In 1979 the Bank Employees Union and Bank Employers Organization, which handles labor negotiations for all the banks on a joint basis, signed the first codetermination agreement in the private employment sector in Sweden. It guarantees employees a voice in decisions concerning computer systems, planning and budgeting, mergers, the opening and closing of offices, and customer services.

In addition, since 1974 employees have been entitled to appoint two members to the banks' boards of directors and one representative to local and regional boards. Although they lack the votes to affect the outcome of decisions, union leaders regard the participation as a valuable way to obtain information. As a matter of fact, none of the union leaders, employees, employers, or public officials interviewed for this study could identify any effect of either codetermination or board representation except a better exchange of information.

Fear in the Land of Security

Statistics indicate that while total employment in Sweden increased 10 percent in the 1970s, it increased more than twice as much in banking. Yet during that time, the number of branches declined by 14.4 percent and the number of CDs increased about tenfold. Nevertheless, according to an OECD study of thirteen countries, the Swedish commercial banks had the lowest annual rate of growth of staff between 1970 and 1977: 0.83 percent, compared to 5.31 percent in the United States.[40] The statistic reflects the impact of computerization, which, in the most impressive example, enabled Sweden's largest bank to handle an 80 percent increase in the volume of work between 1972 and 1982 with only 3 percent more people. One need not look far to find the reason for the commitment to capital spending: between 1970 and 1977, staff costs in the banks increased at an annual rate of over 20 percent. While in the United States the ratio of staff costs to operating costs in banks in 1970 was 53.5 percent, in Sweden it was 64 percent. By 1977, the Swedes had reduced their ratio by 8.5 percent, while the Americans' declined only 0.6 percent. In spite of that success, the upward pressure on operating costs cut profits in the 1971–1977 period to half of what they had been in the 1959–1965 period. Compared to an average 77 percent ratio of profits before tax volume of business in the United States, the Swedish banks' averaged 53 percent.

While profits were falling, the amount of time employees were spending on the job declined to 80 percent as a result of such benefits as the nationwide five-week annual vacation. In response, the banks have hired more part-time workers. Whereas in 1969 part-time employees made up only 7.5 percent of the union's membership, by 1981 that figure was up to 29 percent. By contrast, the Postal Giro, which has been using part-time help since the 1940s, has usually had between 20 to 25 percent of its workers employed on that basis. Because part-timers have the same pay scale and benefits as full-time workers and women prefer part-time work due to high marginal taxes and the desire for more time at home, there is a great demand for the jobs.

As the volume of self-service transactions rose and automated transactions exceeded manual ones for the first time in 1982 at one bank, union leaders expressed fear about the effects of technology on future jobs. Existing jobs are protected by a law that makes it about as difficult to lay off a Swedish worker as it is to fire one in the U.S. Civil Service where, the joke goes, the employee would have to shoot his supervisor at high noon in the presence of three witnesses. When asked why they were not concerned about EFTS when it was introduced, a union man said, "It's hard to worry when you're getting 400 to 500 new members a month."[41] Yet in spite of the security and participation, heightened tensions surfaced in 1981 when, for the first time in Swedish history, there was a nationwide bank strike.

Meanwhile, at the Postal Giro a problem lurks to which Swedes refer in a backhanded way, rather like a shameful family secret, because the giro is a national institution. Over the years, there has been great pride in its international reputation as a leader in the utilization of new technology. Hence, in response to technological advances, the service in 1979 began discussions with its four unions about the need to upgrade its systems and replace old equipment. But although employees have been assured that no one will lose a job, the adoption of new techniques has been blocked because the employees have been unable to agree on which of two systems to implement. In an effort to resolve the impasse, just before Christmas 1982, the project team representing the unions sent a booklet to all workers. It said that there were only two choices—to continue with rising costs and reduced competitive power or improve operations—and stressed that it was a matter of survival. On the back cover was the slogan, "Without our customers we do not have our jobs." Above that, it said, "Merry Christmas and a Happy New Year."[42] But as the negotiations dragged on through 1984, the thoroughly modern Bank Giro was busy stealing the Postal Giro's customers.

Competition for Financial Service Jobs in the United States

Ironically, while fear of fewer banking jobs grew in Sweden, in spite of what is probably the most comprehensive system of mandated employment security measures in the world, in the chancy job environment of the United States, competition mounted for attracting what were described as high-growth financial services firms to locales in order to acquire jobs. In part, the disparity in viewpoints could be attributed to definitional difficulties. These extend even to the FDIC, which in 1983 plaintively asked for comments on what constitutes the financial services industry.[43] While it might strike some as odd that a federal regulatory agency should feel constrained to ask people just what it is supposed to regulate, government people sometimes are the last to know about changes in a major industry. In Sweden in 1982, for example, although bankers knew, some government experts in telecommunications and computerization thought Sweden did not have EFTS because they did not know the definition of the term.

In dealing with employment effects of EFTS, it is essential to understand, first, that many operations that formerly were performed in banks have been moved to other locations because telecommunications permit a geographic mobility that never before existed in the industry. Second, because of that, to achieve the economies of scale necessary to offset the heavy capital investment in computerized systems, certain operations are batch-processed in regional or national centers. Third, because of those two factors, once the systems are up and running, the marginal cost of adding other processing is so small that securities, insurance, and retail firms have found that they can handle payment transactions in addition to their other work processes and at less cost than financial institutions whose systems are dedicated primarily to that work. Hence, nonbank financial service and commercial firms started offering bank products, thereby transforming the financial marketplace and prompting the FDIC's question, a vitally important one that all the banking regulators and Congress should have asked years ago.

Just as the administration, marketing, and processing of credit card operations were shifted in Sweden to separate companies, in the United States the first two functions were handed to Visa and MasterCard and the processing of transactions to large regional bank systems. While that illustrates the first two factors, the third factor now has appeared as Sears provides credit card services for Phillips Petroleum, and J.C. Penney handles electronic payments for two other national oil companies. That used to be considered "banking" work.

The insentience of electronic impulses to state borders has enabled the sharp cost-cutters in the financial supermarkets to move their clerical operations to cities where land, labor, and taxes are lower priced. For those reasons and to avoid the threat of higher future taxes inherent in the crumbling infrastructure of the East, American Express moved its travelers' check operations from New York City to Salt Lake City.

Similarly, when the governor of South Dakota learned of Citicorp's battle with New York State officials over their refusal to raise the state's 12 percent interest rate ceiling in 1980 when the prime rate reached 20 percent, he perceived a chance to bring jobs to his state. He had the legislature remove the state's usury limitations and permit out-of-state bank holding companies to acquire banks for the purpose of conducting credit card operations. Then he put out the welcome mat for the company. Much to the consternation of New

Yorkers, who could not believe that big, slick Citicorp would even consider the invitation, the company bought a bank in Sioux Falls and moved a major portion of its credit operations and over 1,000 jobs to the clean little city. Stunned, New York legislators lifted the ceiling and in effect put on the front porch light and waited for Citi to move back home. But the company, which sees itself as a supplier of communications services, by then was busily installing an earth receiving station at the new card center, linking it to its satellite communications system and thereby bringing the operation within seconds of its Manhattan headquarters.

Citicorp's highly publicized move smarted badly. While total employment in New York City increased only 5 percent between 1977 and 1982 and manufacturing jobs declined 15 percent, bank employment rose 29 percent.[44] Indeed, that solid growth in financial services had helped get the city back on its feet after its brush with bankruptcy in 1975 when there was a mass exodus of corporate headquarters and manufacturing firms. Now the fear that the moneylenders may transfer their clerical back office jobs to less costly suburbs and cities has been gnawing at the Big Apple, as well as such other high-cost urban centers as San Francisco.

The fear of flight grew palpably when South Dakota struck again in 1983 with a law permitting state banks to engage in the insurance business and permitting out-of-state bank holding companies to acquire a single new bank for that purpose. The bill followed a series of meetings of representatives of Citicorp, BankAmerica, and First Interstate Bancorp with state officials after the Garn-St Germain Act in 1982 banned insurance operations by the companies. Devoid of deviousness, the preamble to the South Dakota bill baldly proclaimed that its central purpose was to circumvent federal law and bring more jobs and tax revenues to the state. Even though Prudential-Bache, American Express, Sears, and twenty other companies conduct both banking and insurance business, and insurance firms have crossed industry lines by acquiring nonbank banks and securities firms and by sponsoring money market funds, the insurance interests fussed and flapped over the measure. But while the bill sailed through the legislature, after the state's insurance commissioner publicly expressed skepticism about the number of jobs the law would really create, the governor created one new one immediately by firing him.

After that the insurance industry brought out its big guns in all fifty states and in Washington and, to the battle cry of "The bankers are coming, the bankers are coming," demanded protection. The heels of the lawyers lobbying for the banking and insurance industries drummed a staccato beat up and down the marbled halls of power in the Capitol as they went from office to office, arguing that the national debt could wait until the South Dakota issue was resolved. Relieved to be presented with an issue of a size with which they could deal and with visions of thousands of insurance agents' hands pulling voting levers for them in the 1984 election, lawmakers proclaimed their support for the industry in its battle with the big bankers, who have never been popular in the country anyway. Finally, in January 1984 the Federal Reserve Board lobbed the ball back to the other court by stating in a "tentative judgment" that it could not approve the three companies' bank applications until further consideration by Congress. Back in Sioux Falls, the land developers slid their rolled-up sketches of new suburbs onto the top shelves of closets.

The New Yorkers, however, were not letting any grass grow under their feet. In the following month, the Temporary State Commission on Banking, Insurance and Financial Services, appointed in September 1983, issued a deregulatory report proposing that barriers between the insurance and banking industries be dismantled. While motivated by the goal of maintaining the state's leadership position in financial services and the 300,000 jobs they provide, the work of the commission is an example of public policymaking worth emulating. The study resembled a Swedish one in that the commission was made up of seventeen business people, two representatives of labor and one of consumers, and only three lawyers. The group was given objectives and value constraints; it analyzed the existing regulatory framework and made specific proposals, even though they were not unanimously endorsed, and although the report was comprehensive, it was concise. It differed from the Swedish approach in that there the study would have been ordered years earlier but would have taken longer to complete. It differed from the federal approach in that each segment of the industry was not simply seeking its own advantage in isolation from broader societal objectives.

Because technological advances have eroded barriers and converted erstwhile local markets into national ones, the group warned that failure to conform the state's legal framework to the changing environment could exacerbate the trend of the preceding decade in which the financial industry had grown twice as rapidly nationwide as in New York. To retain a competitive edge, the commission proposed, in addition to the insurance changes, that the state permit the chartering of nonbank banks, end anti-branch/ATM "home office protection," and expand the powers of thrifts. To balance industry interests with consumers', the group proposed "lifeline" accounts to provide basic banking services at minimal cost and advance notification of planned branch closings.

A less subtle come-on has done wonders for the job market in Delaware, where five of New York's largest banking institutions have opened up shop along with dozens of others. By abolishing interest rate ceilings and adopting a sliding-scale tax on bank profits that begins at 8.7 percent and drops to 2.7 percent for those over $30 million, the state has gained 1,800 bank jobs and thereby brought its unemployment rate below the national average for the first time since 1973.[45]

The pervasiveness of the whole hustle for jobs in the industry was revealed in late 1984 when a bank in Boston flexed its muscles by announcing that it planned to relocate its credit card operations to Delaware or New Hampshire because Massachusetts limits the interest on the card accounts to 18 percent while the other states do not.

The high-growth perception of jobs in the industry refers to the new, more highly skilled positions created by advanced technology and the accompanying increases in output, and not to tellers' jobs, about which the Swedish union leaders are concerned. There is, moreover, a vast difference in staffing those jobs in the two nations. In Sweden, where the jobs are seen as highly desirable, the turnover rate is only 3 to 4 percent annually. But in the United States, where turnover averages 33 percent, it is difficult to recruit people for the jobs. Because tellers in busy urban banking offices must contend with customers who are cranky from standing in line, service is indifferent at best and hostile at worst. Hence, as banks in major cities automate branches, customers opt for the ATMs, and tellers are relieved to be assigned to new work. Thus, although U.S. bankers in a 1983 survey reported that they expected ATMs to replace 17 percent of human tellers in the following three years, overall employment is not expected to decrease.[46]

Based on the experience to date in both the United States and Sweden, it appears that while the widespread implementation of EFT services reduces the demand for unskilled labor in financial institutions, it concomitantly increases the demand for more highly skilled individuals familiar with computer technology.

Notes

1. R.V. Jones, "Some Threats of Technology to Privacy," in A.H Robertson, ed., *Privacy and Human Rights* (Manchester: Manchester University Press, 1983), p. 140.

2. "1410 Is Watching," *Time*, August 23, 1963, p. 53.

3. Congressman Cornelius Gallagher, quoted by Alan F. Westin, *Privacy and Freedom* (New York: Atheneum, 1967), p. 315.

4. "The Computer Data Bank: Will It Kill Your Freedom?" *Look*, June 25, 1968, pp. 27–28.

5. Arthur R. Miller, *The Assault on Privacy* (Ann Arbor: University of Michigan Press, 1971), p. 42.

6. Westin, *Privacy*, p. 162. He and Michael A. Baker refuted the accounts in *Databanks in a Free Society* (New York: Quadrangle Books, 1972), pp. 269–279.

7. Charles Ready, "Practical Aspects of the DPC's Report," in Patricia Hewitt, ed., *Computers, Records and the Right to Privacy* (Purley, U.K: Input Two-Nine, 1979), p. 20.

8. Claes-Göran Källner, "Influence of Law and Public Opinion on Data Processing" (paper presented to a meeting of CAPA, June 9, 1977).

9. Interview with DIB official in October 1982.

10. P.G. Vinge, *Experiences of the Swedish Data Act* (Stockholm: Federation of Swedish Industries, 1975), p. 10–11.

11. Westin and Baker, *Databanks,* pp. 244, 341.

12. James B. Rule, *Private Lives and Public Surveillance* (London: Allen Lane, 1973), p. 339.

13. James B. Rule, *Value Choices in Electronic Funds Transfer Policy* (Washington, D.C.: Office of Telecommunications Policy, 1975), pp. 8–11, 32, 36.

14. Ibid., pp. 57–58.

15. Ibid., p. 41.

16. William F. Baxter, Paul H. Cootner, and Kenneth E. Scott, *Retail Banking in the Electronic Age* (Montclair, N.J.: Allanheld, Osmun, 1977), p. 166, quoted by James B. Rule, Douglas McAdam, Linda Stearns, and David Uglow, *The Politics of Privacy* (New York: Elsevier, 1980), p. 149.

17. August Bequai, *The Cashless Society: EFTS at the Crossroad* (New York: John Wiley & Sons, 1981), p. 11.

18. Donn B. Parker, "Vulnerabilities of EFT Systems to Intentionally Caused Losses," in Kent W. Colton and Kenneth L. Kraemer, eds., *Computers and Banking* (New York: Plenum Press, 1980), p. 94.

19. Bequai, *Cashless Society,* p. 11.

20. John Wicklein, *Electronic Nightmare* (New York: Viking Press, 1981), p. 97.

21. John McNulty, "The Information Explosion," in Hewitt, *Computers,* p. 103.

22. Peter H. Schuck, "Electronic Funds Transfer: A Technology in Search of a Market," in Federal Reserve Bank of Boston, *The Economics of a National Electronic Funds Transfer System* (Boston: Federal Reserve Bank of Boston, 1974), p. 155.

23. Sten Walberg, "Bankerna och allmänheten," *Ekonomisk revy* 9 (1980) 401.

24. Swedish Institute, "Swedish Consumer Policy" (Stockholm, 1978), p. 1.

25. Miller, *Assault,* p. 234.

26. Ibid., p. 225.

27. Louis Harris and Associates, Inc., and Alan F. Westin, *The Dimensions of Privacy* (New York: Garland Publishing, 1981), p. 85.

28. *California Bankers Association v. Shultz,* 416 U.S. 21 (1974).

29. Ibid., pp. 89–90.

30. *U.S. v. Miller,* 425 U.S. 435 (1976).

31. Louis Harris and Associates, Inc., *The Road after 1984* (New Haven: Southern New England Telephone, 1984), p. 7.

32. Lynn B. Barr, "Remarks," in Federal Reserve System, *Papers and Comments of the International Conference on Banking and Payment Systems,* Atlanta, April 2–4, 1980, p. 195.

33. Jack Revell, *Banking and Electronic Fund Transfers: A Study of the Implications* (Paris: OECD, 1983), p. 90.

34. Sten Walberg, "The Consequences of New Delivery Systems for Bank Regulators" (Paper presented to the Conference on Retail Banking, London, November 16, 1982).

35. Ministry of Defense, *The Vulnerability of the Computerized Society* (Stockholm: 1979), p. 11.

36. "Mass. Banks Seek to Cut Card Fraud with Crackdown," *American Banker,* December 7, 1979.

37. Bureau of Justice Statistics, *Electronic Fund Transfer Systems and Crime* (Washington, D.C.: Government Printing Office, 1982), p. 116.

38. Ibid., p. 82.

39. Åke Bergqvist, "Bankernas expeditionstider," *Ekonomisk revy* 4 (1959): 270.

40. Statistics in this paragraph from J.R.S. Revell, *Costs and Margins in Banking: An International Survey* (Paris: OECD, 1980), pp. 130, 107.

41. Interview.

42. PGP-projektet, *Viktiga Frågor om jobbet och framtiden* (Stockholm: PostGirot, 1982).

43. FDIC, 12 C.F.R. 332, 333, 337, Advance Notice of Proposed Rulemaking, August 30, 1983.

44. "Handling Money: Some Unlikely Places Benefit from the Boom in Financial Services," *Wall Street Journal*, March 31, 1983.

45. Ibid.

46. "Business Bulletin," *Wall Street Journal*, June 23, 1983, reporting on a survey by Bunker Ramo of 202 bankers.

7

Different Approaches, Different Results

The road Sweden took to the present state of its banking and payment system forked off from that of the United States some years ago. But there remain commonalities in the predominant values in the two nations, which have led to Sweden's being called the "most Americanized" country in Europe. Both prize democracy, are technologically oriented, and have economies that combine private enterprise and welfare systems, albeit in differing proportions. These similarities form a basis for understanding as this chapter shows how Sweden's retail banking and payment system achieved preeminence while that of the United States has been characterized as "still firmly rooted in the 'palaeocartic' age."[1] Based on that analysis, some provocative proposals are presented in an effort to stimulate debate about a comprehensive national policy that would lead to the development of a first-rate system for Americans.

Muddling Through to Excellence

The development of Sweden's retail banking and payment system could be attributed to four primary reasons: (1) its widespread adoption of EFTS began over two decades ago; (2) the implementation of those technological innovations was facilitated by a high degree of intraindustry cooperation and sharing, free of government interference; (3) fierce competition stimulated the creation of extraordinarily convenient customer services; and (4) public policies and regulation protected both users and providers from potential negative effects of the new technology.

In analyzing the first reason, it appears that with the exception of the SIBOL study, the introduction of EFT services was not the result of either brilliant strategic planning or technological prowess. Rather, it was primarily a response to external forces over which the bankers had no control. In fact, some of the cause-and-effect relationships surrounding the evolution of cashless payment mechanisms in Sweden would indicate that the Theory of Unintended Consequences prevailed over planning. Consider, for example, these paradoxes and unanticipated results:

> The banks' failure to develop a secure checking system led to the founding of the Postal Giro in 1925.

> The Postal Giro was meant to reduce the use of cash, but it led to enormous increases in the handling of currency.

> No good usually comes from crime, but much of the early success of the Postal Giro resulted from the need to curb widespread embezzling by civil servants and union leaders.

> Low profit margins imposed on banks by the Riksbank forced them to cooperate to cut costs, which resulted in the early adoption of EFTS.

> Salary accounts produced such huge transaction volumes and heavy customer demands that they drove the banks to early computerization and electronic self-service products.

> The savings banks fought for fifty-five years for the right to offer checking accounts, only to learn their customers did not want them. That forced them to install CDs when they had to close their offices on Saturdays.

> The restrictions on branching, credit, deposit interest, premiums, and service fees compelled bankers to turn to technological innovations as the only way to compete.

> The Bank Employees Union campaigned for decades to get Saturdays off for its members, but when it succeeded, the banks ordered CDs, which, the union now fears, may result in fewer jobs.

> The bankers expected people to use CDs only when the banks were closed. They were flabbergasted when they saw people using them when bank offices were open.

> By guaranteeing the checks of over a million people who had never used them before, the banks unleashed the biggest wave of frauds in Swedish history, which doomed checks as a payment mechanism at retail. This forced them to install more and better CDs to provide cash for shopping and, more recently, to work on a nationwide POS system.

> In their pursuit of salary accounts, the banks promised free checking, but after they had millions of the accounts, the high cost of handling the checks led them to develop a paperless data clearing system and impose fees to discourage excessive use of the payment mechanism.

Banks' profits were halved in the 1970s as staff costs soared over 20 percent annually while time on the job declined to 80 percent. These pressures provided a strong impetus to capital investment, which made EFTS possible.

The Easter Holiday Caper so dramatically demonstrated the vulnerability of off-line units that it spurred the savings banks' move to on-line CDs.

The failure of credit cards to gain widespread use has stimulated R&D for a nationwide POS system.

The armed robberies of welfare disbursement offices fostered the use of direct deposit of government payments.

The recurring threat of nationalization has led the bankers to share their systems and provide reciprocity, thereby increasing customer convenience.

Overall, the high costs of labor were the strongest economic force behind Sweden's early adoption of EFTS, as they have been for the nation's worldwide lead in the use of robots in manufacturing.[2] Nevertheless, of the four reasons, the most significant is the second because without cooperating and sharing, EFTS would not have been developed so early and the smaller financial institutions would not have been able to compete so effectively. The SIBOL study proposed the standardization measures that have facilitated reciprocal services for customers; Bank Giro has provided both an automated clearinghouse and competition for the Postal Giro; and joint efforts have produced competing nationwide CD networks. The banks cooperated to build an infrastructure that ensured equality and permitted economies of scale for early profitability.

Moreover, the banks have pursued these joint efforts free of uncertainty about government intervention because public policy precludes interference in the area. Finally, the convenience enjoyed by customers of all banks, regardless of size, in having access to their funds around the clock every day of the year, from the southernmost part of Sweden to the Arctic Circle, is possible because the government imposes no restrictions on nationwide branching or the sharing of other banks' electronic terminals.

While it was the drive for deposits that led to salary accounts that ushered in retail banking and its mass transactions that required computerization, two changes in public policy stimulated the competition for retail business: the 1968 laws that permitted all banks to offer the same services and the end of the cartels in 1975. On the other hand, because no permission was required from the government for CDs, they represented a way around branching restrictions. By giving territorial protectionism to the thrifts so that they do not compete with one another, the government was partly responsible for their ability to coordinate their efforts. Yet because they did compete with the postal savings bank, the fact that the post offices were open on Saturday was a direct cause of the savings banks' ordering their first CDs. The thrifts' pioneering efforts in electronic retail services spurred responses from the commercial banks, which helped win acceptance of EFTS in that each new service benefited from the synergistic impact of others.

The early diffusion of EFTS in Sweden could have been blocked by the same public outcry about privacy rights that sent U.S. bankers to the bunkers in the 1970s. But the Swedes resolved the problem with the world's first national computer privacy act and a comprehensive credit information act. By relieving consumer fears, setting guidelines for providers, and equalizing costs among them, the approach facilitated the implementation of EFTS. Public confidence in EFTS also was engendered by the soundness of the banking system ensured by the bank inspectorate and by consumer legislation regulating the banks' marketing activities. Thus, while freedom from government intervention in cooperation and sharing was the strongest direct political force behind Sweden's commanding lead in payment services, the high level of government mediation in protecting both providers and users from potential negative effects of the new technology was a powerful indirect force.

The Team That Couldn't Win

To use a football allegory and do some Monday morning quarterbacking, just as there are many heroes in Sweden's win in retail banking, there are scapegoats aplenty for what went wrong in the United States. The most glaring problem was the lack of a good game plan. And since it is the government that charts the plays for the bankers, the brunt of the blame must be laid there. Granted, the bankers fumbled the ball plenty of times, but the Swedish bankers didn't play a flawless game either. The big difference was that all the Swedish players had one coach who drew up a well-charted game plan, and they all played with one set of regulations. Their coach, moreover, knew when to call time-outs to help them and when to keep out. The Americans, by contrast, had five federal coaches and fifty state coaches, all with different game plans and different regulations, which confused the field officials who often were overruled by officials sitting on the bench. Also, while one coach would be calling time-out, another would be telling the team to go for a field goal.

When the whole game of banking was changed in the 1960s by computers, inflation, and the spread of retail banking, U.S. officials did not revise the old rules to permit the industry team to adapt to the changes. Instead they further restricted the players' movements with added protective gear by extending interest rate ceilings on savings accounts to thrifts as well as banks. Thus the officials opened the game to the money market funds, even though they didn't play by the rules at all, who rushed in to pick off one-tenth of the action as market rates rose above the ceilings.

Another problem was that the bank and thrift players were always fighting among themselves, even before they were challenged by the free agents. The thrifts' coach came up with a strong offensive play using ATMs statewide in 1974; but when the banks' coach countered with an ATM plan of his own, the smaller guys on his team got an official on the bench to ban the play because they were afraid they'd get hurt by it. Maybe if they could have got along better, the bankers might have developed EFTS earlier. But the big banks feared that if they worked together or shared systems, they'd be penalized by antitrust officials who always favored the smaller players or by judicial officials who made policy decisions based on old rules because legislative officials could never agree on comprehensive new ones for fear of offending some group of fans. Another stumbling block to efficient systems was set up by state officials who wouldn't let outside players cross into their territory for fear they'd take over.

Anyway, the bankers didn't want to switch to EFT because they feared losing the float on which they were thriving. Although Fed officials spent money on developing EFT, they cancelled out the effects of those efforts by not ending float for fear of losing some of their share of the check collection system. The thrifts weren't much better. Even after the free agents starting scoring, the thrifts were afraid to give up their overly restrictive protective gear, even though they couldn't run in it.

With most everyone afraid to do anything for fear of something or other, the real tigers on the team left. So about all that was left for the game was a bunch of argumentative wimps who couldn't agree on *any*thing. In the whole world, no team like that has ever won.

In Search of Security and Soundness

Like football teams and bridges, the strength of a banking system is revealed only through its performance under stress. On that basis, the United States has never had a strong banking and payment system. The Swedes did not pattern their system on the U.S. one because even then it was marked by runs, collapses, and panics. The free-banking laws enacted by states after the Panic of 1837 to reform abuses in the chartering process ushered in the wild and woolly era of wildcat banking, which soured so many states on banking that some banned it completely and others set up monopolistic state banks. In spite of the chaotic conditions, Congress eschewed dealing with the problem because of its inflammatory political nature until it was finally forced to do so by the need to create funding for the Civil War.

The National Bank Act of 1863 was intended to end state banking by creating a uniform system of national banks, but the state banks refused to convert to national charters, even after Congress tried to bully them into doing so by imposing a tax on their bank notes. The tax succeeded in giving the federal government control over the monetary system, but it did not succeed in eliminating state banks because they turned instead to deposit banking by offering checking accounts. By creating the Office of Comptroller of the Currency to examine banks, the act was meant to ensure a sound system. But with half the banks outside the system, the goal could hardly have been reached with examinations—even if they could have done the job, which was not the case. In fact, because the system did not provide a regulating mechanism for money, the economy was subjected to wild gyrations between booms and busts.

By the turn of the century, the U.S. monetary and banking system was described as "the most barbarous on earth."[3] The impotence of the government in crises was vividly demonstrated in the Panic of 1907, when it took J.P. Morgan to stem a run on New York City banks. But while the condition of the system called for major surgery, Congress responded with the equivalent of a couple of aspirins in the form of a law to deal with emergency currency shortages and created the National Monetary Commission to study the matter.

Because a number of public leaders believed that the unit banking structure was a major source of weakness in the system, they proposed that the United States model its system on Canada's, which, with a few large banks and nationwide branching, enjoyed stability. The commission, however, sailed for Europe, accompanied by some elementary texts on money and banking and a professor who held classes aboard ship for the legislators. But all their efforts were for naught. By the time they presented their plan for reform through centralization, the Democrats, who wanted to limit the power of the bankers through decentralization, had won control of Congress. The newspaperman-congressman who coauthored the Federal Reserve Act attributed the fact that it cleared Congress to the fact that its text was kept secret from everyone but the president and secretary of the treasury because "every other currency bill had been battered to pieces by hostile interests before it could get a start."[4]

The act succeeded in ending currency shortages, but by then, checks had largely displaced currency for large-scale transactions anyway. It also ended the fees banks had been charging for checks drawn on out-of-town banks. To avoid the charges, banks would send such checks to correspondent banks, which often entailed lengthy roundabout routing. By setting up the Fed check-clearing and collection centers, the act, said one of its coauthors, had "done away with the enormous and hazardous 'float' which formerly clogged the mails."[5] But as the volume of checks grew, they clogged the Fed system too. Like other problems involving the U.S. banking system, Fed float was swept under the rug for so long that over the years it too assumed horrendous proportions.

Although Sweden had earlier encouraged the founding of a large number of small banks, when experience showed that such a structure resulted in bank failures and instability, the country adopted a new policy of encouraging fewer and larger banks, which would serve the public through branches. The government also wanted larger banks to support the industrialization process and smooth out seasonal and geographic fluctuations in credit and deposits. Hence, it raised capital requirements, restricted the granting of charters, and encouraged mergers. From eighty-four commercial banks in 1908, the number declined to thirty in 1930 as a result of numerous mergers in the 1920s' depression, and then gradually fell to the present fourteen banks. In response to the poor management in the savings banks, the government encouraged mergers to create stronger units, which resulted in a decrease from 495 in 1926 to 160 in 1983. Moreover, after the collapse of a group of savings banks in the 1920s, regulation of that sector was tightened. Since then, the entire system has remained sound and secure, thus achieving the desired goal.

In the United States, that goal remained only a promise on the lips of politicians who lacked the intestinal fortitude to deal with a basic cause of instability: the fragmented structure of the banking system. The creation of the Federal Reserve System as a central regulating mechanism was just dandy; but without taking the requisite next step of making membership in the system mandatory for all banks, there was no way that the stated goal of ensuring that there would never be another banking crisis could be achieved.

In the first two decades of the century, as federal and state regulators competed to charter banks, they sprang up like kids' lemonade stands on a hot August afternoon. The number of banks more than doubled, with the states winning three-fourths to their ranks by offering less restrictive conditions. Because many banks were poorly managed, they failed; but most of the failures were of state-chartered banks. As the number of failures grew, it engendered contagious fear, which resulted in runs on good banks as well as bad, culminating in the disaster of the early 1930s when people lost some $2.5 billion as 9,000 banks failed. With the surviving banks chastened by the crash, Congress flubbed its chance to create a uniform banking system when, instead of denying FDIC coverage to the state banks that did not join the Federal Reserve System by the deadline, it gave them coverage anyway.

That sustenance of the dual banking system led in the 1970s and 1980s to a repeat performance of the earlier competition in laxity as banks shopped among federal and state authorities for the most complaisant regulators. By then, it was a response to the minefield of deadly old laws and regulations that the bankers had to negotiate to survive in the new era of computerized banking. At a time when the banks should have been strengthening their managerial capabilities to deal with the radical changes in the industry, they instead had to dissipate their resources on lawyers' fees to find loopholes in the laws that denied them direct market responses.

Although the 1930s' laws did not cause any mischief so long as the depression endured, when prosperity returned, the problems created by those solutions to old problems undermined the viability of the industry. Interest rate ceilings were directly responsible for the cannibalization of deposits by unregulated competitors as inflation soared in the 1970s. Because Congress failed to respond to the changing environment, when the banks most needed competitive power, the Glass-Steagall Act impeded product extension and the McFadden Act limited geographic market expansion. Even as electronic technology was revolutionizing the basic nature of banking and annihilating the old barriers to entry, instead of bolstering the industry to withstand incursions by large firms with national operations, Congress restrained the larger banks and prevented the creation of stronger banks by extending its protection of mom-and-pop operations with the bank holding company and merger control laws.

By 1980, although the industry was split into regulated and unregulated sectors, Congress directed its efforts at preserving the old industry structure. The S&Ls, however, fought the removal of deposit rate controls and gave in on the issue in 1982 only in exchange for a promise of government financial assistance. But with 40 percent of the S&Ls operating in the red in early 1984, two years after deregulation many S&Ls came out for reregulation, saying they wanted evolution, not revolution. On Christmas Eve 1984, it was reported that another Illinois bank had failed, the seventy-ninth during the year. While that post-depression record number of failures reflected bad bank management, it no less reflected bad policymaking and regulation. Indeed, the chairman of the House Banking Committee in late 1984 conceded that the regulatory system on which the soundness of the industry depends was "built on the quicksand of secrecy, procrastination, and expedience."[6]

Contrasting Courses in Regulation

The decline in public confidence in the U.S. banking system constitutes a mandate for prompt and effective reform. Fear and anxiety resulting from news stories about failures and government rescues had grown by early 1985 to the point that rumors were enough to trigger a depositor run on an Oklahoma S&L that actually was sound.[7] In fact, all depositors in most failures have been covered up to $100,000. In some cases, however, the FDIC has paid off only a portion of uninsured balances above that amount, based on how much the agency expected to recover from the liquidated bank's assets. As a result of payouts to depositors of failed S&Ls and the costs of assisting mergers, the FSLIC insurance fund fell from $6.3 billion in 1984 to $4.7 billion by early 1985. But that was only a drop in the bucket since the insured deposits in the 3,200 S&Ls covered by the fund totaled $770 billion.

Because the general public views all financial institutions as much the same, depositors' losses in the highly publicized failures of some firms linked to private deposit insurance systems have added to concern about the industry. In California, 12,000 customers who had some $98 million on deposit with a state-regulated thrift association when it failed in April 1984 had received only 12 cents on the dollar by the end of the year as the state began liquidation proceedings that could take five years. Like 66 other such thrifts in the state, the firm had advertised that depositors' accounts were insured up to $50,000 by the California Thrift Guaranty Corporation. But when the thrift collapsed, the fund was found to be grossly underfunded although within state guidelines. The insurance firm had been created by the state but was governed by the industry and was not backed by the credit of the state.

After newscasters announced in late 1983 that the failure of Nebraska's largest industrial bank with deposits of $66.9 million had bankrupted the private fund that insured its deposits, regulators had to freeze certificates of deposit at other industrial banks to prevent runs by a frightened public. The state had chartered 33 such institutions to make consumer loans to lower income people and then created the Nebraska Depository Insurance Guaranty Corporation in 1977 because the firms did not qualify for FDIC coverage. In the wake of the scandal surrounding the failures, the state's banking regulator lost his job, the attorney general was forced to resign, and depositors suffered extensive losses.

The federal government created a dangerous imbalance when it gave banks and thrifts new freedoms with deregulation without providing safeguards for their increased responsibility. With S&Ls pursuing a strategy of rapid growth through speculative loans and investments permitted by lenient state laws, the FHLBB found that S&L problems in 1984 were due more to low asset quality and fraud than to the old problem of mismatched assets and liabilities. For the banks, when the cost of paying interest for deposits forced them to seek new ways to maintain profits, there were only two choices: diversify or make riskier loans. Since the government continued to limit the first option, many took the second, encouraged by the fact that deposit insurance premiums are unrelated to the riskiness of assets and depositors are covered regardless of the cause of insolvencies. Thus, the banks made loans to Third World nations and, to compensate for declining deposits, turned to "hot" money from money brokers who offer deposits in exchange for risky loans. The banks now borrow billions in one-day funds to lend at longer maturities to make speculative profits, the classic error of supporting long-term loans with short-term assets.

With the government standing by to save bankers from their own mistakes, the problem supposedly eliminated by deposit insurance has returned with a vengeance. The danger inherent in the solution adopted in 1933 was illustrated by the credit unions, which enjoyed stability when they were self-insured. But after government insurance was provided, the number of failures grew from 1 in 1971 to 200 in 1980.

In addition to the problem of stupidity there is that of cupidity. Criminal misconduct by bank officers, directors, and insiders was a major contributing factor in 61 percent of bank failures between 1980 and mid-1983, according to a congressional study.[8] An FDIC study of failures between 1960 and 1974 revealed that 31.3 percent were caused by embezzlement and manipulation and an additional 53.8 percent were caused by self-serving loans to bank management or friends of management.[9] Insider loans pose another problem because, as a former assistant U.S. attorney testified in the 1983 congressional hearing into criminal misconduct by bankers, the average citizen likes to know that when he needs a loan, he can go into the bank and obtain one, "confident that persons controlling that bank have not already loaned all the money to themselves."[10]

Regulators, however, have been notoriously unsuccessful in detecting insider abuses even though federal agencies alone employed about 13,000 people in regulating banks, thrifts, and credit unions in 1983 and spent $237 million on examinations in 1982.[11] In two-thirds of the cases in the congressional study, the banking agency either failed to detect the criminal misconduct or failed to report it until after the institution had failed. Even after regulators did learn of the abuses, they took no enforcement action in 80 percent of the cases.

Other criminal misconduct also goes unnoticed. While banks have been required by law to report currency transactions exceeding $10,000 to the Internal Revenue Service since 1974, bank examiners failed to observe that between 1976 and 1983, a vice president of a Chicago bank laundered some $2.5 million from a cocaine operation in which he was involved.[12] A federal court fined the bank $15,000 and placed it on five years' probation to encourage greater vigilance about what was going on since other bank officials had never noticed for seven years that their colleague was exchanging suitcases full of small bills for large ones.

Federal regulators acknowledge that the present examination system is inadequate for today's banking system. If nothing else, the sheer number of institutions and size of the country constitute major stumbling blocks to adequate inspection with the 4,300 federal bank examiners and 1,900 state examiners spending three-fourths of their time traveling. That problem is compounded by the fact that the various federal and state regulators apply different standards in examining banks. The Fed, for example, encourages loans to Third World countries while the FDIC and comptroller's examiners rap bankers' knuckles for making them; the FDIC and FHLBB view brokered deposits as dangerous while the comptroller has not opposed them. These disparities in policies as to what constitutes sound banking practices not only confuse bankers but also have encouraged them to shop for the most accommodating supervision.

In Sweden, the Savings Banks Inspection Board was merged into the Bank Inspection Board in 1962 to ensure consistency in regulating financial institutions. Moreover, the concentration process that the government has encouraged has strengthened the caliber of management and facilitated the monitoring of banking operations so that a BIB auditor can be assigned to each of the large commercial banks. There is no deposit insurance; by granting charters, the government ensures the soundness of institutions and the security of depositors' funds. To achieve those goals, the government supported the banks in the 1920s and 1930s, partly covered depositors' losses in the failures of some thrifts in the 1920s, and through subsidies to industries has sharply reduced banks' losses on loans to them. The banks, in return, must meet capital and liquidity requirements, avoid risky investments including stock ownership, and publicly disclose information about their condition and operating results.

Compared to the rigid U.S. style of regulating, the Swedish approach is more flexible, involves less paperwork, and is based on cooperation with continuing personal contacts to prevent problems. While the banks have been given the freedom of self-regulation in some areas, they also have been made keenly aware of the accompanying burden of responsibility. When officials of one bank violated some standards, the retribution was severe. Unlike the chairmen of Continental Illinois and Financial Corporation of America who, after leading their firms to the brink of disaster, received severance payments of $500,000 and $2 million respectively, the president of the Swedish bank was deposed in disgrace. Other top executives were asked to leave, and those remaining had their salaries cut in half.

The effectiveness of Swedish regulation is attested to by the fact that in a 1981 survey, respondents chose banks as the type of business in which they had the greatest confidence.[13] Moreover, regulation emerged as an important reason for the banks' trustworthy image among the Swedish people.

Pragmatic Proposals for Reform

After more than 120 years of fruitless efforts, it is apparent that a sound and secure banking system for the United States cannot be achieved solely through regulation as it has been in Sweden. The problem is rooted in the inability of legislators and regulators to take the necessary actions for political reasons and in basic weaknesses in the regulatory and deposit insurance systems. Hence, I propose the following measures.

The federal government should vigorously prosecute whitecollar crime in banking to restore a greater measure of soundness to the system. Not only is managerial dishonesty the number-one cause of bank failures, but the extent of insider crime dwarfs that of the more publicized crimes by outsiders. FBI crime figures for federal violations alone in 1982 reveal that while $38.3 million was taken from banks, thrifts and credit unions in robberies, burglaries, and larcenies, $333.3 million was taken through fraud and embezzlement.[14] The cost to consumers can only be conjectured from the fact that commercial banks alone pay over $1 billion a year for insurance coverage.

This proposal requires not only a commitment from top law enforcement officials but also a stepped-up effort on the part of examiners and greater disclosure of information about insider crime to see if publicity could not serve as something of a deterrent to those who seem to have cast-iron consciences when it comes to honesty. In addition, new legislation should be enacted to provide stiffer penalties than the present maximum of $5,000 and/or imprisonment for five years for an officer who loans himself $1 million illegally compared to the twenty years' penalty for a thief who is not on the institution's payroll. Certainly one form of crime endangers the security of the bank no less than the other.

State regulations and chartering requirements for all financial institutions should conform to national standards. While this will be politically unpopular, stability cannot be achieved until this step is taken. In fact, a banking crisis to rival that of the 1920s looms if an incipient competition in laxity is not halted. As the states compete for jobs and tax revenues, some plan to permit their banks to expand into new services to gain an advantage over banks in other states. Since each move by one state elicits responses from others, a bidding war could ensue, with banks expanding into more and more areas with less and less supervision. Once started, the process would be difficult, if not impossible, for the federal government to stop. While the dual banking system was based on deference to states' rights, the responsibility accompanying the privilege has so often been breached that the time has come to subordinate sectionalism to the benefit of society as a whole.

Uniform standards should be adopted by federal and state banking examiners along with a program of shared supervision to eliminate duplication which is costly both to the agencies and to the banks. Standardization also could reduce traveling so that examiners would spend more time behind bank desks and less time behind the steering wheel of a car.

Interstate banking should be legalized. To say it should be permitted would be perpetuating a sham. It has long been enjoyed by businesses, which can make deposits or borrow anywhere in the country; only individuals have been denied such freedom of choice. Among the damages caused by banning this economically beneficial practice have been less convenience and higher costs resulting from anticompetitive behavior; the hindrance to earlier diffusion of EFTS; the failures of banks whose flow of funds lacked the smoothing effects of wider operations and of those that could not merge with banks in other states; the money lost to the industry from the incursion of nonfinancial competitors that could operate nationwide; and the waste of resources on nonbank banks and other euphemisms for out-of-state branches. Although such bans were originally based on the flawed populist argument of the value of keeping deposited funds in the community, they have fostered instability by forcing banks to turn to risky out-of-state brokered funds when needed.

The regulation of all U.S. banks, S&Ls, and savings banks should be vested in one federal agency that is free of political influence to achieve the integrity, coherence, and conformity needed for effective supervision. The agency would consolidate the regulatory activities of the FDIC, the Comptroller of the Currency, the Federal Reserve, and the Federal Home Loan Bank system. At least for the present, the regulation of the credit unions should remain intact because it is working well. The Federal Reserve should be represented on the board of the new agency because of its special role in conducting monetary policy and as the lender of last resort. But with its direct supervisory role removed, the conflict between the Fed's regulatory policies and its monetary and payments processing policies would be resolved. After state regulatory and examination standards are brought into conformity with the uniform national standards, and as geographic limitations on banking disappear, the state regulatory systems may be merged into the national system in the interest of efficiency.

The measure could reduce the costs of bureaucratic bloat which, at the federal level alone, resulted in regulators employing on a per capita basis 5.3 times more people in 1984 than did the lean, mean Swedish BIB. While $290 million was spent to regulate finance and banking in the United States at the federal level in 1980 when deregulation of the industry began, an estimated $428 million was spent in 1984 to produce unprecedented confusion.[15]

The consolidation would solve the problem inherent in the fact that while the Fed regulates bank holding companies, an agency regulating banks owned by those companies has no authority over the parents or their nonbanking affiliates. With all information about banks and holding companies in the records of one agency, problems no longer would slip between agencies, and bankers would no longer be able to conceal illegal loan transactions by moving such loans from bank to bank in the industry's version of musical chairs.

The proposal also would solve the problem of regulators who, because they are responsible for the welfare of their constituency, act on behalf of its best interests rather than those of the public. With the Conference of State Bank Supervisors collecting over 90 percent of its multimillion-dollar operating budget from the annual dues of the banks, the regulators' role as trade associations for the industry is apparent. Congressional investigators discovered that, in the club-like atmosphere between bank regulators and the people they regulate, conduct that should be criminally prosecuted earns only a tap on the knuckles. While a thief who walks into a bank with a note for a teller and gets less than $1,000 faces a relentless hunt by the FBI and up to twenty years in prison, a bank president who misappropriates $1 million is usually asked by the regulatory agency to sign an agreement which in effect says, "Please don't do this anymore."

All financial institutions, both state- and federally-chartered, with the exception of credit unions, should be required to have federal deposit insurance through the FDIC. The FDIC thus would displace the FSLIC and the private funds operating in ten states that guarantee some $30 billion in deposits in S&Ls, savings banks, and industrial banks. Although private insurance has worked well for the credit unions, and Massachusetts has had an excellent history with it, the importance of public confidence in the banking system is so great that it should not be jeopardized by any more collapses of funds like those in California and Nebraska. Customers trust private systems that have official-appearing names and often use the state seal in advertising; yet those funds do not have the backing of the state. Technically, FDIC insurance is not backed by the full faith and credit of the U.S. government either. But through access to the Fed's discount window, it implicitly has the backing of the U.S. Treasury, which is a psychological deterrent to fear-induced runs.

Because this proposal strikes at the heart of the duality issue, it can be expected to encounter considerable opposition. After the Federal Reserve in late 1983 issued a regulation that would have required many state institutions to obtain FDIC coverage, the Division of S&L Associations of the Ohio Department of Commerce succeeded in having the ruling overturned in a U.S. Appeals Court decision. The Ohio supervisor of S&Ls branded the Fed Action as "arrogant," and said it would "cripple the non-Federal depository insurers in the independent state regulatory systems."[16] The state executive described the Ohio Deposit Guarantee Fund that insures 72 state-chartered thrifts as preferable to the FDIC because it permits its members to pay as much as 11 percent interest on passbook accounts.

Freed of its regulatory responsibilities, the FDIC would concentrate its efforts on examining and monitoring financial institutions only for insurance purposes, thereby resolving the conflict between the goals of the regulatory and insurance functions. The agency could act like a private insurer, responding to market forces as it sought to minimize losses. With a nationwide focus on troubled institutions, the FDIC could better detect linkages such as those that plagued Seafirst and Continental Illinois in the aftermath of the collapse of Oklahoma's Penn Square Bank.

The insurance premiums of the financial institutions should be related to risk, just as automobile insurance is based on one's driving ability and record. This would remove the inequity from the present situation in which good bankers pay too much and poor ones, too little.

Brokered deposits should not be insured by the FDIC because they encourage excessive risk-taking and can contribute to failures. This raises the cost of banking services since the cost of losses and insurance premiums is passed on to the customers. The FDIC was created to protect the funds of small depositors, not profit-seekers.

All of the nation's largest banks—those too big to fail—should have a government auditor assigned full-time to monitor their operations. This is simply a quid pro quo for the government's assurance that it will not let any of them fail.

Financial institutions should be required to disclose more information about their operations, including nonperforming loans. While the argument against this is that people would become unduly alarmed because "they don't understand," the American people now are more knowledgeable about finance than ever before in history. If the makers of food products must disclose ingredients so that consumers can make more informed choices, bankers should not be subject to more lenient standards.

Financial institutions should be permitted to diversify into securities, insurance, real estate, and travel services to compensate for their increased costs from deposit rate deregulation, continuing decline in deposits, and loss of payments processing to nonfinancial firms. While many banks have failed as a result of risky loans, none has ever failed as a result of offering different services. Europeans have enjoyed banks that are financial supermarkets for years; in Europe and Canada even cooperative and savings banks offer mutual funds. This proposal recognizes that what formerly was a group of discrete industry segments has been transformed into one financial services industry, as securities firms have entered banking through money market funds and limited service banks and banks have offered discount brokerage services. With after-tax returns of 22 percent for discount brokers in 1983, compared to 11.6 percent after-tax return on equity for banks and BHCs, the profits could strengthen the industry. Consistent with the Swedish experience, an economist at the Federal Reserve Bank of Boston has found that, providing the banks act only as agents, their securities activities can increase their safety and soundness rather than increase risks.[17]

All depository institutions should be permitted to offer the same services, as in Europe and Canada. Until deregulation in Canada in 1967, depository institutions were losing their market share of savings to life insurance companies and pension funds; afterward, they regained their competitive strength by introducing innovative products.

Depository institutions should launch campaigns to sign up salary accounts to counter the incursions into their deposit bases by outsiders. In recent years those accounts have made up about one-quarter of the Swedish banks' deposits.

The government should consider requiring that all institutions handling payments be licensed in order to control the activities of nonfinancial firms, as does Germany. The criteria could be based on capital and professional qualifications and include an insurance requirement.

The regulatory agency should develop a system of fewer, stronger banks by assisting mergers as an alternative to a long series of costly failures that are inevitable because there are too many banks to survive in a deregulated environment. Although some industry analysts have predicted that in the future the United States would have only 25 to 35 banking organizations, the European experience indicates that a few large banks plus a number of regional and small banks provide the optimal customer service, with the large ones offering the advantages of vast resources and the smaller ones providing personal services with low operating costs through centralization, provided that they establish electronic linkages with other financial services' providers. As this book has shown, it is not the number of firms in the market that ensures effective competition; it is what they do. Sweden's oligopolistic market is far stronger and more competitive than the fragmented U.S. market.

Financial institutions should be permitted to coordinate their operations and cooperate technologically without fear of government intervention. In particular, thrift institutions should be allowed to compete in groups as they so effectively do in Europe. This would produce greater stability by strengthening smaller institutions and create a climate in which technological innovation could flourish. The Swedish model shows that it is possible to have uniform, shared delivery systems while maintaining sharp competition between institutions.

All banking laws, including those affording territorial protectionism, should be reviewed and then expunged or revised to reflect the realities of electronic banking.

Financial institutions should issue identification/credit cards bearing a photo, signature, watermarked magnetic stripe and/or microchip to eliminate most check and credit card crime.

Microchip cards should be used for small purchases, telephone calls, highway tolls, parking meters, and public transit to reduce crime and operating costs and enhance convenience.

Financial institutions should be permitted to offer check guarantee cards to reduce the loss of millions of dollars each year by retailers and increase consumer convenience. It is mind-boggling that this is forbidden in the United States while Eurocheque cards can be used in twenty different countries to cash checks, in POS and ATM terminals, and even at toll stations on French highways.

Need for Public-Mandated Reform

At the heart of the current crisis in banking is the lack of a comprehensive, well-analyzed national policy for what the shape of the financial services industry in the United States should be. Congress knows what needs to be done, but institutional changes are politically difficult to implement. As the chairman of the Senate Banking Committee said during debate on banking legislation in 1984, "I'm sick and tired of the greed, hypocrisy and selfishness. . . . I'm getting to the point where I don't care which way it goes."[18] Nor can the existing regulatory agencies do it because it is in their own vested interests to preserve the status quo. Moreover, it is Congress and the agencies that created the quagmire of laws and regulations into which the industry is sinking.

In the past, the best interests of the public have been sacrificed to special interest groups that contribute hundreds of thousands of dollars through political action committees to the campaign coffers of congressional banking committee members. What is needed now is an independent public commission to develop a framework for the financial services industry that would be best for the U.S. public and the national economy rather than what is best for the industry, the legislators, or the regulators. Both long-term and short-term goals must be articulated, with strategies predicated on meeting the needs of the present and the future, not on putting out long-smoldering fires. The role of the government, moreover, must be clearly enunciated because in an era of electronic banking, with technological obsolescence occurring ever sooner, it is imperative that financial institutions be able to plan their capital investments in hardware and software and schedule product development free of uncertainty. Finally, the plan also must have mechanisms built in for continual monitoring and evaluating and for flexibility so that it can be adjusted for changing conditions.

With the concept of money itself transformed from paper to electronic impulses, the U.S. public should demand that the government adopt a wholly new policy based on a combination of market forces and government regulation to create a strong and efficient industry. The cutting edge of technology is opening up opportunities at a revolutionary pace. The United States needs a strong, advanced banking and payment system to support the needs of the nation, its consumers, and its businesses as they move into the twenty-first century.

Notes

1. Patrick Frazer and Dimitri Vittas, *The Retail Banking Revolution* (London: Michael Lafferty Publications, 1982), p. 39.

2. Jack Baranson, *Robots in Manufacturing: Key to International Competition* (Mt. Airy, Md.: Lomand Publications, 1983).

3. Carter Glass, *An Adventure in Constructive Finance* (New York: Arno, 1975), p. 60.

4. Ibid., p. 93.

5. Ibid., pp. 301–302.

6. Representative Fernand J. St Germain, quoted in "The Regulatory Maze Is Part of Banking's Problem," *Business Week,* October 29, 1984, p. 110.

7. "Sooner Federal S&L Has Run on Deposits at Its Tulsa Offices," *Wall Street Journal,* January 11, 1985.

8. U.S. Congress, House Committee on Government Operations, *Federal Response to Criminal Misconduct by Bank Officers, Directors, and Insiders (Part 2), Hearings before a Subcommittee of the Committee on Government Operations.* 98th Cong., 2d sess., 1984, p. 4.

9. Ibid., p. 283.

10. Theodore J. MacDonald in statement, U.S. Congress, House Committee on Government Operations, *Federal Response to Criminal Misconduct by Bank Officers, Directors, and Insiders (Part 1), Hearing before a Subcommittee of the Committee on Government Operations.* 98th Cong., 1st sess., 1983, p. 3.

11. Task Group on Regulation of Financial Services, *Blueprint for Reform* (Washington, D.C.: Government Printing Office, 1984), pp. 18, 29.

12. "Probation, Fine Levied on National Republic Bank in Cocaine Case," *Wall Street Journal,* August 31, 1983.

13. Survey conducted by Swedish Petroleum Institute, reported by Gunnar von Sydow, "Attityder till banker," *Ekonomisk revy* (December 1981): 451–454.

14. U.S. Congress, House Committee on Government Operations, *Federal Response (Part 2)*, pp. 2036–2042.

15. Murray L. Weidenbaum, "Regulatory Reform: A Report Card for the Reagan Administration," *California Management Review* 26, no. 1 (Fall 1983): 17.

16. "States Can Keep Own Insurance," *National Thrift News*, Vol. 9, Issue 1, October 8, 1984.

17. Steven D. Felgran, "Bank Entry into Securities Brokerage: Competitive and Legal Aspects," *New England Economic Review* (November–December 1984): 12–33, which includes data on relative profits.

18. Senator Jake Garn, quoted in "U.S. Congress Edges toward Bank Bill to Clear Up Confusion in Industry," *Wall Street Journal*, April 23, 1984.

Glossary of Acronyms and Banking Terms

ABA American Bankers Association

ACH automated clearinghouse

ATM automated teller machine; can perform functions in addition to dispensing cash

autogiro preauthorized automatic transfer between giro accounts

Bankomat Swedish network of cash dispensers owned by commercial and cooperative banks

BHC bank holding company

BIB Bank Inspection Board (Sweden)

CD cash dispenser; also may give account balance

Comptroller of the Currency U.S. Treasury Department official appointed to supervise the national banks

Datex Nordic public data network

DIB Data Inspection Board (Sweden)

DIDMCA Depository Institutions Deregulation and Monetary Control Act (1980)

ECR electronic cash register

EDP electronic data processing

EFTS electronic funds transfer system(s)

FDIC Federal Deposit Insurance Corporation

Fed Federal Reserve System

FHLBB Federal Home Loan Bank Board, which oversees S&Ls

FSLIC Federal Savings and Loan Insurance Corporation

Glass-Steagall Act Banking Act of 1933

GNP gross national product

IBAA Independent Bankers Association of America

ITS Iowa Transfer System

krona (pl., kronor) Swedish monetary unit, which for convenience throughout book equals one-fifth U.S. dollar

MICR magnetic ink character recognition system for making bank documents computer readable

NCEFT National Commission on Electronic Fund Transfers

NOW negotiable order of withdrawal account, similar to a checking account

OBHC one-bank holding company

PK Bank (Post-och-Kreditbank) commercial bank owned by the Swedish government

POS point-of-sale system

Riksbank Sweden's central bank

SDP Social Democratic party (Sweden)

SIBOL R&D project in which all Swedish banks participated from 1969 to 1972

SPADAB Swedish savings banks' jointly owned computer center

STA Swedish Telecommunications Administration

T&E card travel and entertainment card, such as American Express

Selected Bibliography

Aldom, Robert S.; Purdy, Alan B.; Schneider, Robert T.; and Whittingham, Jr., Harry W. *Automation in Banking.* New Brunswick, N.J.: Rutgers University Press, 1963.

American Bankers Association. *Critical Issues in Bank Cards: Seminar.* Washington, D.C.: American Bankers Association, 1980.

Anton, Thomas J. *Administered Politics.* Boston: Martinus Nijhoff, 1980.

————. *Governing Greater Stockholm: A Study of Policy Development and System Change.* Berkeley: University of California Press, 1975.

Arthur D. Little, Inc. *The Consequences of Electronic Funds Transfer.* Cambridge, Mass.: Arthur D. Little, Inc., 1975.

Bank for International Settlements. *Payment Systems in Eleven Developed Countries.* Basel: BIS, 1980.

Baxter, William F.; Cootner, Paul H.; and Scott, Kenneth E. *Retail Banking in the Electronic Age.* Montclair, N.J.: Allanheld, Osmun, 1977.

Bender, Mark G. *EFTS. Electronic Funds Transfer Systems.* Port Washington, N.Y.: Kennikat Press, 1975.

Bequai, August. *The Cashless Society: EFTS at the Crossroad.* New York: John Wiley & Sons, 1981.

Bergqvist, Åke. "Bankernas expeditionstider." *Ekonomisk revy* 4 (1959): 266–270.

Bergström, Hans. "Affärsbankernas rätt att öppna avdelningskontor." *Ekonomisk revy* 9 (1959): 604–613.

Black, Harold, and Dugger, Robert H. "Credit Union Structure, Growth and Regulatory Problems." *Journal of Finance* 36, no. 2 (May 1981): 529–538.

Brisman, Sven. *Sveriges affärsbanker.* 2 vols. Stockholm: Svenska Bankföreningen, 1924–1934.

Browaldh, Ernfrid. "Konkurrensen på den svenska kreditmarknaden." *Ekonomisk revy* (1955): 355–371.

————. "The State and the Private Banking System." Supplement to Svenska Handelsbank's *Index* (September 1946).

Bureau of Justice Statistics. "Electronic Fund Transfer and Crime." Special Report NCJ-92650. February 1984.

"Checkar och legitimation." *Ekonomisk revy* 6 (1968): 342–343.

Clayton, G. "The Swedish Post Giro." *Bankers Magazine* (London) (September 1956): 229–232.

Colton, Kent W., and Kraemer, Kenneth L., eds. *Computers and Banking.* New York: Plenum Press, 1980.

Del Mar, Alexander. *History of Monetary Systems.* London: Effinghams Wilson, Royal Exchange, 1895.

Dunham, Constance. "The Growth of Money Market Funds." *New England Economic Review* (September–October 1980): 20–34.

Eisenmenger, Robert W.; Munnell, Alicia H.; and Weiss, Steven J. "Pricing and the Role of the Federal Reserve in an Electronic Funds Transfer System." In Federal Reserve Bank of Boston. *The Economics of a National Electronic Funds Transfer System.* Boston: Federal Reserve Bank of Boston, 1974.

"Electronic Banking." *Business Week,* January 18, 1982, pp. 70–80.

Ernsell, Olov. "Checklöneräkningen—ett räntabilitets problem." *Ekonomisk revy* 2 (1965): 90–97.

European Financial Marketing Association. *Texts of the Presentations, Amsterdam Conference.* Paris: EFMA, 1977.

———. *Texts of the Presentations, Monte-Carlo Conference.* Paris: EFMA, 1982.

Federal Reserve Bank of Boston. *The Economics of a National Electronic Funds Transfer System.* Conference Series No. 13. Boston: Federal Reserve Bank of Boston, 1974.

Federal Reserve System. *Papers and Comments of the International Conference on Banking and Payment Systems.* Washington, D.C.: Board of Governors of the Federal Reserve System, 1980.

Felgran, Steven D. "Bank Entry into Securities Brokerage: Competitive and Legal Aspects." *New England Economic Review* (November–December 1984): 12–33.

———. "Shared ATM Networks: Market Structure and Public Policy." *New England Economic Review* (January–February 1984): 23–38.

Flannery, Mark J., and Jaffee, Dwight M. *The Economic Implications of an Electronic Monetary Transfer System.* Lexington, Mass.: D.C. Heath, 1973.

Ford, William F. "Banking's New Competition: Myths and Realities." *Federal Reserve Bank of Atlanta Economic Review* (January 1982): 4–11.

Frazer, Patrick, and Vittas, Dimitri. *The Retail Banking Revolution.* London: Michael Lafferty Publications Ltd., 1982.

Freese, Jan. "Swedish Data Policy." *Current Sweden,* no. 212 (March 1979).

Friedman, Milton, and Schwartz, Anna J. *A Monetary History of the United States, 1867–1960.* Princeton: Princeton University Press, 1963.

Gambs, Carl M. "The Cost of the U.S. Payments System." *Journal of Bank Research* (Winter 1976): 240–244.

Glass, Carter. *An Adventure in Constructive Finance.* New York: Arno, 1975.

Government of Canada. *Changing Times: Banking in the Electronic Age.* Ottawa: Government of Canada, 1979.

Gunnarsson, Bo. "Data Clearing: A Swedish EFT System in Operation." *Magazine of Bank Administration* (July 1978): 6.

———. "Elektroniska betalningsjänster nu och i framtiden." *Svenska Bankföreningen,* November 4, 1982.

Hammond, Bray. *Banks and Politics in America.* Princeton: Princeton University Press, 1957.

"Handling Money: Some Unlikely Places Benefit from the Boom in Financial Services." *Wall Street Journal,* March 31, 1983.

Harris and Associates, Inc., Louis. *The Road after 1984.* New Haven: Southern New England Telephone, 1984.

————, and Westin, Alan F. *The Dimensions of Privacy.* New York: Garland, 1981.

Heckscher, Eli F. "The Bank of Sweden in Its Connection with the Bank of Amsterdam." In *History of the Principal Public Banks,* edited by J.G. Van Dillen. London: Frank Cass & Co., 1934.

————. *An Economic History.* Translated by Göran Ohlin. Cambridge: Harvard University Press, 1954.

Hendrickson, Robert A. *The Cashless Society.* New York: Dodd, Mead & Co., 1972.

Hewitt, Patricia, ed. *Computers, Records and the Right to Privacy.* Purley, U.K.: Input Two-Nine, 1979.

Hildebrand, Karl-Gustaf. *Banking in a Growing Economy.* Translated by D. Simon Harper. Stockholm: Svenska Handelsbanken, 1971.

Hondius, Frits W. *Emerging Data Protection in Europe.* New York: North American-Holland Elsevier, 1975.

Hopton, David. *Electronic Fund Transfer Systems: The Issues and Implications.* Bangor Occasional Papers in Economics 17. Cardiff: University of Wales Press, 1979.

Hultin, Gösta. "Re-organization of the Banking Activities of the Swedish Postal Administration." *Union Postale,* no. 6 (1975): 110–116A.

"Interstate Banking: The Big Gamble That Congress Will Make It Legal." *Business Week,* November 12, 1984, pp. 142–143.

Ivestedt, Ragnar. "Den svenska betalningsvolymens sammansättning." *Ekonomisk revy,* no. 2 (April 1945): 89–100.

Jalakas, Rudolf. "The Question of a State Commercial Bank in Sweden." Svenska Handelsbank's *Index* (June 1949): 1–7.

James, Marquis, and James, Bessie R. *Biography of a Bank.* New York: Harper & Row, 1954.

Janson, Åke. "Något om sparbankerna och deras verksamhet." *Ekonomisk revy* 8 (1960): 602–608.

Johnson, Roger T. *Historical Beginnings . . . The Federal Reserve.* Boston: Federal Reserve Bank of Boston, 1982.

Källner, Claes-Göran. "Influence of Law and Public Opinion on Data Processing." Paper presented to a meeting of CAPA, June 9, 1977.

Karlsson, Harry. "Elektronisk betalningsförmedling och konsumentskyddet." *Institutet för Rättsinformatik-rapport* (1981).

"Kontantlösa Samhället—ett Fiasko!" *Ny Teknik* (Stockholm), September 25, 1980.

Law & Business, Inc. *The State Banking Revolution and the Federal Response: New Frontiers of Financial Service Expansion.* Clifton, N.J.: Law & Business, Inc., 1984.

Lipis, Allen H. "Costs of the Current U.S. Payments System." *Magazine of Bank Administration* (October 1978): 27–31.

McLeod, Robert W. *Bank Credit Cards for EFTS: A Cost-Benefit Analysis.* Ann Arbor: University of Michigan Research Press, 1979.

Miller, Arthur R. *The Assault on Privacy.* Ann Arbor: University of Michigan Press, 1971.

Ministry of Defense. *The Vulnerability of the Computerized Society.* Stockholm, 1979.

Minsky, Hyman P. *California Banking in a Growing Economy: 1946–1975.* Berkeley:

Institute of Business and Economic Research, University of California, 1965.

Mitchell, George W. "EFT Issues and Outlook: Technology, Innovation and Banking." Paper presented at the Conference on Contemporary Issues in Cash Management, Bank Administration Institute, New Orleans, September 7–10, 1982.

Montgomery, Arthur. "Affärsbankerna i Sveriges ekonomiska historia 1880–1955." *Ekonomisk revy* (1955): 343–354.

Montgomery, George A. *The Rise of Modern Industry in Sweden*. London: P.S. King & Son, Ltd., 1939.

"Några synpunkter på checken som betalningsmedel." *Ekonomisk revy* 1 (February 1944): 182–183.

National Commission on Electronic Fund Transfers. *EFT in the United States: Policy Recommendations and the Public Interest*. Washington, D.C.: NCEFT, 1977.

———. *EFT and the Public Interest*. Washington, D.C.: NCEFT, 1977.

———. *International Payments Symposium*. Washington, D.C.: NCEFT, 1977.

"The New Sears." *Business Week*, November 16, 1981, pp. 140–146.

Nora, Simon, and Minc, Alain. *The Computerization of Society*. Report to the President of France. Cambridge: MIT Press, 1978.

Nordens Centrala Sparbanksorgans Delegation. *Savings Banks in the Nordic Countries*. Borås, Sweden: NCSD, 1981.

Organization for Economic Cooperation and Development. *Policy Issues in Data Protection and Privacy*. OECD Informatics Studies, Vol. 10. Paris: OECD, 1976.

Palmquist, Gunnar. *Segrande samverkan*. Stockholm: Svenska Bankmannaförbundet, 1962.

PGP-projektet. *Viktiga frågor om jobbet och framtiden*. Stockholm: PostGirot, 1982.

Phillips, Almarin. "Competitive Policy for Depository Financial Institutions." In *Promoting Competition in Regulated Markets*, edited by Almarin Phillips. Washington, D.C.: Brookings Institution, 1975.

Plenk, Helfried. "How Important Are POS Systems?—How Rapidly Will They Spread in Europe?" *Savings Banks International*, no. 4 (1981): 7–10.

Porat, Marc U. *The Information Economy: Definition and Measurement*. Washington, D.C.: Government Printing Office, 1977.

Postal Giro. *This Is the Swedish Postal Giro*. Stockholm: Postal Giro, 1982.

"Probation, Fine Levied on National Republic Bank in Cocaine Case." *Wall Street Journal*, August 31, 1983.

"The Problems Continental Illinois' Rescue Is Creating." *Business Week*, June 4, 1984, pp. 108–112.

Pyle, David H. "The Losses on Savings and Deposits from Interest Rate Regulation." *Bell Journal of Economics and Management Science* 5 (Autumn 1974): 614–622.

"The Regulatory Maze Is Part of Banking's Problem." *Business Week*, October 29, 1984, p. 110.

The Report of the President's Commission on Financial Structure and Regulation. Washington, D.C.: Government Printing Office, 1972.

Revell, J.R.S. *Cost and Margins in Banking: An International Survey*. Paris: OECD, 1980.

———. *Banking and Electronic Fund Transfers: A Study of the Implications*. Paris: OECD, 1983.

Richardson, Dennis W. *Electric Money: Evolution of an Electronic Funds Transfer*

System. Cambridge: MIT Press, 1970.

Robertson, A.H., ed. *Privacy and Human Rights*. Manchester: Manchester University Press, 1973.

Rule, James B. *Private Lives and Public Surveillance*. London: Allen Lane, 1973.

————. *Value Choices in Electronic Funds Transfer Policy*. Washington, D.C.: Office of Telecommunications Policy, 1975.

————; McAdam, Douglas; Stearns, Linda; and Uglow, David. *The Politics of Privacy*. New York: Elsevier, 1980.

Samuelsson, Kurt. *From Great Power to Welfare State*. London: George Allen & Unwin, 1968.

————. *Postbanken—postsparbank och postgiro (1884–1925–1974)*. Stockholm: Postverkets tryckeri, 1978.

Sharkey, Robert P. *Money, Class and Party*. Baltimore: Johns Hopkins, 1959.

Söderström, Lars. "What Swedish Savings Banks Learned from Their POS Experiment." Paper presented at International Savings Banks Institute Tenth International Automation Conference, Lyon, France, May 3–7, 1982.

Sommarin, Emil. *Vårt sparbanksväsen 1834–1892*. Lund: Gleerup, 1942.

————. *Vårt sparbanksväsen 1893–1945*. Lund: Gleerup, 1945.

Sparbankernas Information. *Savings Banks in Sweden*. Stockholm: Sparfrämjandet, 1979.

Stålnert, Helena. "Handla penninglöst—är det så vi ska ha det?" *Råd & Rön*, no. 1 (1980): 10–12.

"States Can Keep Own Insurance." *National Thrift News*, Vol. 9, Issue 1, October 8, 1984.

Streeter, Bill. "Paperless Back Office Is a Reality in Sweden." *ABA Banking Journal* (May 1981): 73–78.

————. "DP Shop Blends Technical and Business Expertise." *ABA Banking Journal* (June 1981): 106–110.

Svenska Bankföreningen. *The Swedish Credit Market*. Stockholm: Svenska Bankföreningen, 1983.

"Sweden Regulates Those Snooping Data Banks." *Business Week*, October 6, 1973, pp. 93–95.

Swedish Bankers Association. *The Swedish Banking Experience*. Stockholm: Swedish Bankers Association, 1981.

Tangney, Eugene M. "EFTS Impact on Banking and the Consumer." Paper presented at the IBM Executive Banking Conference, Fort Lauderdale, September 26, 1978.

Task Group on Regulation of Financial Services. *Blueprint for Reform*. Washington, D.C.: Government Printing Office, 1984.

Thomson, F.P. *Money in the Computer Age*. Oxford: Pergamon Press, 1968.

Thunholm, Lars-Erik. "Samordnad banklagstiftning." *Ekonomisk revy* 10 (1967): 560–563.

————. *Svenskt kreditväsen*. 10th ed. Stockholm: Rabén & Sjögren, 1969.

U.S. Congress. House. Committee on Government Operations. *Federal Response to Criminal Misconduct by Bank Officers, Directors, and Insiders (Part 1). Hearing before a Subcommittee of the Committee on Government Operations*. 98th Cong., 1st sess., 1983.

U.S. Congress. House. Committee on Government Operations. *Federal Response to Criminal Misconduct by Bank Officers, Directors, and Insiders (Part 2). Hear-*

ings before a Subcommittee of the Committee on Government Operations. 98th Cong., 2d sess., 1984.

"U.S. Congress Edges toward Bank Bill to Clear Up Confusion in Industry." *Wall Street Journal,* April 23, 1984.

Vaughan, James A., and Porat, Avner M. *Banking Computer Style.* Englewood Cliffs, N.J.: Prentice-Hall, 1969.

Veith, Richard H. *Multinational Computer Nets.* Lexington, Mass.: D.C. Heath, 1981.

Vinge, P.G. *Experiences of the Swedish Data Act.* Stockholm: Federation of Swedish Industries, 1975.

von Sydow, Gunnar. "Attityder till banker." *Ekonomisk revy* (December 1981): 451–454.

Walberg, Sten. "Brott och säkerhet i banklokaler." Paper presented at annual meeting of the Swedish Savings Banks Association, Stockholm, October 19, 1978.

———. "Banktillsyn i omvandling." *Ekonomisk revy* 8 (1980): 340–346.

———. "Bankerna och allmänheten." *Ekonomisk revy* 9 (1980): 401–406.

———. "The Consequences of New Delivery Systems for Bank Regulators." Paper presented to the Conference on Retail Banking, London, November 16, 1982.

Weidenbaum, Murray L. "Regulatory Reform: A Report Card for the Reagan Administration." *California Management Review* 26, no. 1 (Fall 1983): 8–24.

West, Robert C. *Banking Reform and the Federal Reserve, 1863–1923.* Ithaca: Cornell University Press, 1977.

Westin, Alan F. *Privacy and Freedom.* New York: Atheneum, 1967.

———, and Banker, Michael A. *Databanks in a Free Society.* New York: Quadrangle Books, 1972.

White, George C. *White Paper* (March–April 1982).

———. "Commentary: Corporate Electronic Payment Alternatives." *Journal of Cash Management (January–February 1984): 50–51.*

Wicklein, John. *Electronic Nightmare.* New York: Viking Press, 1981.

Wilhelmsson, Karl. *Svenska postgirot 1925–1949.* Stockholm: Postverkets tryckeri, 1950.

———. *70 år i sparandets tjänst.* Stockholm: Postverkets tryckeri, 1954.

Yavitz, Boris. *Automation in Commercial Banking.* New York: Columbia University and Free Press, 1967.

Index

About the Author

Mary L. King, who earned her Ph.D. in business administration at the University of Washington, is an associate professor of management and marketing at San Francisco State University. She has done marketing and production for a broadcasting company in Denver, where she also was hostess of a daily television show; has run her own public relations-advertising firm; has served as an information officer for the U.S. Small Business Administration in Denver and Washington, D.C.; and as a marketing officer of one of the nation's largest bank holding companies, has worked on the development of EFT services. In addition to watching bankers, she enjoys bird watching.